DIVERSITY
& the College Experience

Research-Based Strategies for Appreciating Human Differences

Aaron Thompson
Eastern Kentucky University

Joseph B. Cuseo
Marymount College

Kendall Hunt
publishing company
4050 Westmark Drive • P O Box 1840 • Dubuque IA 52004-1840

Book Team

Chairman and Chief Executive Officer   Mark C. Falb
President and Chief Operating Officer   Chad M. Chandlee
Vice President, Higher Education   David L. Tart
Director of National Book Program   Paul B. Carty
Editorial Development Manager   Georgia Botsford
Senior Editor   Lynne Rogers
Vice President, Operations   Timothy J. Beitzel
Assistant Vice President, Production Services   Christine E. O'Brien
Senior Production Editor   Charmayne McMurray
Permissions Editor   Elizabeth Roberts
Cover Designer   Jeni Chapman

Copyright © 2009 by Kendall Hunt Publishing Company

ISBN 978-0-7575-6101-6 Student Edition
ISBN 978-0-7575-6103-0 Special Edition

All rights reserved. No part of this publication may be reproduced,
stored in a retrieval system, or transmitted, in any form or by any
means, electronic, mechanical, photocopying, recording, or otherwise,
without the prior written permission of the copyright owner.

Printed in the United States of America
10 9 8 7 6 5 4 3

Contents

Chapter 5   Making the Most of Diversity in College and Beyond   145

 # Preface

Plan and Purpose of This Book

There are three primary purposes or goals of this book:

1. to promote your understanding and appreciation of diversity
2. to demonstrate how experiencing diversity can strengthen your learning, personal development, and career success, and
3. to supply you with specific strategies for making the most of diversity in college and beyond.

We believe that college can and should be done *strategically*. Consequently, you will find that specific action strategies appear throughout the book. We also provide solid reasons and evidence for each strategy suggested because it is important that you not only know *what* to do, but *why* to do it. When you understand the reasoning behind a suggested strategy, you will be more motivated to take action on that strategy and put it into practice.

Our practical recommendations are *research-based*; thus, you will find references cited throughout the body of the text. We have included this documentation to assure you that our practical suggestions are supported by empirical research. You will find a balanced blend of references that include older, "classic" studies and more recent, "cutting edge" research. The combination of the old and the new serves to demonstrate how the ideas presented in the text have withstood the test of time (and evidence).

Chapter 1. What Is Diversity?

Since the word "diversity" means different things to different people, this chapter takes the important first step toward any meaningful discussion of diversity by clarifying the meaning of diversity, so that we are all "on the same page." The chapter defines diversity and key diversity-related concepts, such as: race, culture, ethnicity, humanity, and individuality.

Chapter 2. Major Forms and Dimensions of Diversity

Diversity comes in a variety of forms, including ethnic and racial diversity, gender and sexual diversity, socioeconomic diversity, religious diversity, generational diversity, and individual diversity. The chapter describes these major forms of diversity, their historical development, current relevance, and future implications.

Chapter 3. The Benefits of Experiencing Diversity

The first two chapters focus on describing what diversity is; this chapter moves from "What?" to "Why?" (Why take diversity seriously?) The chapter outlines the multiple benefits of diversity, which include not only the global ideals of human rights, social justice, and international harmony, but also the educational, vocational, and personal benefits of diversity for individuals who experience it.

Chapter 4. Stumbling Blocks and Barriers to Diversity: Stereotypes, Prejudice, and Discrimination

This chapter identifies and describes different barriers to diversity that continue to plague our world, such as stereotyping, bias, prejudice, and discrimination. The chapter examines the possible causes of prejudice and discrimination, and proposes a model for overcoming bias that involves a sequence of four key steps: awareness, acknowledgement, acceptance, and action.

Chapter 5. Making the Most of Diversity in College and Beyond

In this final chapter of the text, you are provided with a strategic plan for making the most of diversity, which consists of specific, action-oriented steps that can be taken inside and outside the classroom, and in life after college. Implementing this plan will increase the educational impact of your college experience and enrich the quality of your personal life. It will do the same for diverse groups of people that you interact with in college and beyond.

Sequencing of Chapter Topics

The chapters that comprise this text are arranged in an order that asks and answers the following five questions:

1. What is diversity?
2. What are diversity's major forms or dimensions?
3. Why is diversity worth pursuing?
4. What blocks or barriers must be overcome before the benefits of diversity can be fully experienced?
5. How can you make the most of diversity in college and beyond?

Process and Style of Presentation

How information is presented is as important as *what* information is presented. When writing this text, we made an intentional attempt to deliver information in a manner that would: (a) deepen your learning, (b) strengthen retention (memory) of what you have learned, and (c) stimulate your motivation to learn. We tried to do this by incorporating the following principles of learning, memory and motivation throughout the text.

- At the *start* of each chapter, we begin with an **Activate Your Thinking** exercise designed to energize or activate ideas and feelings you may already have about the upcoming material. This pre-reading exercise serves to "warm up" and "wind up" your brain, preparing it to make connections between the ideas you will encounter in the chapter and the ideas you already have in your head. It is an instructional strategy that implements one of the most powerful principles of human learning: we learn most effectively by relating what we are trying to learn to what we already know or what is already stored in our brain.

- During each chapter, we periodically interrupt your reading with a **Pause for Reflection** that asks you to reflect on, and think deeply about, the material you have just read. These timely pauses should help you stay alert and remain mentally active throughout the reading process. The pauses interrupt and intercept the attention loss that normally takes place when the brain is required to receive and process information for an extended period of time—such as it is required to do when you are reading. These periodic reflections should also deepen your understanding of the material because they encourage you to *write* in response to what you read. Writing in response to reading stimulates greater reflection and deeper thinking than simply underlining or highlighting words.

- At the *end* of each chapter, we include **Exercises** that ask you to reflect on the knowledge you acquired from the chapter and transform that knowledge into informed action. As we point out in Chapter 5, deep learning and wisdom are not achieved solely by the *acquisition of* knowledge, but through the *application* of knowledge, i.e., putting it into practice.

The strategic positioning of the Activate Your Thinking exercises at the start of the chapter, followed by the Pauses for Reflection interspersed throughout the chapter and application Exercises at the conclusion of each chapter are intended to create a powerful learning sequence that has a meaningful beginning, middle, and end. The different learning activities you engage in at these three times should ensure that your attention is focused and your mind is active at three key points in the reading process: *before*, *during*, and *after*.

- Information is presented in a *variety of formats* that include diagrams, pictures, cartoons, advice from college students, words of wisdom from famous and successful people, and personal experiences drawn from the authors' background as students, professors, and advisors. This variety of formats allows information to be delivered through multiple channels and sensory modalities, which increases the number of routes through which information reaches your brain and the number of places in your brain where that information is registered and stored.

Listed below is a more detailed description of the book's key learning and motivational features.

- **"Snapshot Summary" Boxes.** Throughout the text, you will find boxes that contain summaries of key concepts and events. These boxed summaries are designed to pull together ideas related to the same topic and put them in the same place—physically, which helps you put them in the same place—mentally.

- **"Did You Know?" Boxes.** Included at different points in the text are boxes titled "Did you know?" These boxes contain interesting facts, historical developments, myths, fallacies, and realities. This supplemental information is designed to support and embellish the key concepts discussed in the body of the text.

- **"Remember" Cues.** Periodically, you will encounter the word "Remember" in **red**, followed by information that appears in **boldface** type. This is a cue or clue that the information appearing in boldface is especially important to attend to and remember.

- **Words of Wisdom.** Dispersed throughout the text are quotes from famous and influential people. These quotes relate to and reinforce key concepts that are being discussed at that point in the chapter. You can learn a lot from the first-hand experiences and actual words of "real people." You will find quotes from accomplished individuals who have lived in different historical periods and who have specialized in different professional fields. The wide-ranging cultures, timeframes, and fields of study represented by the people who have issued these quotes demonstrate that their words of wisdom are timeless and universal. It is our hope that their words will inspire you to aspire to the same level of diversity appreciation attained by these successful and influential people.

- **Personal Experiences.** In each chapter, you will find personal experiences from the authors. We have learned a lot from being college students ourselves, from our professional experiences working with students as teachers and advisors, and from our life experiences. By sharing our experiences with you, we hope to personalize and humanize the text. We also hope that learning about our experiences with diversity will enable you to better appreciate and learn from your own experiences with diversity (even if it's by learning not to make the same mistakes we did!)

- **Student Perspectives.** You will discover comments and advice from college students throughout the text. Research repeatedly shows that students learn a great deal from their peers. You can learn from both their diversity-related success stories and stumbling blocks.

- **Concept Maps: Verbal-Visual Aids.** Diagrams and concept maps are included in the text that relate to and reinforce ideas contained in the reading. These visual images are designed to strengthen your learning of concepts presented in print by organizing and transforming abstract (verbal) ideas into concrete (visual) form. This should improve your comprehension and retention of these ideas by laying down two different memory tracks in your brain: verbal (words) and visual (images).

- **Cartoons: Emotional-Visual Aids.** You will find a sizable supply of cartoons sprinkled throughout the text. These humorous illustrations are included to provide you with a little entertainment, but, more importantly, they are intended to help you remember the concept illustrated by the cartoon by reinforcing it with a visual image (drawing) and an emotional experience (humor). If the cartoon manages to trigger some laughter, your body will release adrenalin—a hormone that travels to your brain and promotes memory storage. Furthermore, laughter stimulates your brain to release endorphins—a brain chemical that reduces stress and elevates mood!

Ultimately, we hope that the information contained in this book, and the manner in which it is delivered, will ignite and sustain your interest in diversity and enhance your ability to relate to people from diverse backgrounds. Keep in mind that the skills discussed in this book go beyond the college experience; they are life skills. Learning from and through diversity is a lifelong process. If you strive to apply the ideas discussed in this text and continue to use them throughout your lifetime, you should improve the quality of the world we live in, while simultaneously strengthening your prospects for success in any professional or personal path you choose to follow.

Sincerely,

Aaron Thompson & Joe Cuseo

Acknowledgments

I would like to thank all of my former teachers and professors who gave me many breaks when I may not have deserved them and for believing in me and protecting me when I did deserve them. I would also like to thank my current and former employers for both giving and denying me opportunities which helped shaped the person I am today. Diversity as I know it comes from many of these experiences. I also want to thank my forefathers and foremothers who paved the way for me and my children. Thanks to my wife and children who listen to my spouting of endless data and what the world would be like if "we all could just get along." I would also like to thank Rhonda Goode who has been a constant in the process of writing this book and many other items that keep me on track. Thanks to Paul Carty and Lynne Rogers at Kendall Hunt who are professionals who know how to work with authors. Last but not least (only in height), I would like to thank my co-author Joe Cuseo. He knows how to take knowledge to a different level and work well with his co-author while doing it.

Aaron Thompson

I would like to thank the original members of the San Francisco Giants and the original blues musicians who showed me that I could identify with (and advocate for) people of all colors. Thanks also to my college professors who awakened me to the prevalence of prejudice, the need for tolerance, and the value of diversity. Last, but not least, thanks to co-author, Aaron Thompson for tolerating my intensity and compulsivity. For a team of two, we exhibit considerable diversity with respect to race, religiosity, and verticality.

Joe Cuseo

About the Authors

Aaron Thompson is a Professor of Sociology in the Department of Educational Leadership and Policy Studies at Eastern Kentucky University. Thompson has a Ph.D. in Sociology in areas of Organizational Behavior and Race and Gender relations. Thompson has researched, taught and/or consulted in areas of diversity, leadership, ethics, multicultural families, race and ethnic relations, student success, first-year students, retention, cultural competence and organizational design throughout his personal career. He has over 30 publications and numerous research and peer reviewed presentations. Thompson has traveled over the U.S. and has given more than 300 workshops, seminars and invited lectures in areas of race and gender diversity, living an unbiased life, overcoming obstacles to gain success, creating a school environment for academic success, cultural competence, workplace interaction, leadership, organizational goal setting, building relationships, the first-year seminar, and a variety of other topics. He has been or is a consultant to educational institutions (elementary, secondary and postsecondary), corporations, non-profit organizations, police departments, and other governmental agencies. His latest co-authored books are *Thriving in College and Beyond: Research-Based Strategies for Academic Success and Personal Development*, *Focus on Success* and *Black Men and Divorce* and two books relating to diversity that will be published in 2009: *Humanity, Diversity, & the Liberal Arts: The Foundation of a College Education* (summer reading), and *Infusing Diversity into the College Experience: Research-Based Strategies for Teaching and Learning about Human Differences*.

Aaron Thompson

Joe Cuseo holds a doctoral degree in Educational Psychology and Assessment from the University of Iowa. Currently, he is a Professor of Psychology at Marymount College (California) where for 25 years he has directed the first-year seminar, a course required of all new students. He is a regular columnist for a bimonthly newsletter published by the National Resource Center for The First-Year Experience & Students in Transition, and has received the Resource Center's "outstanding first-year advocate award." He is also a 13-time recipient of the "faculty member of the year award" on his home campus, a student-driven award based on effective teaching and academic advising. He has made numerous presentations and authored many articles and monographs on the first-year experience, college success, and student diversity. He is co-author of the textbook, *Thriving in College and Beyond: Research-Based Strategies for Academic Success & Personal Development*, and two books relating to diversity that will be published in 2009: *Humanity, Diversity, & the Liberal Arts: The Foundation of a College Education* (summer reading), and *Infusing Diversity into the College Experience: Research-Based Strategies for Teaching and Learning about Human Differences*.

Joe Cuseo

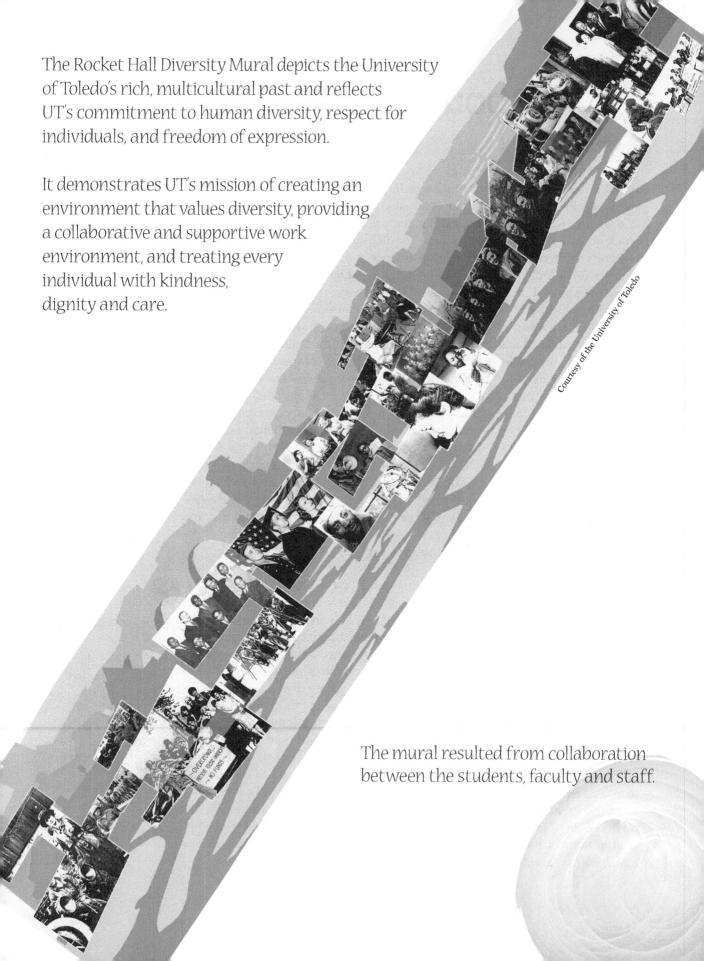

The Rocket Hall Diversity Mural depicts the University of Toledo's rich, multicultural past and reflects UT's commitment to human diversity, respect for individuals, and freedom of expression.

It demonstrates UT's mission of creating an environment that values diversity, providing a collaborative and supportive work environment, and treating every individual with kindness, dignity and care.

Courtesy of the University of Toledo

The mural resulted from collaboration between the students, faculty and staff.

What Is Diversity?

Purpose

"Diversity" means different things to different people. Thus, the first step toward a meaningful discussion of diversity is to clarify what diversity actually means so that everyone is on the "same page." The purpose of this chapter is to clearly define diversity and delineate its key components.

Activate Your Thinking

Complete the following sentence:

When I hear the word "diversity," the first thoughts that come to my mind are . . .

The Spectrum of Diversity

The word diversity derives from the Latin root "diversus," meaning various. Thus, human diversity refers to the variety of differences that exist among individuals and groups of people who comprise humanity (the human species). In this book, we use the word "diversity" to refer primarily to differences among groups of people that, together, make up the whole of humanity. The relationship between diversity and humanity is represented visually in Figure 1.1.

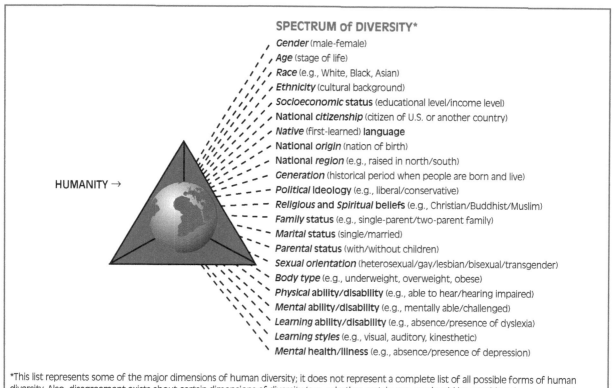

SPECTRUM of DIVERSITY*

HUMANITY →

- *Gender* (male-female)
- *Age* (stage of life)
- *Race* (e.g., White, Black, Asian)
- *Ethnicity* (cultural background)
- *Socioeconomic* status (educational level/income level)
- National *citizenship* (citizen of U.S. or another country)
- *Native* (first-learned) language
- National *origin* (nation of birth)
- National *region* (e.g., raised in north/south)
- *Generation* (historical period when people are born and live)
- *Political* ideology (e.g., liberal/conservative)
- *Religious* and *Spiritual* beliefs (e.g., Christian/Buddhist/Muslim)
- *Family* status (e.g., single-parent/two-parent family)
- *Marital* status (single/married)
- *Parental* status (with/without children)
- *Sexual orientation* (heterosexual/gay/lesbian/bisexual/transgender)
- *Body type* (e.g., underweight, overweight, obese)
- *Physical* ability/disability (e.g., able to hear/hearing impaired)
- *Mental* ability/disability (e.g., mentally able/challenged)
- *Learning* ability/disability (e.g., absence/presence of dyslexia)
- *Learning styles* (e.g., visual, auditory, kinesthetic)
- *Mental* health/illness (e.g., absence/presence of depression)

*This list represents some of the major dimensions of human diversity; it does not represent a complete list of all possible forms of human diversity. Also, disagreement exists about certain dimensions of diversity (e.g., whether certain groups should be considered races or ethnic groups).

Figure 1.1 Humanity and Diversity

WORDS OF WISDOM

"We are all brothers and sisters. Each face in the rainbow of color that populates our world is precious and special. Each adds to the rich treasure of humanity."

MORRIS DEES, CIVIL RIGHT LEADER AND CO-FOUNDER OF THE SOUTHERN POVERTY LAW CENTER

The relationship between humanity and human diversity is similar to the relationship between sunlight and the spectrum of colors. Just as sunlight passing through a prism is dispersed into all the different groups of colors that make up the visual spectrum, the human species spread across planet earth is dispersed into various groups of people that make up the spectrum of humanity.

As you can see in Figure 1.1, groups of people can differ from one another in a wide variety of ways, including physical features, religious beliefs, mental and physical abilities, national origins, social backgrounds, gender, sexual orientation, and in a variety of other dimensions.

Pause for Reflection

Look back to the diversity spectrum on the first page of this chapter and review the list of groups that make up the spectrum. Do you notice any groups that are missing from the list that should be added, either because they have distinctive cultures or because they have been targets of prejudice or discrimination?

Equal rights and social justice are key aspects of diversity; however, they are not the only aspects. In fact, in a national survey of American voters the vast majority of respondents agreed that diversity is more than just political correctness (National Survey of Voters, 1998). While diversity may still be viewed narrowly by some people as strictly a "political" issue, in this book we take a broader view of diversity, which not only includes the political issue of equal rights and social justice, but also considers diversity to be a key *educational* issue—an integral element of the college experience that can have a powerful impact on promoting your learning, personal development, and career success.

REMEMBER: Diversity is a human issue that embraces and benefits all people; it is not a code word that stands for "some people."

Since diversity has been interpreted (and misinterpreted) in different ways by different people, we will begin by defining some key terms related to diversity which should lead to a clearer understanding of its true meaning and value.

What Is Race?

A *racial group (race)* refers to a group of people who share some distinctive physical traits, such as skin color or facial characteristics. The United States Census Bureau (2000) identifies three races: white, black, and Asian. However, as Anderson & Fienberg (2000) caution us, racial categories are social–political constructs (concepts) that are not scientifically based, but socially determined. There continues to be disagreement among scholars about what groups of people actually constitute a human "race," or whether totally distinctive races truly exist (Wheelright, 2005).

There are no specific genes that differentiate one race from another. In other words, there is no way you could do a blood test or any type of "internal" genetic test to determine a person's race. Humans have simply decided to categorize people into "races" on the basis of certain external differences in physical appearance, particularly the color of their outer layer of skin. The U.S. Census Bureau could just as easily divide people into categories of human groups based on such physical characteristics as eye color (e.g., blue, brown, green) or hair texture (e.g., straight, wavy, curly, frizzy).

The expression "white race" did not exist until Americans introduced it in the 18th and 19th centuries. Up to that point in history, the term was not used anywhere else in the world. The term was created by English settlers to distinguish themselves from Native Americans and African Americans whom they deemed to be "uncivilized" and "savages."

The success of the cotton industry increased the need for Native American land and African American slaves. As a result of these needs, white Anglo-Protestant elite created and disseminated the idea of a privileged "white race." This was also seen as a means to provide privilege to British and European immigrants who did not own property. Immigrants who initially defined themselves as German, Irish, or Italian slowly began to refer to themselves as "white" as they began to move up to higher levels of socioeconomic and political status (Feagin & Feagin, 2003).

Personal Experience

My father stood approximately six feet tall and had light brown straight hair. His skin color was that of a Western European with a very slight suntan. My mother was from Alabama and she was dark in skin color with high cheekbones and long curly black hair. In fact, if you did not know that my father was of African American descent, you would not have thought of him as black. All of my life I have thought of myself as African American and all of the people who are familiar with me thought of me as an African American. I have lived half of a century with that as my racial description. Several years ago after carefully looking through records available on births and deaths in my family history, I discovered that I had fewer than 50% of African lineage. Biologically, I am no longer black. Socially and emotionally, I still am. Clearly, race is more of a social concept than a biological concept.

—Aaron Thompson, *Professor of Sociology and co-author of this text*

There are far more similarities than differences between us regardless of skin tone. Copyright © 2009 Monkey Business Images. Under license from Shutterstock, Inc.

The differences in skin color that now exist among humans is likely due to biological adaptations that evolved over long periods of time among groups of humans who lived in different geographic regions. These differences in skin tone helped different groups of humans survive in different environmental regions where they were living and breeding. For instance, darker skin tones developed among humans who inhabited and reproduced in hotter regions nearer the equator (e.g., Africans), where darker skin may have enabled them to adapt and survive in that environment by providing their bodies with better protection from the potentially damaging effects of the sun (Bridgeman, 2003) and better ability to use the sun's source of vitamin D (Jablonski & Chaplin, 2002). In contrast, lighter skin tones were more likely to develop among humans inhabiting colder climates more distant from the equator (e.g., Scandinavians) to allow their bodies to absorb greater amounts of sunlight that was less plentiful and direct.

While humans may display diversity in skin color or tone, the biological reality is that all members of the human species are remarkably similar. There is much less genetic variability among humans than members of other animal species. The fact is that over 98% of the genes of humans from different racial groups are exactly the same (Bridgeman, 2003; Molnar, 1991). This large amount of genetic overlap accounts for the many similarities that exist among humans, regardless of what differences in color appear at the surface of our skin. For example, all humans have similar external features that give us a "human" appearance and clearly distinguish us from other animal species; all humans have internal organs that are similar in structure and function; and, no matter what the color of our outer layer of skin, all humans bleed in the same color.

Personal Experience

I was proofreading this chapter while sitting in a coffee shop in Chicago O'Hare airport when I looked up from my work for a second and saw what appeared to be a white girl about 18 years old. As I lowered my head to return to work, I did a double-take to look at her again, because something about her seemed different or unusual. When I looked at her more closely the second time, I noticed that although she had white skin, the features of her face and hair apeared to be those of an African American. After a couple of seconds of puzzlement, I figured it out: she was an *albino* African American. That satisfied me for the moment, but than I began to wonder: Would it still be accurate to say she was "black" even though her skin was not black? Would her hair and facial features be sufficient for her to be considered or classified as black? If yes, then what about someone who had a black skin tone, but did not have the typical hair and facial features characteristic of black people? Is skin color the defining feature of being African American or are other features equally important? I was unable to answer these questions, but I found it amusingly ironic that all of these thoughts were taking place while I was working on a book dealing with diversity. Later, again on the plane ride home, I thought again about the albino African American girl and realized that she was a perfect example of how classifying people into "races" is not based on objective, scientifically determined evidence, but on subjective, socially-constructed categories.

—Joe Cuseo, *Professor of Psychology and co-author of this text*

Pause for Reflection

What race do you consider yourself to be? Would you say you identify strongly with your race, or are you rarely conscious of it?

What Is Culture?

"Culture" can be broadly defined as a distinctive pattern of beliefs and values that are learned by a group of people who share the same social heritage and traditions. In short, culture is the whole way in which a group of people has learned to live (Peoples & Bailey, 2008); it includes style of speaking (language), fashion, food, art, music, values, and beliefs. The following list is a snapshot summary of key dimensions or components of culture that members of a group may share, and which may differentiate them from other cultures.

Key Components of Culture ——————————————→ SNAPSHOT SUMMARY

Language: How members of the group communicate through written or spoken words, dialect, and nonverbal communication (body language).

Space: How group members arrange themselves with respect to the dimension of physical distance (e.g., how closely they position themselves in relation to each other when they communicate).

Time: How the group conceives of, divides, and uses time (e.g., the speed or pace at which they conduct business).

Aesthetics: How the group appreciates and expresses artistic beauty and creativity (e.g., visual art, culinary art, music, theater, literature, and dance).

Family: The group's attitudes and habits with respect to parents and children (e.g., styles of parenting and caring for aging parents).

Finances: How the group meets its members' material wants and its cultural habits with respect to spending and saving money.

Science and technology: The group's attitude toward and use of science or technology in its day-to-day activities (e.g. whether or not the culture is technologically "advanced").

Philosophy: The group's ideas or views on wisdom, goodness, truth, and the meaning or purpose of life (e.g., dominant ethical viewpoints or values).

Religion: The group's beliefs about a supreme being and the afterlife (e.g., heaven, hell, reincarnation).

Sometimes, the terms "culture" and "society" are used interchangeably as if they have the same meaning, however they refer to different aspects of humanity. *Society* refers to a group of people who are organized under the same social system. For example, all members of American society are organized under the same system of government, justice, and education. On the other hand, culture is what members of a certain group of people actually have in common with respect to their traditions and lifestyle, regardless of how their society or social system has been organized (Nicholas, 1991). Cultural differences can exist within the same society (multicultural society), within a single nation (domestic diversity), or across different nations (international diversity).

What Is an Ethnic Group?

An *ethnic group (ethnicity)* is a group of people who share the same culture. Thus, culture refers to *what* an ethnic group shares in common, and an ethnic group refers to a group of people *who* share the same culture. Unlike a racial group, whose members share physical characteristics they are born with and which have been passed on biologically, an ethnic group's shared characteristics have been passed on through *socialization* (i.e., common characteristics that have been *learned* or acquired through shared social experiences).

The primary ethnic groups in the United States include Hispanic Americans (Latinos), Native Americans (American Indians), European Americans, African Americans (also classified as a racial group), and Asian Americans (also classified as a racial group). Ethnic *subgroups* also exist within each of these major ethnic groups. For example, Hispanic Americans include people who have cultural roots in Mexico, Puerto Rico, Central America, South America, etc.; Asian Americans include cultural descendents from Japan, China, Korea, Vietnam, etc.; and European Americans include descendents from Scandinavia, England, Ireland, Germany, Italy, etc.

Currently, European Americans represent the *majority* ethnic group in the United States because they account for more than one-half of the American population. Native Americans, African Americans, Hispanic Americans, and Asian Americans are considered to be ethnic *minority* groups because each of these groups represents less than 50% of the American population.

Culture is a distinctive pattern of beliefs and values that develop among a group of people who share the same social heritage and traditions.

Pause for Reflection

What ethnic group(s) do you belong to or identify with? What cultural values do you think are shared by your ethnic group(s)?

Like the concept of race, whether a particular group of people is defined as an ethnic group can be arbitrary, subjective, and interpreted differently by different groups of people. For instance, according to the U.S. Census, Hispanic is not defined as a race; it is considered to be an ethnic group. However, among those who checked "some other race" in the 2000 Census, 97% were

STUDENT
SPERSPECTIVE

"I'm the only person from
my race in class."

HISPANIC STUDENT COMMENTING
ON WHY HE FELT UNCOMFORTABLE
IN HIS CLASS ON RACE, ETHNICITY,
AND GENDER

Hispanic. This fact has been viewed by Hispanic advocates as a desire for their "ethnic" group to be reclassified as a race (Cianciotto, 2005). Currently only white, black, and Asian are recognized as races by the U.S. Census Bureau. The Census Bureau wanted to remove the "some other race" category from the 2010 Census; however, Hispanic advocacy groups argued that the elimination of the category would exclude Hispanics who do not consider themselves to be white, black, or Asian (Cianciotto, 2005). This disagreement illustrates how difficult it is to conveniently categorize groups of people into particular racial or ethnic groups. The United States will continue to struggle with this issue because the ethnic and racial diversity of its population is growing and members of different ethnic and racial groups are forming cross-ethnic and interracial families. Thus, it is becoming progressively more difficult to place people into distinct categories of race or ethnicity. For example, by 2050 the number of people who will identify themselves as being of two or more races is projected to more than triple, from 5.2 million to 16.2 million (U.S. Census Bureau, 2008).

Personal Experience As a child of a black man and a white woman, someone who was born in the racial melting pot of Hawaii, with a sister who's half Indonesian but who's usually mistaken for Mexican or Puerto Rican, and a brother-in-law and niece of Chinese descent, with some blood relatives who resemble Margaret Thatcher and others who could pass for Bernie Mac, family get-togethers over Christmas take on the appearance of a U.N. General Assembly meeting. I've never had the option of restricting my loyalties on the basis of race, or measuring my worth on the basis of tribe.

—Barack Obama (2006)

What Is Humanity?

It is important to realize that human *variety* and human *similarity* exist side-by-side. Diversity is a "value that is demonstrated through mutual respect and appreciation of similarities and differences" (Public Service Enterprise Group, 2009). Experiencing diversity not only enhances our appreciation of the unique features of different cultures, it also provides us with a larger perspective on the universal aspects of the human experience that are common to all people, no matter what their particular cultural background happens to be. For example, despite our racial and cultural differences, we express our emotions with the same facial expressions (see Figure 1.2).

Other human characteristics that anthropologists have found to be shared across all groups of people in every corner of the world include storytelling, poetry, adornment of the body, dance, music, decoration of artifacts, families, socialization of children by elders, a sense of right and wrong, supernatural beliefs, explanations of diseases and death, and mourning of the dead (Pinker, 1994). These are universal experiences common to all humans, even though different ethnic groups may express these human experiences in different ways.

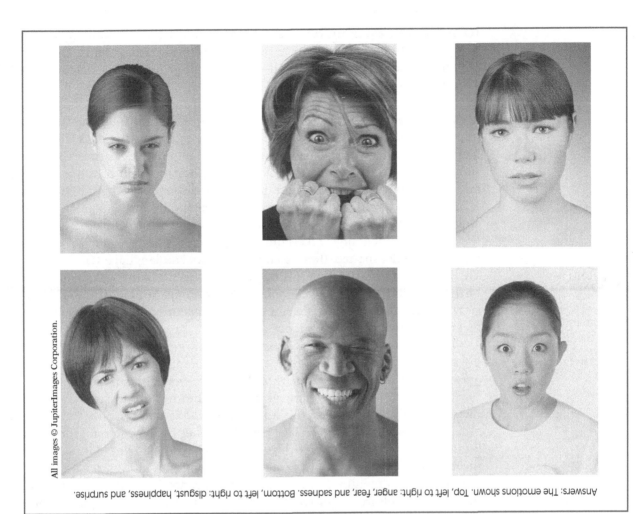

Answers: The emotions shown, Top, left to right: anger, fear, and sadness. Bottom, left to right: disgust, happiness, and surprise.

Figure 1.2 Humans all over the world display the same facial expressions when experiencing certain emotions. See if you can detect the emotions being expressed in the following faces. (To find the answers, turn your book upside down.)

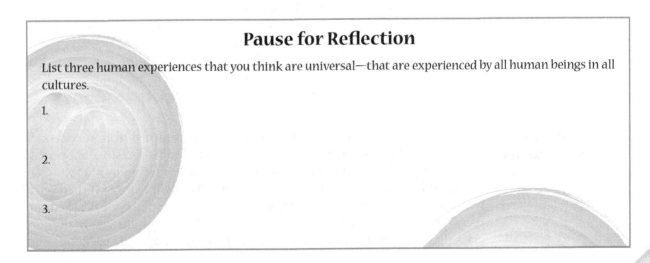

Pause for Reflection

List three human experiences that you think are universal—that are experienced by all human beings in all cultures.

1.

2.

3.

REMEMBER: Diversity represents variations on the common theme of humanity. Although people have different cultural backgrounds, they are still cultivated from the same soil—they are all grounded in the common experience of being human.

Human languages provide an excellent example of the interplay between humanity and diversity. Although humans across the world speak different languages, the fact is that newborn babies in all cultures babble with the same sounds. The determination of which sounds they will continue to use and eventually speak as a language depends on the language they are exposed to in their culture. Infants will eventually speak only in the sounds of the language(s) they are exposed to in their particular culture; the other sounds they used while babbling will eventually drop out of their vocabulary because their culture doesn't use those sounds in its spoken language (Oller, 1981). The fact that all humans express themselves with the same set of sounds at birth (our universal "language") reflects our common humanity; the wide variety of languages that are spoken by different groups of humans reflects the diversity of our cultural experiences.

Thus, cultures associated with various ethnic groups may be viewed simply as variations on the same theme: being human. You may have heard the question: "We're all human, aren't we?" The answer to this important question is "yes and no." Yes, we are all the same, but not in the same way. One metaphor for understanding this apparent paradox is to visualize humanity as a quilt in which all humans are joined together by the common thread of humanity—we are all human beings, yet the different patches that makes up the quilt represent diversity—the distinctive or unique cultures that comprise our common humanity. The quilt metaphor acknowledges the identity and beauty of all cultures. It differs from the old American "melting pot" metaphor—which viewed differences as something that should be melted down or eliminated, or the "salad bowl" metaphor—which suggests that America is a hodgepodge or mishmash of different cultures thrown together without any common connection. In contrast, the quilt metaphor suggests that the cultures of different ethnic groups should be recognized and celebrated. However, these differences can be woven together to create a unified whole—as in the Latin expression: "E pluribus Unum" ("Out of many, one")—the motto of the United States, which you will find printed on all its coins.

To appreciate diversity and its relationship to humanity is to capitalize on the power of our differences (diversity) while still maintaining our collective strength through unity (humanity).

WORDS OF WISDOM

"We are all the same, and we are all unique."

GEORGIA DUNSTON, AFRICAN-AMERICAN BIOLOGIST AND RESEARCH SPECIALIST IN HUMAN GENETICS

Personal Experience When I was 12 years old and living in New York, I returned from school one Friday afternoon and my mother asked me if anything interesting happened at school that day. I mentioned to her that the teacher went around the room, asking students what we had for dinner the night before. At that moment, my mother began to become a bit agitated and nervously asked me: "What did you tell the teacher?" I said: "I told her and the rest of the class that I had pasta last night because my family always eats pasta on

Thursdays and Sundays." My mother exploded and yelled back at me: "Why couldn't you tell her that we had steak or roast beef!" For a moment, I was stunned and couldn't figure out what I had done wrong or why I should have lied about eating pasta. Then it suddenly dawned on me: My mother was embarrassed about being an Italian American. She wanted me to hide our family's ethnic background and make it sound like we were very "American." After this became clear to me, it later became clear to me why her maiden name was changed from the very Italian-sounding "DeVigilio" to the more American-sounding "Vigilis" to avoid discrimination.

I never forgot this interchange with my mother because it was such an emotionally intense experience. For the first time in my life, I became aware that my mother was ashamed of being a member of the same group to which every other member of my family belonged, including me. After her outburst, I felt a combined rush of astonishment and embarrassment. However, these feelings didn't last long because my mother's reaction eventually had the opposite effect on me. Instead of making me feel inferior or ashamed about being Italian-American, my mother's reaction that day caused me to become more aware of, and take more pride in, my Italian heritage.

As I grew older, I also grew to understand why my mother felt the way she did. She grew up in America's "melting pot" generation—a time when different American ethnic groups were expected to melt down and melt away their ethnicity. They were not to celebrate diversity; they were to eliminate it.

—Joe Cuseo, *Professor of Psychology and co-author of this text*

REMEMBER: By learning about diversity (our differences), we simultaneously learn more about our commonality—our shared humanity.

What Is Individuality?

It is important to keep in mind that *individual* differences *within* the same racial or ethnic group are *greater* than the average differences between different groups. For example, although we live in a world that is very conscious of differences between races, the fact is that differences among individuals of the same racial group in physical attributes (e.g., height and weight) and their behavior patterns (e.g., personality characteristics) are greater than the average differences between racial groups (Caplan & Caplan, 1994).

As you proceed through this book, keep in mind the following distinctions among humanity, diversity, and individuality:

- **Diversity:** We are all members of *different groups* (e.g., our gender and ethnic groups).
- **Humanity:** We are all members of the *same group* (the human species).
- **Individuality:** Each of us is a *unique person* who is different than all other people in any group to which we may belong.

WORDS OF WISDOM

"We have become not a melting pot but a beautiful mosaic."

JIMMY CARTER, THIRTY-NINTH PRESIDENT OF THE UNITED STATES AND WINNER OF THE NOBEL PEACE PRIZE

Diversity and the College Experience

WORDS OF WISDOM

"Every human is, at the same time, like all other humans, like some humans, and like no other human."

CLYDE KLUCKHOLN, AMERICAN ANTHROPOLOGIST

There are more than 3,000 public and private colleges in the United States. They vary in terms of size (small to large), location (urban, suburban, rural), and mission (research universities, comprehensive state universities, liberal arts college, and community colleges). This variety makes the American higher education system one of the most diverse and accessible systems in the world. The diversity of educational opportunities in American colleges and universities reflects the freedom of opportunity in the United States as a democratic nation (American Council on Education, 2008).

Our diverse system of higher education is becoming more diverse with respect to the groups of people enrolled in it. The ethnic and racial diversity of students in American colleges and universities is rapidly rising (see Figure 1.3). In 1960, Whites comprised almost 95% of the total college population; in 2005, the percentage decreased to 69%. At the same time, the percentage of Asian, Hispanic, black, and Native American students attending college increased (*Chronicle of Higher Education*, 2003).

The rise in ethnic and racial diversity on American campuses is particularly noteworthy when viewed in light of the historical treatment of minority groups in the United States. Traditionally, the dominant culture in the U.S. has been white, European, male, and wealthy. In the early 19th century, education was not a right, but a privilege available only to those who could

The college classroom provides an excellent environment to experience diversity. View your campus as a sea of diverse individuals and thought, taking in the richness each person has to offer. Copyright © 2009 Brian Chase. Under license from Shutterstock, Inc.

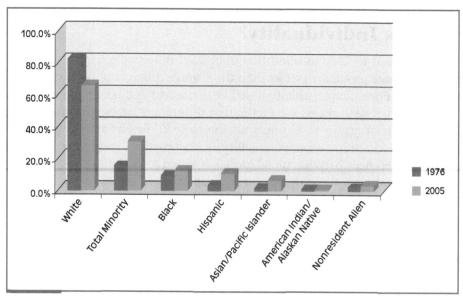

Figure 1.3 College Enrollment Fall 1976–Fall 2005 Comparison.
Source: National Center for Education Statistics, 2008.

afford to attend private schools and it was delivered largely to and by Protestants of European descent. Later, white immigrants from other cultural backgrounds began migrating to the U.S. and public education was then made mandatory, with the idea that education would "Americanize" these new immigrants and obliterate their own cultural identities in the process (Luhman, 2007). Members of certain minority groups were left out of the educational process altogether or were forced to be educated in racially segregated settings. For example, Americans of color were once taught in separate, segregated schools that were typically inferior in terms of educational facilities. It was not until the groundbreaking Supreme Court ruling in *Brown vs. Board of Education* that the face of education was changed for people of color. On May 17, 1954, the United States Supreme Court ruled that "separate educational facilities are inherently unequal." The decision made it illegal for Kansas and 20 other states to deliver education in segregated classrooms.

WORDS OF **W**ISDOM

"Of all the civil rights for which the world has struggled and fought for 5,000 years, the right to learn is undoubtedly the most fundamental."

W.E.B. DUBOIS, AFRICAN AMERICAN SOCIOLOGIST, HISTORIAN, AND CIVIL RIGHTS ACTIVIST

Personal Experience

My mother was a direct descendent of slaves and moved with her parents from the deep south at the age of 17. My father lived in an all-black coal mining camp, into which my mother and her family moved in 1938. My father remained illiterate because he was not allowed to attend public schools in eastern Kentucky.

In the early 1960s my brother, my sister, and I were integrated into the white public schools. Physical violence and constant verbal harassment caused many other blacks to forgo their education and opt for jobs in the coal mines at an early age. But my father remained constant in his advice to me: "It doesn't matter if they call you n____; but don't you ever let them beat you by walking out on your education."

My dad would say to me, "Son, you will have opportunities that I never had. Many people, white and black alike, will tell you that you are no good and that education can never help you. Don't listen to them because soon they will not be able to keep you from getting an education like they did me. Just remember, when you do get that education, you'll never have to go in those coal mines and have them break your back. You can choose what you want to do, and then you can be a free man."

Being poor, black, and Appalachian did not offer me great odds for success, but constant reminders from my parents that I was a good and valuable person helped me to see beyond my deterrents to the true importance of education. My parents, who could never provide me with monetary wealth, truly made me proud of them by giving me the gifts of insight and aspiration for achievement.

—Aaron Thompson, *Professor of Sociology and co-author of this text*

American colleges are also becoming more diverse in terms of gender and age. In 1955, only 25% of college students were female; in 2000, the percent-

The ethnic and racial diversity of students in American College is increasing.

© Stockbyte.

age had jumped to almost 66% (*Postsecondary Education Opportunity*, 2001). College students 24 years of age or older has also grown to 44% of the total student body (*Chronicle of Higher Education*, 2003).

In addition to greater diversity among college students with respect to race, ethnicity, and age, you are also likely to find students on your campus from different nations. From 1990 to 2000, the number of international students attending American colleges and universities increased by over 140,000 (Institute of International Education, 2001).

Today, colleges and universities intentionally recruit a student body that is rich with diversity. In fact, the popular magazine *U.S. News and World Report* now ranks colleges and universities in terms of their "campus diversity." Although this is a significant development, the magazine merely ranks colleges in terms of the total number of students from diverse groups that are present on campus. However, as Hill (1991) notes: "The mere presence of persons of other cultures and subcultures [on campus] is primarily a political achievement, not an intellectual or educational achievement. Real educational progress will be made when multiculturalism becomes inter-culturalism" (p. 45). Thus, the key is to interact with people from these different cultures so you can convert *multi*culturalism into *inter*-culturalism.

The wealth of diversity on college campuses today represents an unprecedented educational opportunity. You may never again be a member of a community that includes so many people from such a variety of backgrounds with

Pause for Reflection

1. What diverse groups do you see represented on your campus?

2. Are there groups on your campus that you did not expect to see, or to see in such large numbers?

3. Are there groups on your campus that you expected to see but do not see, or see in smaller numbers than you expected?

whom to interact. Seize this opportunity! You're now in the right place at the right time to experience the people and programs that can infuse diversity into your college experience and enrich the quality of your college education.

Summary

Diversity refers to the wide variety of differences that exist among individuals and groups who comprise humanity (the human species). Humans can and do differ from one another in multiple ways, including physical features, religious beliefs, mental and physical abilities, national origins, social backgrounds, gender, and sexual orientation. Diversity is concerned with the important political issue of securing equal rights and social justice for all people, but diversity also represents an *educational* issue—an integral element of the college experience that can enrich learning, personal development, and career preparation.

Racial diversity involves grouping humans into categories that are not scientifically based, but are socially determined. There are no specific genes that differentiate one race from another; there is no "blood test" or genetic marker that can be used to detect a person's race. Humans have simply decided to classify themselves into "racial" categories on the basis of certain external differences in physical appearance, particularly the shade of their outer layer of skin.

An ethnic group is a group of people who share a distinctive culture (i.e., a particular set of shared traditions, customs, and social heritage). Unlike a racial group, whose members share physical characteristics that they were born with; an ethnic group's shared characteristics have been *learned* through shared social experiences. Thus, *ethnic diversity* refers to different groups of people with different cultural characteristics. Cultural differences can exist within the same society (multicultural society), within a single nation (domestic diversity), or across different nations (international diversity).

Appreciating diversity not only involves respecting and valuing human differences, but also human similarities. Diversity represents variations on the common theme of humanity. Although people have different cultural backgrounds, their group differences emerge from the same soil; they are all grounded in the common experience of being human. Thus, experiencing diversity not only enhances our appreciation of the unique features of different cultures, it also provides us with a larger perspective on the universal aspects of the human experience that are common to all of us—no matter what our particular cultural background happens to be.

Embedded within humanity and diversity is *individuality*. Studies show that individual differences *within* the same racial or ethnic group are *greater* than the average differences between groups. The key distinctions among humanity, diversity, and individuality may be summarized as follows:

- **Diversity:** All humans are members of *different groups* (e.g., different gender and ethnic groups).

- **Humanity:** All humans are members of the *same group* (the human species).
- **Individuality:** Each human is a *unique person* who differs from all members of any group to which he or she may belong.

Diversity among college students with respect to ethnicity, race, and gender is greater now than at any other time in the nation's history. This rich diversity represents an unprecedented educational opportunity. By planning to intentionally infuse diversity into your college experience, you can increase the power of your college education and your prospects for future success.

Chapter 1 Exercises

1.1 Diversity Spectrum

Turn back to the diversity spectrum on the first page of this chapter and look over the list of groups that make up the spectrum. Do you notice any groups that are missing from the list that should be added, either because they have distinctive cultures or because they have been targets of prejudice and discrimination?

1.2 Multi-Group Self-Awareness

We are members of different groups at the same time, and our membership in these groups can influence our personal development and self-identity. In the figure below, the shaded center circle represents yourself, and the six non-shaded circles represent six different groups that you belong to, which you feel have influenced your personal development.

Fill in these circles with the names of those groups to which you belong that have had the most influence on your personal development. You can use the diversity spectrum that appears on the first page of this chapter to help you identify different groups. Do not feel you have to come up with six groups to fill all six circles. What is most important is to identify those groups that you think have had significant influence on your development and personal identity.

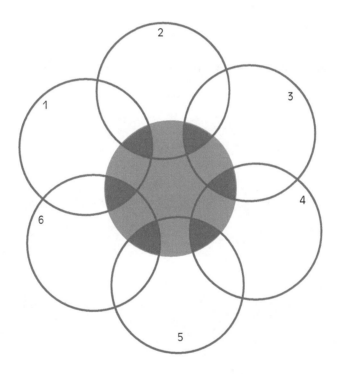

After identifying your groups, take a moment to reflect on the following questions:

a. Which one of your group memberships has had the greatest influence on your personal identity? Why?

b. Have you ever felt limited or disadvantaged by being a member of any group(s)?

c. Have you ever felt that you experienced advantages or privileges because of your membership in any group(s)?

1.3 Social Identities

In the boxes under columns 1 and 2 of the following grid, rate each of the identities that are listed on a scale from 1–10 (10 being the highest), and provide a written response to the questions in columns 3 and 4.

Identity	1 How important do you consider this piece of your identity?	2 If someone sees you but does not know you personally, how obvious is this piece of your identity to them?	3 Is this identity regarded in a positive manner by society at large?	4 Is this identity regarded in a negative manner by society at large?
Race or ethnicity				
Gender				
Socio-economic class				
Sexual orientation				
Religion				
Generation				
National region (where you were raised)				
Marital status				

1.4 Sudden Realization

You meet someone sitting at a party, and after talking with this person for several hours, you realize that you really like this person and you have a lot in common. The attraction is mutual, so you both exchange phone numbers. As you both leave the party, the other person gets into a motorized wheelchair (that you had not noticed previously) and motors away.

What thoughts and feelings would cross your mind immediately after you discover this person has a physical disability?

Would you still give the person a call? Why?

Source: University of New Hampshire, 2001

1.5 Switching Group Identity

If you were to be born again as a member of a different racial or ethnic group:

a. What group would you want it to be? Why would you choose this group?

b. With your new group identity, what things would change in your personal life?

c. What things would remain the same in your life despite the fact that your group identity has changed?

d. What group would you not want to be born into? Why would you prefer not to be a member of this group?

Source: Adapted from University of New Hampshire, 2001

Major Forms and Dimensions of Diversity

2

Purpose

Diversity comes in different dimensions and forms. The purpose of this chapter is to describe some of the major dimensions of diversity, their historical development, and current relevance.

Activate Your Thinking

Would you say that you identify more closely with your *race, ethnic group,* or *gender*?

Ethnic and Racial Diversity

America is rapidly becoming a more racially and ethnically diverse nation. In 2008, the minority population in the U.S. stood at 34% of the total population, which was an all-time high. The population of ethnic minorities is growing at a much faster rate than the white majority. This trend is expected to continue and, by the middle of the 21st century, the minority population will have grown from one-third of the U.S. population to more than one-half (54%), with more than 60% of the nation's children expected to be members of minority groups (U.S. Census Bureau, 2008).

By 2050, the U.S. population is projected to be more than 30% Hispanic (up from 15% in 2008), 15% Black (up from 13% in 2008), 9.6% Asian (up from 5.3% in 2008), and 2% Native Americans (up from 1.6% in 2008). The Native Hawaiian and Pacific Islander population is expected to more than double between 2008 and 2050. During the same timeframe, the percentage of Americans who are white will decline from 66% (2008) to 46% (2050). As a result of these population trends, ethnic and racial minorities will become the "new majority" because they will constitute the majority of Americans by the middle of the 21st century (see Figure 2.1).

As a result of this increasing diversity, "cultural competence"—the ability to understand cultural differences and to interact effectively with people from different cultural backgrounds—has become an important skill that is essential for success in today's world (Pope et al., 2005).

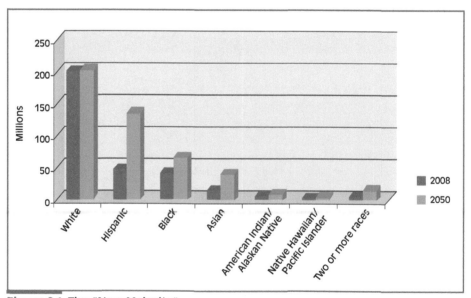

Figure 2.1 The "New Majority"

Native Americans (American Indians)

Lest we forget, there is only one ethnic group who can truly be called American "natives"; they are the American Indians. Although white is the majority group in America, all current white Americans are descendents of immigrants who migrated to the United States from other countries. Thus, all of America's ethnic and racial groups are either recent immigrants or descendants of immigrants who settled in North America many years ago.

Native Americans have contributed much to the history of the United States that you see today. In fact, the names of approximately one-half of all the states in America originate from Indian languages: Alabama, Alaska, Arizona, Arkansas, Connecticut, Hawaii, Illinois, Iowa, Kentucky, Massachusetts, Michigan, Minnesota, Mississippi, Missouri, Nebraska, New Mexico, North Dakota, Ohio, Oklahoma, South Dakota, Tennessee, Texas, Utah, Wisconsin, and Wyoming (NativeAmericans.com, 2008).

25,000+ Native Americans speak the Navajo language.
Copyright © 2009 by Mona Makela. Under license from Shutterstock, Inc.

Famous Firsts by Native Americans

1000: First to bring and adapt corn to the northeast part of North America were the Iroquois people, who also acted as guides, interpreters, and teachers for European settlers and Pilgrims

1868: First Non-Caucasian commissioner of Indian affairs and first Native American to hold federal office, Ely Samuel Parker

1912: First Olympic gold medal winner in the pentathlon and decathlon events, Jim Thorpe—who was voted by Associated Press writers as "the greatest athlete of the first half of the 20th century"

1969: First Pulitzer Prize in fiction, N. Scott Momaday, for *House Made of Dawn*

1974: First winner of PGA Tour, Rod Curl

1987: First woman to lead a major tribe, Wilma Mankiller, Cherokee Nation of Oklahoma

1992: First U.S. Senator, Ben Nighthorse Campbell

1993: First Assistant Secretary of Indian Affairs (also first woman to hold office), Adda E. Deer

DID YOU KNOW . . .
American Indian Heritage Month is celebrated annually in November **?**

Native Americans now comprise slightly less than 1% of the entire population of the United States, and they come from more than 550 different tribes that differ with respect to socioeconomic conditions, levels of education, geographic locations, and traditional customs.

A common misconception regarding Native Americans is that they all speak the same language. The reality is that there were approximately 1,000 languages spoken by Native Americans prior to the arrival of Europeans, and the number today remains closer to 250.

Native Americans have a long tradition of respect for and connection with nature. It could be said that they were the first ecology-minded Americans and the first group to appreciate the connection between humankind and the natural world. Native American culture reminds us to balance the

WORDS OF **W**ISDOM

May the sun bring you new energy by day; may the moon restore you by night. May the rain wash away your worries; may the breeze blow strength into your being. May you walk gently through the world and know its beauty all the days of your life.

APACHE INDIAN BLESSING

"Everyone is a house with four rooms: a physical, a mental, an emotional, and a spiritual. Most of us tend to live in one room most of the time but unless we go into every room every day, even if only to keep it aired, we are not complete."

NATIVE AMERICAN PROVERB

human quest for manipulation and control the physical environment with respect for the beauty and value of nature. The search for a connection between the self and the larger world or universe is now considered to be an important component of spirituality (National Wellness Institute, 2005).

Myths and Realities about Native Americans

Myth: African Americans were the only people who were ever enslaved in the New World.

Fact: Millions of Native Americans were also enslaved, particularly in South America. In the American colonies in 1730, nearly 25% of the slaves in the Carolinas were Cherokee, Creek, or other Native Americans.

Myth: Most American Indians live on reservations.

Fact: Only about 36% of Native Americans live on reservations.

Myth: All American Indians share the same culture.

Fact: Although there are many similarities among Native Americans, there are more than 560 tribes in the United States, each of which has distinctive cultural characteristics.

Myth: Americans Indians are financially well off because of their non-taxable income derived from casino revenue.

Fact: Only 39.3% of tribes operate casinos and only 8.2% of the total Native American population earns money generated by legal gambling.

Pause for Reflection

When you think about the history of Native Americans in the United States, what thoughts immediately come to mind?

As a group, what do you think Native Americans should be most proud of?

Hispanic Americans (Latinos)

Hispanics originate from many different countries. Based on a national survey conducted by the U.S. Census Bureau in 2006, Hispanic Americans in the U.S. have the following origins: Mexican (65.5%), Puerto Rican (8.6%), Central American (8.2%), South American (6%), Cuban (3.7%), and other Hispanic (8%; U.S. Census Bureau, 2006). Because of their Latin American origins, Hispanic Americans are also referred to as Latinos. More specifically, a person with Latino heritage is a descendant of a family from Mexico, the Caribbean, Central America, or South America. The term Hispanic refers to people who come from a country where Spanish is spoken.

Although many people associate the growth of the Hispanic population in the U.S. with recent immigration, their heritage dates back very far. Hispanic heritage in the United States is centuries old, predating the arrival of many European immigrants by many years; colonies of Spanish and American Indians have been traced back to the early 1500s. Spanish settlements in the part of the United States that we now call the Southwest and the Florida peninsula existed before the Puritans landed at Plymouth Rock in 1620. Puerto Rico was annexed into the U.S. during the late 19th century and Puerto Ricans were granted American citizenship in 1917 (U.S. Diplomatic Mission to Germany).

There are now 48 million American citizens of Hispanic origin (including the 3.8 million residents of Puerto Rico), nearly half of whom reside in the states of California and Texas. Currently, Hispanics constitute 15% of the U.S. population, making them the largest minority population in the United States. They are also the fastest growing minority-group population; it is projected that the Hispanic population will nearly triple between 2008 and 2050 and will account for one-third of the American population by the middle of the 21st century (U.S. Census Bureau, 2008).

California and Texas have the largest Hispanic populations in the U.S. Copyright © 2009 by Monkey Business Images. Under license from Shutterstock, Inc.

Famous Firsts by Hispanic Americans

1822: First member of U.S. Congress, Joseph Marion Hernandez, delegate from the Florida territory

1865: First Medal of Honor recipient, Philip Bazaar, Chilean member of U.S. Navy

1866: First Admiral in U.S. Navy, David G. Farragut

1871: First Major League Baseball Player, Esteban Bellan

1872: First novel written in English and published in the U.S., *Who Would Have Thought It?* by Maria Amparo Ruiz

1876: First U.S. Representative, Romualdo Pacheco, representative from California. He served four months before an opponent succeeded in contesting the election results. Pacheco was elected again in 1879.

1919: First World Series Baseball Player, Adolfo "Dolf" Luque, relief pitcher for the Cincinnati Reds

1927: First professional football player, Ignacio "Lou" Molinet

1928: First U.S. Senator, Octaviano Larrazolo, finished term of New Mexico Senator Andieus Jones who had died in office

1941: First professional football player drafted from college, Joe Aguirre

1950: First Oscar (Best Actor), Jose Ferrer, in *Cyrano de Bergerac*

1952: First, Oscar (Best Supporting Actor), Anthony Quinn in *Viva Zapata*

1956: First Rookie of the Year, Luis Aparicio, shortstop, Chicago White Sox

1959: First Nobel Prize in Physiology or Medicine, Severo Ochoa, for synthesis of ribonucleic acid (RNA)

1961: First Oscar (Best Supporting Actress), Rita Moreno, in *West Side Story*

1968: First Nobel Prize in Physics, Luiz Walter Alvarez, for discoveries about subatomic particles

1970: First professional football player inducted into the Hall of Fame, Tom Fears

1971: First #1 professional football drafted from college, Jim Plunkett

1973: First Baseball Hall of Fame Inductee, Roberto Clemente, Pittsburg Pirates, who died in a plane crash while delivering emergency aid packages to earth quake victims in Nicaragua.

1973: First Tony (Best Director), Jose Quintero, for *A Moon for the Misbegotten*

1975: First Tony (Best Supporting Actress), Rita Moreno, in *The Ritz*

1976: First U.S. Army General, Richard E. Cavazos

1986: First male astronaut, Franklin Chang-Diaz

1988: First U.S. Cabinet Member, Lauro F. Cavazos, Secretary of Education

1990: First U.S. Surgeon General, Antonia Coello Novello, who also was the first woman to hold the position

1990: First Pulitzer Prize for Fiction, Oscar Hijuelos, *The Mambo Kings Play Songs of Love*

1991: First female astronaut, Ellen Ochoa

2003: First Pulitzer Prize for Drama, Nilo Cruz, *Anna in the Tropics*

2005: First U.S. Attorney General, Alberto Gonzales

D ID YOU KNOW . . .

Hispanic Heritage Month is celebrated annually in September ?

Pause for Reflection

Prior to reading this book, did you think of Hispanics as a racial group or an ethnic (cultural) group?

As a group, what do you think Hispanic Americans should be most proud of?

African Americans (Blacks)

Americans who are categorized as black in today's society display a wide range of physical traits. Their skin color extends from ebony to a shade paler than many whites. A small number of black Americans are actually black, most are some shade of brown (Feagin & Feagin, 2003). Although most of the nation's immigrants chose to come to the United States of their own accord, the vast majority of African Americans were brought to America against their will to perform forced labor or be sold as slaves.

Privilege is defined as an advantage given to or enjoyed by a person or group. There are several ways in which privilege has been assigned to selected groups and denied other groups. Few examples of privilege are as explicit as the process of black slavery in North America. Once African American slaves were brought to America, they were not given the same rights as the other immigrants.

Under slave law, blacks and their children were the property of slave owners. Although there were many freed married blacks, family units under slavery existed at the slave-master's discretion. People could marry, but could not own property because slaves, themselves, were considered "property." Slave owners could break up marriages at any time by merely selling one or both of the partners to different owners. Thus, white privilege came at the expense of black oppression.

After slavery, whites created formal and informal laws (known as Jim Crow laws) that continued their control of black labor that they once owned outright. For instance, blacks could not attend the same schools, vote, eat the same restaurants, or use the same restrooms as whites. Such laws were enacted after the Civil War and continued to foster an ideology that blacks were subordinate and inferior to whites (Thompson, 2009).

Myths and Realities about African Americans

Myth: Black people couldn't or didn't resist slavery.

Fact: The weight of historical evidence suggests that enslaved black people throughout the new world developed a culture of continual resistance. In every community, some slaves ran away, committed suicide, or died fighting back. In Jamaica, Surinam, and Brazil, slaves escaped to the mountains and established independent free communities. In Haiti, black people ended slavery by defeating both the Spanish and the French armies. In the United States, slaves fled north and west to freedom and organized several slave rebellions. In addition, the continual agitation of black people like Frederick Douglass helped spark the Civil War, which ended slavery in the United States.

Myth: Most lynchings started when a black man was accused of a sexual incident involving a white woman.

Fact: Sexually motivated lynchings made sensational national headlines; however, carefully-conducted research revealed a more complicated story. In 1892, crusading African American journalist Ida B. Wells published *Southern Horrors*, which investigated hundreds of lynchings. Wells found that more than 70% of the lynchings occurred when the victims tried to vote, demanded their rights, purchased land, or owned successful businesses. Between 1920 and 1950, the NAACP also investigated scores of lynchings and those investigations supported Well's conclusions.

Source: Ruffins & Ruffins (1997).

Today, African Americans now enjoy the same legal rights as whites in the United States. However, it is important to remember that less than 50 years ago African Americans did not have the same human rights as other U.S. citizens, and discrimination toward blacks continues today. The manner

African Americans have strong familial ties that are rooted in Africa and the history of slavery in the U.S. Copyright © 2009 by Monkey Business Images. Under license from Shutterstock, Inc.

by which Africans in the Americas were exploited and stereotyped has left a long-standing mark on the economic and social system in the United States. For instance, black Americans and their families continue to face institutional racism. Racism can occur at an individual or institutional level. *Institutional racism* is a more subtle and indirect form of racism that is rooted in organizational policies and practices that have the effect of disadvantaging certain racial or ethnic groups. For example, institutional racism manifests itself in race-based discrimination in mortgage lending, housing, and bank loans. The term "redlining" was coined in the late 1960s to describe the practice of marking a red line on a map to indicate an area where banks would not invest or lend money; many of those areas were neighborhoods inhabited predominantly by African Americans (Shapiro, 1993). Additional studies show that black patients, compared to white patients of the same socioeconomic status, are less likely to receive breast cancer screening, follow-up visits after hospitalization for mental illness, and eye examinations if they have diabetes (Schneider, Zaslavsky, & Epstein, 2002).

Institutional racism also takes place with respect to employment. As demonstrated in Figure 2.2, African American males earn less than white Americans, even if they have attained exactly the same level of education.

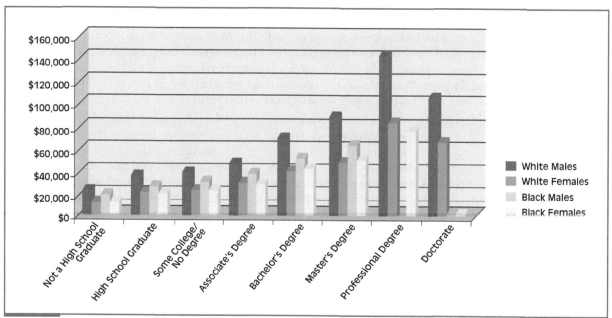

Figure 2.2 Median Income by Level of Highest Degree by Race and Sex, 2005

Famous Firsts by African Americans

1773: First published poet, Phillis Wheatley, *Poems on Various Subjects, Religious, and Moral*

1821: First male patent holder, Thomas L. Jennings, dry-cleaning process

1823: First male college graduate: Alexander Lucius Twilight, Middlebury College

1837: First male physician (M.D.): James McCune Smith, University of Glasgow

1856: First college president, Daniel A. Payne, Wilberforce University, Ohio

1859: First published novelist, Harriet Wilson, *Our Nig*

1862: First female college graduate: Mary Jane Patterson, 1862, Oberlin College

1864: First female physician (M.D.), Rebecca Lee Crumpler, New England Female Medical College

1869: First male U.S. Diplomat, Ebenezer D. Bassett Haiti

1870: First male U.S. Representative, Joseph Rainey, 1870, South Carolina

1870: First male U.S. Senator, Hiram Revels, 1870, Mississippi

1876: First male Ph.D., Edward Bouchet, Yale

1900: First Congressional Medal of Honor winner, Sgt. William H. Carney, for bravery during the Civil War

1917: First combat pilot, Eugene Jacques Bullard

1921: First female Ph.D.'s, Georgiana Simpson, University of Chicago; Sadie Tanner Mossell Alexander, University of Pennsylvania; Eva Beatrice Dykes, Radcliffe College

1940: Inventor of the Blood Bank, Dr. Charles Drew

1940: First U.S Military General, Benjamin O. Davis, Sr.

1946: First male Federal Judge, William Henry Hastie

1950: First Nobel Peace Prize Winner, Ralph J. Bunche, for mediating the Arab-Israeli truce

1950: First Pulitzer Prize Winner, Gwendolyn Brooks, for poetry

1958: First male Grammy Award winner, Count Basie

1958: First female Grammy Award winner: Ella Fitzgerald

1965: First female U.S. Diplomat, Patricia Harris, Luxembourg

1966: First U.S. Cabinet Member, Robert Weaver, Secretary of the Department of Housing & Urban Development

1966: First female Federal Judge, Constance Baker Motley

1967: First U.S. Supreme Court Justice, Thurgood Marshall

1967: First male astronaut, Robert H. Lawrence, Jr.

1969: First female U.S. Representative, Shirley Chisholm, New York

1977: First U.S. Representative to the United Nations, Andrew Young

1989: First Chairman of the Joint Chiefs of Staff, Colin Powell

1992: First female U.S. Senator, Carol Mosely Braun, Illinois

1992: First female astronaut, Mae Jemison

1993: First Nobel Prize Winner for Literature, Toni Morrison

2005: First female Secretary of State, Condoleezza Rice

2008: First elected President of the United States, Barack Obama

Did you know . . .

Black History Month is celebrated annually in February?

Pause for Reflection

What would you say is the major advantage of being Black in today's world?

As a group, what do you think African Americans should be most proud of?

Did You Know

African Americans were the originators of blues music. The roots of the blues are grounded in the experiences of black slaves in the Deep South, particularly the Mississippi Delta. Most musicologists believe that the music can be traced to the work experiences of the first black slaves who, while toiling the hot plantation fields, uttered moans, shouts, and hollers to provide themselves with emotional release from the drudgery of slave labor and to communicate with other slaves working many yards away. Thus, the blues is an original American musical genre, which distinguishes it from many other forms of music played in the United States that were imported in part, or wholesale, from European countries.

After World War I, Blacks migrated from the rural south, searching for better jobs and a better life in the more industrialized northern cities, and the blues migrated with them. By the end of World War II, Chicago had replaced the Mississippi Delta as the home of the blues. The softer, slower, and gentler acoustic blues played in the country gave way to the new, urban blues, which were played louder—due to instrumental amplification, and faster—perhaps reflecting the faster tempo of city life, and rougher—perhaps reflecting the rougher style of inner-city life as well as the amplified (electric) guitar's capacity for reverb, feedback, and other forms of sound distortion. The cranked-up, sped-up, and roughed-up style of urban blues that emerged primarily in Chicago during the late 1940's provided the roots that influenced the later development of amplified "rock and roll" in the 50's, "acid rock" (psychedelic music) in the 60's, "heavy metal" in the 70's, and "hard rock" in the 80's.

Internationally the blues has enjoyed great popularity in western European countries, from which came the "British invasion" of bands, such as the Beatles and Rolling Stones—a band whose name derives from a blues song recorded by Muddy Waters—a famous blues musician. In fact, when the Beatles came to America, among the first questions they asked American reporters was if they could see Muddy Waters (to which, American reporters naively replied: "Where's that?"). Blues has also become popular in Japan, where blues bands play to enthusiastic Japanese audiences who, in many cases, do not fully understand the lyrics, but still feel the emotional intensity and raw instrumental power of the blues.

To think that this music, which now moves people all over the world and has influenced virtually all major forms of contemporary American music, was created by the original African Americans—imported slaves who were socially segregated, economically impoverished, educationally deprived, and illiterate—whose musical skills were entirely self-taught and whose original instruments were entirely self-made—is an astonishing accomplishment. It is also a powerful tribute to the resiliency and creativity of the original African American culture. The blues legacy should neither be overlooked nor underrated simply because their roots are in slavery. Now permanently etched in America's musical memory and continually influencing different musical forms, the blues remain a major artistic contribution of African American people to American culture.

Sources: Charter (1975), Jones (1963), Leadbitter (1971), and Palmer (1981)

Asian Americans

The U.S. Census Bureau continues to define Asians as a single "race." However, Asians come from a wide variety of origins. In addition to Chinese and Japanese Americans, Asian Americans also include citizens who have immigrated to the United States from:

East Asia (e.g., Hong Kong, Mongolia, North Korea, South Korea, and Taiwan);
Southeast Asia (e.g., Cambodia, Malaysia, Philippines, and Vietnam);
South Asia (e.g., India, Bangladesh, and Nepal);
Central Asia (e.g., Afghanistan, Tajikistan, and Sri Lanka); and
Pacific Islands (e.g., Polynesia, Micronesia, and Melanesia).

Asian culture stresses strong kinship and familial ties. Copyright © 2009 by Monkey Business Images. Under license from Shutterstock, Inc.

As a result of discrimination and prejudice, Asian immigrants were not allowed to marry whites, own homes, obtain an education, or live in certain areas. These limitations resulted in the first "Chinatowns" being created, but not from a desire of Asians to live exclusively with one another. Rather, they were forced to create their own restaurants, businesses, and housing areas because they were excluded from the general population (AsianNation.org, 2008).

Myths and Realities about Asian Americans

Myth: All Asians share the same culture.
Fact: Asian Americans and Pacific Islanders come from diverse origins and have a wide variety of cultural backgrounds.
Myth: In college, Asians major exclusively in the fields of science, technology, engineering, and math (i.e., STEM subjects).
Fact: Asian American and Pacific Islander students pursue a broad range of academic fields of study.
Myth: Asian college students are concentrated in prestigious colleges and universities, and are outperforming all other racial and ethnic groups.
Fact: Asian American and Pacific Islander students enroll most heavily in their local public two-year and four-year institutions, and the risk for dropping out of college is as high among certain Asian groups as it is for other minority groups.

Asians are America's second-fastest growing group (after Hispanics). The Asian population in the U.S. is projected to increase by 213% between the years of 2000 and 2050, compared to a total population increase of 49% over the same time period. By 2050, 8% of the total U.S. population will identify themselves as Asians. After Spanish, the most widely spoken non-English language in the U.S. is an Asian language—Chinese, which is spoken by 2.5 million Americans (AsianNation.org, 2008).

Famous Firsts by Asian Americans

1921: First movie star, Anna May Wong, in *Bits of Life*

1932: First female aviator, Katherine Sui Fun Cheung

1951: First host of a network TV series, Anna May Wong, *The Gallery of Madame Lie Tsong*

1956: First male U.S. Representative, Dalip Singh Saund, California

1959: First U.S. Senator, Hiram Fong, Hawaii

1964: First female U.S. Representative, Patsy Takemoto Mink, Hawaii

1971: First Mayor of Major U.S. City, Norman Yoshio Mineta, San Jose, California

1971: First Federal Court Judge, Herbert Choy

1974: First Governor, George R. Ariyoshi, Hawaii

1976: First star of a network sitcom, Pat Morita, in *Mr. T and Tina*

1984: First Oscar (Best Supporting Actor), Haing Ngor, in the *The Killing Fields*

1985: First astronaut, Ellison Onizuka (died in the '86 Challenger disaster)

1989: First anchor of a national radio program, Emil Guillermo, NPR's *All Things Considered*

1989: U.S. Ambassador, Julia Chang Bloch, Ambassador to Kingdom of Nepal

1992: First to be selected in the first round of professional football league draft, Eugene Chung, New England Patriots

1993: First nightly news anchor, Connie Chung, CBS

2000: First Member of Presidential Cabinet, Norman Yoshio Mineta, Secretary of Commerce

DID YOU KNOW . . .

Asian Pacific American Heritage Month is celebrated annually in May?

Pause for Reflection

When you think about the history of Asian Americans in the United States, what thoughts or events come to mind?

What do you think Asian Americans should be most proud of?

Gender and Sexual Diversity

Women

Although women are not a minority group in terms of their overall population, they have faced significant prejudice and discrimination throughout history. The Women's Rights Movement began in 1848 when a young housewife and mother from New York by the name of Elizabeth Cady Stanton, along with four female friends, organized a convention that was held in Seneca Falls, N.Y. In preparation for the event, Stanton used the Declaration of Independence as a guide to draft her own "Declaration of Sentiments." Thus, she tied the women's rights movement directly to the rights of citizens outlined by the nation's founding fathers. Her Declaration of Sentiments specified the following injustices:

- Women could not vote.
- Married women were legally dead in the eyes of the law.
- Women had to follow laws they had no part in drafting.
- Married women had no property rights.
- Husbands had legal power over and were responsible for their wives to a degree where they could imprison or beat them with impunity.
- Divorce and child custody laws gave no rights to women.
- Women had to pay property taxes even though they had no representation in the levying of these taxes.
- Many professional occupations were closed to women completely and when they were allowed to work, the compensation was only a fraction of what a man would earn.
- Women were barred from entering medical and law professions.
- Women could not be admitted to any college or university to further their education.
- With only a few exceptions, women were not permitted to participate in the affairs of the church.
- Women were deprived of self-confidence and self-respect, making them totally dependent on men.

As a result of the success of the initial convention in 1848, other conventions were held regularly between 1850 and the start of the Civil War. Prominent women in the movement traveled the country speaking on behalf of equal rights for the next forty years. The movement encountered intense opposition, and it took more than 70 years before women secured the right to vote in 1920 (National Women's History Project, 1998).

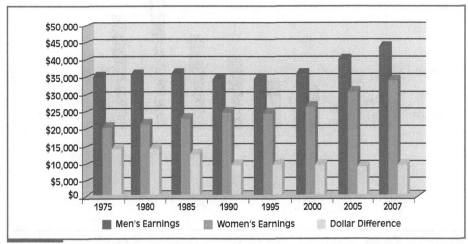

Figure 2.3 Wage Gap
Source: National Committee on Pay Equity, 2008

Women continue to overcome professional barriers (glass ceilings) in today's society. Copyright © 2009 by Chiyacat. Under license from Shutterstock, Inc.

Although women have earned the right to vote and many now hold professional positions that were in the past dominated by men, women still experience inequities with respect to employment compensation. In 1963, women earned 59 cents to every dollar earned by men, which prompted President John F. Kennedy to sign the Equal Pay Act into law, making it illegal for employers to pay unequal wages to men and women who perform the same jobs. In 2004, women still earned only 77 cents to every dollar earned by men. In 2005, the median annual earnings of women ages 15 and older were $31,858 compared to $41,386 for their male counterparts (National Women's Law Center, 2007). Females with graduate degrees earn only slightly more than males with a high school diploma: $41,995 for women vs. $40,822 for men (Rose & Hartmann, 2004).

Wage gaps continue to persist in many professional occupations as well. In 2005, the median weekly income earned by women in the same occupation as men was significantly lower. For example, females earn only a percentage of male salaries in the following professions:

- Physicians: 61%
- Sales: 63%
- Construction: 79%
- Computers and Mathematics: 86%

(National Committee on Pay Equity, 2008).

A study conducted of management positions in ten industries which together employ over 70% of women in the American workforce, found that the wage gap actually increased between 1995 and 2000 (National Women's Law Center, 2007). American females today still earn less than American males, even if they have attained the same level of education (see Figure 2.4).

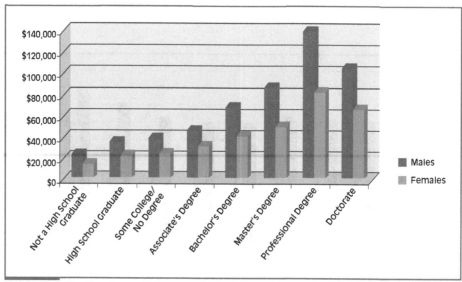

Figure 2.4 Median Income by Level of Highest Degree by Sex, 2005
Source: National Women's Law Center, 2007

Although laws have been created to equalize pay for men and women, segregation of males and females into separate careers continues to take place. Certain fields are dominated by one sex (e.g., most nurses are female, most engineers are male, and there has never been a female President or Vice President of the United States). Women make up approximately 25% of the labor force in the fields of science, technology, engineering, and mathematics (STEM) careers (U.S. Census Bureau, 2005). Although women have made great gains in certain employment in fields once dominated by males, females still remain a small minority in STEM occupations—which also tend to be some of the highest paid professions. Figure 2.5 depicts the percentage of women represented in various professional fields.

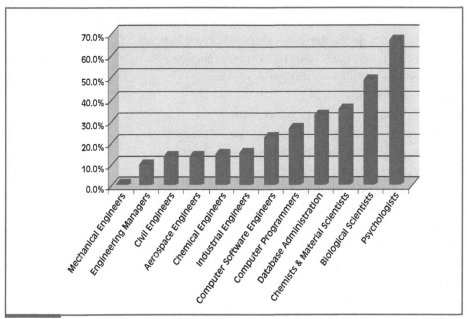

Figure 2.5 Percentage of Women in Selected Occupations
Source: CPST, *Professional Women and Minorities*, 2007

Pause for Reflection

Are females likely to be represented in equal numbers as males in the career field(s) you are considering? Why do you think this is so?

Famous Firsts by American Women

1650: First published American writer, Anne Bradstreet, *The Tenth Muse Lately Sprung Up in America*

1707: First professional artist, Henrietta Johnston

1766: First publisher in America, Mary Katherine Goddard, *Providence Gazette* newspaper

1809: First patent holder, Mary Kies, method of weaving straw with silk

1849: First physician (M.D.), Elizabeth Blackwell

1853: First ordained minister, Antoinette Blackwell

1866: First dentist, Lucy Hobbs, Ohio College of Dental Surgery

1869: First lawyer, Arabella Mansfield

1872: First presidential candidate, Victoria Claflin Woodhull, nominated by the National Radical Reformers

1887: First Mayor, Susanna Medora Salter, Argonia, Kansas

1896: First film director, Alice Guy Blaché, *La Fee aux Choux (The Cabbage Family)*

1914: First to conduct a symphony orchestra, Mary Davenport-Engberg, Bellingham Washington

1916: First to be elected to the U.S. House of Representatives, Jeannette Rankin, Montana

1921: First to receive a Pulitzer Prize for Fiction, Edith Wharton, *The Age of Innocence*

1925: First to serve as a State Governor, Nellie Tayloe Ross, Wyoming

1932: First to fly solo across the Atlantic, Amelia Earhart

1932: First to be elected to U.S. Senate, Hattie Wyatt Caraway, Arkansas

1933: First member of a presidential cabinet, Frances Perkins, Secretary of Labor

1934: First to serve as director of a major corporation, Frances Perkins, Coca-Cola

1946: First to be canonized as a saint, Mother Maria Frances Cabrini

1964: First woman nominated for president by a major party, Margaret Chase Smith

1970: First female jockey to ride in the Kentucky Derby, Diane Crump

1972: First Rabbi, Sally Jean Priesand

1981: First U.S. Supreme Court Justice, Sandra Day O'Connor

1983: First astronaut, Sally K. Ride

1984: First to run for vice president on a major political party, Geraldine Ferraro, Democrat

1990: First U.S. Surgeon General, Dr. Antonia Novello

1991: First Mayor of a Major City, Sharon Pratt Dixon, Washington, DC (Dixon was also African American)

1992: First to be elected to U.S. Senate, Carol Moseley-Braun, Illinois

1993: First U.S. Attorney General, Janet Reno

1997: First Secretary of State, Madeleine Albright

2000: First former First Lady to be elected to National Office, Hillary Clinton, New York

2006: First to win the Indianapolis 500 automobile race, Danica Patrick

2007: First Speaker of U.S. House of Representatives, Nancy Pelosi

DID YOU KNOW . . .
Women's History Month is celebrated annually in March?

Pause for Reflection

What would you say are the major pros and cons of being a woman in America today?

As a group, what do you think women should be most proud of?

Gay, Lesbian, Bisexual, and Transgender (GLBT) People

Although the debate continues as to whether gay and lesbian households should be considered "legal" families, the reality is that nearly 600,000 same-sex couples reside in the United States. It is estimated that there are 6–9 million children in America who live in a household where there are two gay or lesbian parents (Stein, Perrin, and Potter, 2004). In the United States, there are approximately 3 million GLBT people over the age of 55, and by 2030, that number is expected to double. Despite their sizable numbers, GLBT people continue to face prejudice and discrimination. A survey of 24 federal senior-citizen agencies in the United States revealed that 50% would not welcome GLBT seniors if their sexual orientation were known (National Gay and Lesbian Task Force Summit, 2005). In a study of 14 college campuses, it was found that 36% of all GLBT undergraduate students experienced harassment

More and more gay and lesbian couples are adopting children in the U.S. today. Copyright © 2009 by Galina Barskaya. Under license from Shutterstock, Inc.

within the past year. The study also found that 51% concealed their sexual orientation or gender identity to avoid intimidation (Rankin, 2003).

The GLBT population is currently undergoing its own civil rights movement, trying to gain the same rights and respect that women and minority groups fought to attain. It appears as if they are making headway. For example, a recent survey of GLBT college students revealed that, although 43% rated the overall campus climate as homophobic, 64% agreed that their work place or classroom accepted them as GLBT people and 72% felt that their college provided visible resources on GLBT issues and concerns (Rankin, 2003).

Myths and Realities about Gays and Lesbians (Homosexuals)

Myth: Homosexuality is a type of mental illness and can be cured by appropriate psychotherapy.

Fact: In 1973 the American Psychiatric Association removed homosexuality from its list of official mental illnesses. In 1974, the American Psychological Association did the same, and went further to state that: "Homosexuality, per se, implies no impairment in judgment, stability, reliability, or general social or vocational capacities."

Myth: People who are lesbian, gay, and transgender can usually be identified by certain mannerisms or physical characteristics.

Fact: There is as much variation among GLBT people in mannerisms and physical characteristics as there are among heterosexuals. Only a small percentage of GLBT people display stereotypical mannerisms and characteristics. The fact is that heterosexuals also display some characteristics that are stereo-typically "gay."

Myth: The majority of child molesters are gay or lesbian.

Fact: Studies repeatedly show that, the vast majority of child molestation (over 90%) is performed by heterosexual males.

To gain a complete and accurate understanding of diversity and its effects, it is important to remember that each human is a unique individual, yet at the same time, is a member of multiple groups. The effects of belonging to different groups do not operate independently; instead, they work together in a combinatorial fashion to affect an individual. For instance, a person's sexual orientation/identity and race/ethnicity produce a combined effect on individuals who simultaneously belong to both of these groups. Evidence for this combinatorial effect is demonstrated by the results of a survey of approximately 1,200 gay and bisexual Hispanic males, in which 64% of the respondents reported that in addition to experiencing prejudice from society as a whole about their sexual orientation, they also experienced racism from white members of the gay, lesbian bisexual, transgender (GLBT) community (Cianciotto, 2005). Similar findings surfaced from a survey of 2,700 black GLBT people conducted in 2000, in which it was found that many of the respondents faced a double dose of discrimination because of their race/ethnicity and sexual orientation (Dang, Frazer, 2004).

Personal Experience In the 2008 election, the majority of California voters supported a proposition that made gay marriages illegal. A larger percentage of Black and Hispanic American voters supported this proposition than did Whites. When Black and Hispanic voters were asked how they could vote to deny rights to a minority group (gays and lesbians) when their own racial or ethnic minority group had to fight for equal rights, their most common response was: Gays and lesbians *choose* to be who they are; we were born into our group.

I have always been puzzled by the idea that we choose our sexual orientation or identity. Why would someone choose to be a member of a group that was so often the target of intense prejudice and discrimination? Why would someone voluntarily run the risk of not being accepted by family and friends, and having fewer rights and opportunities?

I've also wondered why I never made a conscious choice to be heterosexual. If sexual orientation were a matter of choice, why didn't I ask myself at puberty: Should I choose to be straight or gay? That question never entered my mind; I was just naturally attracted to members of the opposite sex—just as it was natural for me to be right-handed rather than left-handed. I've always suspected that it was the same for people who were gay or lesbian—they were naturally (biologically) attracted to members of the same sex, rather than consciously choosing to be gay. I've also thought that we choose one thing over another (e.g., mustard over mayonnaise) after we have experienced both options and decide we like one better than the other. Virtually all gays and lesbians I've known in my life have told me that they were aware that they had a "different" sexual orientation *before* they ever had a homosexual or heterosexual experience, and despite being surrounded by heterosexual family members and friends. This suggests to me that their sexual orientation was not a matter of personal choice, but a matter of natural predisposition.

When I checked the research on sexual orientation, the results matched my personal experience: The vast majority of gays report knowing they were gay before actually experimenting with homosexual or heterosexual activity and despite being surrounded by heterosexual role models (Pillard & Bailey, 1998). My research on sexual orientation also led me to discover that same-sex relationships were widespread in the animal kingdom—at all levels of the evolutionary ladder—ranging from insects to mammals (Driscoll, 2008). These findings lead me to the conclusion that it is normal or "natural" for a percentage of any living species to be attracted to members of the same sex.

—Joe Cuseo, *Professor of Psychology and co-author of this text*

Pause for Reflection

What does the expression "gay" mean to you?

Today the term "gay" is used more frequently than the older term "homosexual." Do you think one of these terms is less offensive or prejudicial than the other?

Socioeconomic Diversity

Two primary criteria used to define socioeconomic status (SES) are *income* level and level of *education*. Each of these components of SES will be discussed in this section.

Diversity in Income

According to U.S. Census figures, the wealthiest 20% of the American population controls approximately 50% of the total American income, and the poorest 20% controls 4% of the nation's income. Sharp differences in income levels exist between people of different race, ethnicity, and gender. A recent survey revealed that black households had the lowest median income in 2007 ($33,916), compared to a median income of $54,920 for non-Hispanic White households (Current Population Survey Annual Social and Economic Supplement, 2008). A greater percentage of people of color live in poverty (U.S. Census Bureau, 2000), and people who live in poverty are more likely to be targets of discrimination (Lott, 2002).

Poverty remains a persistent problem in the United States. In 2007, 12.5% or 37.3 million people in the U.S. lived in poverty, making America one of the most impoverished of all developed countries in the world (United Nations, 2008). Minority groups experience poverty at a higher rate than the white majority group. For example, the poverty rate in 2007 for whites was 8.2%, for Asians it was 10.2%, for Hispanics it was 21.5%, and for Blacks it was 24.5% (U.S. Census Bureau, 2008). All racial and ethnic groups experience poverty but it is more egregious among certain groups.

In 2007, 85% of the U.S. population were natives and 12.5% were foreign born. The poverty rate for natives was at 11.9%; for Americans who were born in other countries it was 16.5%. Among those born in foreign countries, who were naturalized citizens, the poverty rate was 9.5%; the rate for non-citizens was 21.3% (U.S. Census Bureau, 2008).

Poverty also strikes Americans unequally in different geographic regions. In the South (where the majority of the African American population resides), the poverty rate is 14.2%. Poverty rates in the other regions of the country are as follows: the Northeast (11.4%), the Midwest (11.1%), and the West (12%) (U.S. Census Bureau, 2008).

Personal Experience   When I was 4 years old and living in the mountains of Kentucky, it was safe for a young lad to walk the railroad tracks and roads alone. My mother knew this and would send me to the general store to buy a variety of small items we needed for our household. Since we had very little money, she was aware of the fact that we had to be cautious and only spend money on the staples we needed to survive. I could only purchase items from the general store that I could carry back home by myself and the ones my mother strictly ordered me to purchase. Most of these items cost less than a dollar and many times you could buy multiple items for a dollar in the early 1960s. At the store, I would hand my mother's handwritten list to the owners and would pick the items for me. On the checkout counter there were jars with different kinds of candy or gum. You could buy two pieces for $.01. I didn't think there would be any harm in rewarding myself with two pieces of candy after doing a good deed. After all, I could devour the evidence of my disobedience on my slow walk home. Upon returning home, my mother being the protector of the vault and the sergeant-of-arms in our household, would count each item I brought home to make sure I had been charged correctly. She always found that I was missing one cent!

Growing up in poverty wasn't fun but we managed to eat. What we ate had to be reasonable in price and bought in bulk. Every morning my mother fixed rice or oatmeal for breakfast along with wonderful buttermilk biscuits. Every night she fixed pinto beans and cornbread for dinner. We also had fresh vegetables from the garden and apples, hickory nuts, and walnuts from surrounding trees. Meat was not readily available and was only eaten when we killed a chicken or hog that we had raised.

—Aaron Thompson, *Professor of Sociology
and co-author of this text*

WORDS OF WISDOM

"The most important thing I got out of college was self-confidence. All my life, I heard subtle and not so subtle messages that I was inferior, and even if I wasn't that I couldn't really succeed like a white person could. College taught me I could. Besides, going to college was the key to a good job—a one-way ticket out of the ghetto and the means to give something back to my community. Now I have a real reason to have black pride. I think the most important thing I learned in college was that we must fight for equality not just by demonstrating, but by showing the world that we can."

AFRICAN AMERICAN COLLEGE GRADUATE, QUOTED IN NEMKO (1988)

Pause for Reflection

What would you say is the factor that is most responsible for poverty in:

a.   the United States?

b.   the world?

Diversity in Level of Education

Approximately 35% of todays 18- to 24-year-olds are non-white, making it the most diverse generation in American history (The Echo Boomers, 2004). Although there is more racial and ethnic diversity among college students to-

day than at any other time in the history of the United States, the college enrollment rates for minority groups are still consistently lower than those of majority students. For instance, 69% of majority students graduating from high school go on to college, compared to 55% of black high school graduates and 58% of Hispanic high school graduates (National Center for Education Statistics, 2008).

In 2007, 29% of the U.S. population reported having completed a bachelor's degree. Among Americans 25 years and older, the percentage of different groups attaining a bachelor's degree was as follows: Asians (52%), non-Hispanic Whites (32%), Blacks (19%), and Hispanics (13%) (U.S. Census Bureau, 2008).

The justice system has served as a mechanism to provide civil rights for many Americans from all population groups. Copyright © 2009 by James Steidl. Under license from Shutterstock, Inc.

A Timeline of Key Historical Events — → SNAPSHOT SUMMARY
Relating to Diversity and Equality in America

1619   The first 20 Africans are sold to settlers in Virginia as "indentured servants." This started the path to slavery in the U.S.

1789   The U.S. Constitution is adopted. Slaves are counted as 3/5 of a person for means of representation.

1818   African American slave, Molly Williams, is the first-known woman firefighter. Owned by a member of Oceanus Engine Company #11 in New York City, Williams helped the crew during blizzard.

1831   Nat Turner leads slave revolt in Virginia.

1838   Over 18,000 Cherokees are forcibly removed from their land and resettled west of the Mississippi.

1848   First Women's Rights Convention meeting in Seneca Falls, N.Y. Elizabeth Cady Stanton proposes a constitutional amendment giving women the right to vote.

1851   Sojourner Truth, an African American woman, gave her famous "Ain't I a Woman?" speech at the Women's Rights Convention in Akron, Ohio. The Women's Rights Movement grew in large part out of the antislavery movement.

1861   The Civil War begins.

1863   President Lincoln signs the Emancipation Proclamation. The proclamation declares "that all persons held as slaves" within the rebellious states "are, and henceforward shall be free."

1865   The Civil War ends. Lincoln is assassinated. The Freedmen's Bureau is established to help former slaves. Ku Klux Klan forms in Tennessee. The 13th Amendment to the Constitution is ratified, stating that "neither slavery nor involuntary servitude . . . shall exist."

1867   Over 2,000 Chinese workers on the Central Pacific Railroad strike for better pay.

1868   The 14th Amendment is ratified, making African Americans full citizens of the U.S., prohibiting states from denying equal protection or due process of law. Women petition to be included but are turned down.

1870   The 15th Amendment is ratified, guaranteeing the right to vote will not be denied on account of race. First segregation law is passed in Tennessee, mandating separation of African Americans from whites on trains. By 1885, most Southern states have laws requiring separate schools.

1873   In *Bradwell v. Illinois*, the Supreme Court affirms that states can restrict women from the practice of any profession to preserve family harmony and uphold the "Law of the Creator."

1875   Congress passes the first Civil Rights Act, requiring equal accommodations for blacks with whites in public facilities other than schools.

   Congress passes the Chinese Exclusion Act, restricting the immigration of all Chinese laborers for 10 years and requiring Chinese to carry identification cards. (Renewed in 1892 for an additional 10 years.)

1883   The Civil Rights Act of 1875 is voided by the Supreme Court.

1886   Women's Suffrage Amendment asking for voting rights and the privilege of being heard on the floor of Congress reaches the Senate floor. It is defeated.

1896   Supreme Court rules on *Plessy v. Ferguson*, upholding "separate but equal" accommodations under Jim Crow laws. The National Association of Colored Women is founded and becomes a major vehicle for attempted reforms on behalf of women and people of color for the next 40 years.

1909   Women garment workers strike in New York for better wages and working conditions. Over 300 shops eventually sign union contracts.

   The National Association for the Advancement of Colored People (NAACP) is founded.

1910   The Mexican Revolution brings an influx of immigrants to the U.S. seeking safety and employment.

1916   Jeannette Ranking (R-Mont.) becomes the first woman elected to Congress.

1917   During WWI, many women enter into jobs working in industries such as mining, chemical manufacturing, auto and railway plants, streetcar conducting and mail delivery.

1920   The 19th Amendment gives women the right to vote and is ratified by the required 36 states. When African American women try to register to vote in most Southern states, they face property tax requirements, literacy tests and other obstacles.

1921   Emergency Immigration Restriction Law introduces a quota system that favors northern and western Europeans.

1924   Congress passes the Indian Citizenship Act, granting U.S. citizenship to Native Americans. Several nations, including the Hopi and the Iroquois, decline citizenship in favor of retaining sovereign nationhood.

1942   Following the bombing at Pearl Harbor, U.S. government interns over 110,000 Japanese Americans in "relocation Camps" encircled by barbed wire.

1947   Jackie Robinson becomes the first African American to play major league baseball.

1948   The Women's Armed Services Integration Act grants women permanent status in the Army, Navy, Marine Corps and Air Force.

1954   In *Brown v. Board of Education* of Topeka, Kansas, the Supreme Court rules that deliberate public school segregation is illegal.

1955   Fourteen-year-old Emmitt Till from Chicago, who was visiting his family in Mississippi, is kidnapped, brutally beaten, shot, and dumped in the Tallahatchie River for allegedly whistling at a white woman. Two white men, J. W. Milam and Roy Bryant, are arrested for the murder and acquitted by an all-white jury. They later boast about committing the murder in a *Look* magazine interview. The case becomes a cause célèbre of the civil rights movement.

   In Montgomery, Alabama NAACP member Rosa Parks refuses to give up her seat at the front of the "colored section" of a bus to a white passenger, defying a southern custom of the time. In response to her arrest, the Montgomery black community launches a bus boycott. The boycott lasts for more than a year, until the buses are desegregated Dec. 21, 1956.

1957   Central High School in Little Rock, Arkansas, meets with legal resistance and violence. Nine African American students attend the school with the presence of federal troops.

1960   Four black students from North Carolina Agricultural and Technical College in Greensboro, NC begin a sit-in at a segregated Woolworth's lunch counter. Although they are refused service, they are allowed to stay at the counter. The event triggers many similar nonviolent protests throughout the South. Six months later, the original four protesters are served lunch at the same Woolworth's counter. Student sit-ins would be effective throughout the Deep South in integrating parks, swimming pools, and theaters.

1961   More than 1000 volunteers from different races, known as the "Freedom Riders," took bus trips through the South to test out new laws that prohibit segregation in interstate travel facilities, including bus and railway stations. They were attacked by angry mobs along the way.

1962   Cesar Chavez leads the United Farm Workers Union to win bargaining power for Mexican Americans.

1963   Martin Luther King, Jr. delivers his "I Have a Dream" speech at the March on Washington.

1964   Congress passes the Civil Rights Act, protecting citizens against discrimination and segregation.

   Patsy Mink (D-HI) is the first Asian American woman elected to the U.S. Congress.

1965   President Johnson signs executive order requiring federal agencies and contractors to take "affirmative action" in overcoming employment discrimination. President also signs the Immigration Act, which eliminates race, creed and nationality as a basis for admission to the U.S.

Malcolm X, black civil rights leader, is assassinated.

1966   The National Organization for Women (NOW) is established to fight for political equality.

1967   Congress passes the Age Discrimination Act of 1967, prohibiting employment discrimination against older Americans.

1968   Martin Luther King, Jr. is assassinated. Unrest and civil disorders erupt in 124 cities across the country.

President Johnson signs the Civil Rights Act of 1968, aimed at curbing discrimination in housing.

Senator Robert Kennedy is assassinated.

The American Indian Movement (AIM) is founded in Minneapolis.

1969   Police raid the Stonewall Inn, a Greenwich Village bar catering to homosexuals, resulting in two nights of rioting and the beginning of the Gay Rights Movement.

1972   Title IX of the Education Amendment prohibits gender discrimination in educational programs or activities that receive federal assistance.

1973   The Civil Service Commission eliminates height and weight requirements, which have discriminated against women applying for police, park service and firefighting jobs.

In *Roe vs. Wade*, the Supreme Court strikes down most states' restrictive abortion laws, greatly expanding a woman's right to legal abortion.

Congress passes section 504 of the Vocational Rehabilitation Act barring discrimination against disabled people under any program or activity receiving federal funds.

1975   President Ford signs law admitting women to military academies. The American Medical Association calls for the repeal of all state laws barring homosexual acts between consenting adults.

1976   Title IX goes into effect, opening the way for women's increased participation in athletic programs and professional schools.

1978   In the Regents of the University of California v. Bakke case, the Supreme Court upholds affirmative action principles but rejects fixed racial quotas as unconstitutional. Bakke had been denied a slot in medical school and claimed to be a victim of reverse discrimination when a minority student with lower test scores gained admission through affirmative action.

The Pregnancy Discrimination Act amends the 1964 Civil Rights Act to ban employment discrimination against pregnant women.

1982   The Equal Rights Amendment falls three states short of ratification. The amendment would have written into the Constitution equal pay for equal work, a guarantee of social opportunity and a ban on sexual bias.

The Supreme Court rules that children of undocumented immigrants have a right to free public schooling.

1984   The Supreme Court holds that states have the right to outlaw homosexual acts between consenting adults.

1986   The Supreme Court declares that sexual harassment is a form of illegal job discrimination. Coined in 1975, the term sexual harassment is defined as "uninvited and unwelcome verbal or physical conduct directed at an employee because of his or her sex."

1990   Congress passes the Americans with Disabilities Act, banning discrimination against people with disabilities.

1993   President Clinton pursues his policy of lifting the ban prohibiting gays from serving in the military. Faced with congressional opposition, Clinton announces a "don't ask, don't tell, don't pursue" policy, which falls short of allowing or protecting lesbians and gay men in the military.

1995   Air Force Lt. Col. Eileen M. Collins becomes the first woman pilot of a space shuttle.

1996   Proposition 209 passes in California, abolishing the state's affirmative action programs in hiring, contracting and educational admissions.

2003   In a 5–4 decision, the Supreme Court of the United States upholds the University of Michigan Law School's policy, ruling that race can be one of many factors considered by colleges when selecting their students—because it furthers "a compelling interest in obtaining the educational benefits that flow from a diverse student body."

2007   James Bonard Fowler, a former state trooper, is indicted for the murder of Jimmie Lee Jackson 40 years after Jackson's death. The 1965 killing leads to a series of historic civil rights protests in Selma, Alabama.

2008   Barack Obama becomes the first black president of the United States.

Source: PBS.ORG, 2008

Personal Experience

At the time of the writing of this book, there are high emotions going into the presidential election of 2008. This is the first time that an African American is the candidate for a major party and, as it turned out, the first time an African American was elected President of the United States. As a person who grew up in an environment and times where history books only discussed African Americans in terms of slave roles, this is very much a historic occasion. As an African American who is the great grandson of slaves, this is a time that I did not think I would see in my lifetime. However, the success of this candidate reached across many diverse lines: generational, racial, ethnic, religious, socioeconomic, political party affiliation, etc. Although we have a long way to go to break down all the barriers that keep us separated in this country, I am an American who is very proud today to see a new chapter added to the American Dream. In fact, all of America should be proud that we expressed our diversity in action and moved America one step forward in our global family.

—Aaron Thompson, *Professor of Sociology and co-author of this text*

Religious Diversity

In 2007, humans around the world reported the religious affiliations depicted in Figure 2.6.

Among those who reported being Christian, 17% reported that they were Roman Catholic, 5.8% Protestant, 3.5% Orthodox, and 1.3% Anglican (*The World Factbook*, 2008).

In the United States, approximately 90% of Americans report having a religious preference (Gallup, 2004). While all of the world religions are represented in the United States, most Americans report that they are Christians or Jews (Luhman, 2007). More specifically, 49% of Americans report being Protestant, 23.7% Catholic, 2.2% Jewish, 0.5% Muslim, 0.5% Buddhist, and 0.4% Hindu (Kosmin, Mayer,

Religious beliefs are as diverse as cultural values among individuals. Copyright © 2009 by Magdalena Kucova. Under license from Shutterstock, Inc.

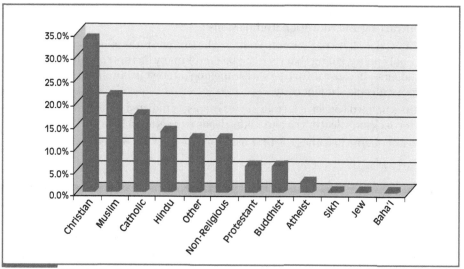

Figure 2.6 World Religions, 2007
Source: The World Factbook, 2008

& Keyser, 2001). The top ten religious bodies in the United States are represented in Figure 2.7.

In a study conducted by the Pew Forum on Religion and Public Life, the majority of Americans report that they are tolerant of other religions and do not believe that their religion is the only path to salvation (America.gov, 2008).

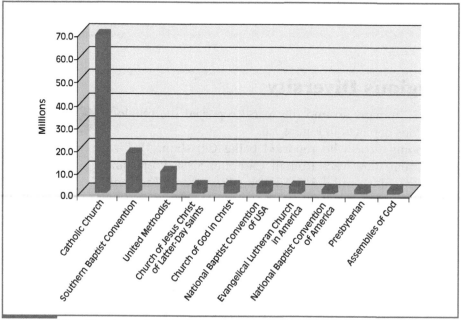

Figure 2.7 Top Ten Organized Religions, 2005
Source: 2005 Yearbook of American and Canadian Churches

Pause for Reflection

Are you a member of an organized religion? Why or why not?

How do you think the majority of students on your campus would have answered the above questions?

Generational Diversity

Humans are also diverse with respect to the generation in which they grew up. Generation refers to a group or cohort of individuals born and raised during the same historical period. As a result of their common historical experience, members of the same generation may develop certain personal characteristics, values, and attitudes related to the influential events that took place in the world during their formative years of development (e.g., childhood, adolescence, and young adulthood). Since each generation experiences different historical events, it is likely that these different events shape their personalities in different ways. For example, people who grew up during the Great Depression (1920s and '30s)

As life expectancy increases, people of multiple generations will be working side by side. Copyright © 2009 by Andresr. Under license from Shutterstock, Inc.

may be more likely to develop the habit of being financially conservative and not wasting anything, especially food. The generation born after World War II experienced significant political and world events, such as Vietnam and the human rights movement, which may make them more likely to question or distrust authority. The generation born during the late '60s and '70s was the first to see the American family shattered by high divorce rates and to witness the beginning of the AIDS crisis. For these reasons, this generation may be the most pessimistic or skeptical of all generations. Americans born between the '80s and the beginning of the 21st century were the first to view a mass murder of students in a school setting (Columbine) and the 9/11 terrorist attack on the United States, which may explain why this may be the most sheltered generation of our time.

Listed below is a more detailed description of generational diversity, the key historical events that occurred during the period in which each generation grew up, and the characteristics that have been associated with each generation.

- The *"Traditional Generation," aka the "Silent Generation"* (born during the years 1922–1945). This generation was influenced by events such as the Great Depression and World War I and II. Characteristics associated with this generation include loyalty, patriotism, respect for authority, valuing logic and discipline, and resistance to change.

- The *"Baby Boomer" Generation* (born during the years 1946–1964). This generation was influenced by events such as the Vietnam War, Watergate, and the human rights movement. Characteristics associated with this generation include idealism, need for personal fulfillment, and concern for equal rights.

    Note: In 2030, all baby boomers will be 65 and older, and they will account for nearly 1 of every 5 U.S. residents. The 65 and older age group is expected to more than double in number, from 38.7 million (2006) to 88.5 million (2050). During the same time period, the 85 and older population is likely to more than triple, from its current number of 5.4 million to 19 million. In contrast, the percentage of the population in the "working ages" (18 to 64) is projected to decline from 63% in 2008 to 57% in 2050.

- *"Generation X"* (born during the years 1965–1980). This generation was influenced by Sesame Street, creation of MTV, AIDS, and the soaring divorce rates—producing the first generation of "latchkey" children—children who used a key hung around their neck or placed under a mat to let themselves into their home after school (because their single parent was working). The characteristics associated with this generation include self-reliance, resourcefulness, and being comfortable with change.

- *"Generation Y," aka "Millennials"* (born between 1981–2002). This generation was influenced by the 9/11 terrorist attack on the United States, the shooting of students at Columbine, and the collapse of the Enron corporation. The characteristics associated with this generation include a preference for working and playing in groups, being fully immersed in technology, and a willingness to engage in volunteerism or service to the community (hence, they are sometimes referred to as the "civic generation"). Millennials tend to regard themselves as special because they received unprecedented attention from their parents. They are also the most ethnically diverse generation in American history, which may explain why they are thought to be the most open to diversity and see it as a positive experience. Both Generation X and Generation Y seek to have a balance between work and life; unlike their parents who devoted a lifetime to one company, these generations see moving and change as a necessity (Lancaster & Stillman, 2002).

Pause for Reflection

Look back at the characteristics associated with your generation. Would you say that they accurately reflect your personal characteristics?

Are there any particular characteristics that clearly do (or do not) reflect who you are?

I have a 24-year-old daughter who is a third grade school teacher. During a weekend visit she decided to develop her lesson plans for the following week. Sitting at my desk in front of the computer I noticed that she was talking in a microphone to someone on my computer (some sort of device that uses the computer as a telephone and even allows her to see the person with whom she is talking). Anyway, while in the throws of that conversation, I noticed she was also texting on her cell phone. Moreover, she was completing the lesson plans and screaming at her brothers and sisters for being too loud while she was working. I have determined that the Generation Y crowd is multi-talented and way beyond my academic reaches. However, I have figured out how to text and use email while listening to music on my multi-talented telephone. The gap is closing!

—Aaron Thompson, *Professor of Sociology
and co-author of this text*

Individual Diversity (Individual Differences)

Regardless of one's group membership, each individual within a group has personal characteristics that make him or her unique. Due to differing genetic makeups and personal life experiences, individuals of the same group will differ from one another in a large variety of ways. Some of the more important ways in which this individual diversity is experienced and expressed are summarized in the following snapshot summary.

 ## Key Dimensions of Individual Diversity —————▶ SNAPSHOT SUMMARY

Personal Interests: What an individual *likes* to do or *enjoys* doing.

Personal Values: What an individual finds *important*, *cares* about, believes in, or considers to be a high priority.

Self-Concept: How individuals view themselves. Two components of self-concept, in particular, can have a dramatic impact on an individual's development and success:

Self-Esteem: How individuals *feel* about themselves (e.g., positive, negative, or neutral) and their level of *self-confidence* in different situations (e.g., academic, social, or occupational)

Self-Efficacy: The degree to which individuals believe they are in control of their own fate. For instance: Do they think their success depends largely on their own effort and that they have the power to change things for the better? Or, do they believe that personal success depends largely on factors beyond their control (e.g., their past or present circumstances) and that they cannot change or improve the quality of their life (e.g., due to lack of ability or resources).

Aptitudes or Talents: An individual's ability or potential to do certain things *well* (e.g., intellectual, social, or emotional intelligence).

W ORDS OF
ISDOM

"Do what you value; value what you do."

SIDNEY SIMON, VALUES CLARIFICATION AND IN SEARCH OF VALUES

Learning Styles: How an individual *prefers* to learn, that is, the way in which a person prefers to:

Receive information (e.g., reading from books or listening to speakers),
Perceive information (e.g., through sight, sound, or touch), and
Process information: how an individual prefers to deal mentally with information once it has been received or perceived (e.g., studying about it alone, or talking about it with others in study groups).

Personality Traits: Individual differences in *temperament, emotional* characteristics and *social* tendencies (for example, whether the individual tends to be an introvert or extrovert).

"Never desert your line of talent. Be what nature intended you for and you will succeed."

SYDNEY SMITH, 18TH-CENTURY ENGLISH WRITER, AND DEFENDER OF THE OPPRESSED

Many psychological and educational tests and inventories have been developed to measure individual differences and allow you to compare your results with others. This *comparative perspective* can give you an important reference point for assessing whether your preferences or personal characteristics are high, average, or low in relation to your peers. By seeing how your results compare with others, you can gain greater awareness of your distinctive traits, tendencies, strengths, and weaknesses. For example, on a learning styles test, you can determine whether your preference for learning through concrete, hands-on experience is higher or lower than other college students. Or, on a career-interest inventory, you can get feedback on how your interest in different careers compares with other people who have taken the same inventory.

Different offices or centers on your campus are likely to have self-assessment instruments available, which you can take to assess your personal characteristics. For instance, you could go to the:

- Learning Center (Academic Support Center)—for instruments that assess your learning styles and learning habits,
- Career Development Center—for instruments that assess your personal interests, aptitudes, and values, and
- Personal Counseling Center—for instruments that assess your personality traits, temperament, emotional tendencies, and social characteristics.

Take advantage of the self-assessment instruments that are available on your campus. You can use the results to increase your self-awareness, and you can use your increased self-awareness to improve the quality of your learning strategies, educational decisions, and life choices. You can begin this process of self-assessment by reading and responding to the following information about individual differences.

Multiple Intelligences: Individual Differences in Natural Talents or Abilities

Intelligence was once considered to be a single, general intellectual trait that could be detected and measured by an IQ (Intelligence Quotient) test. Today, the singular word "intelligence" has been replaced by the plural word "intelligences" because humans display intelligence or mental ability in many ways other than intellectual performance on paper-and-pencil tests.

Based on studies of gifted and talented individuals, experts in different lines of work, and a variety of other sources, Howard Gardner (1983, 1993) had identified multiple types of human intelligence.

Pause for Reflection

As you read about the different forms of intelligence included in the following snapshot summary, rate yourself in terms of how strong or talented you think you are with respect to each type of intelligence, using the following scale:

1 = very weak   2 = weak   3 = average   4 = above average   5 = very strong

---

Forms of Multiple Intelligence ⟶ SNAPSHOT SUMMARY

Linguistic Intelligence: Ability to communicate through words or language. For example: verbal skills in the areas of speaking, writing, listening, or reading.

Logical–Mathematical Intelligence: Ability to reason logically and succeed in tasks that involve mathematical problem-solving. For example, skillful at making logical arguments and using logical reasoning; or, the ability to think effectively with numbers and make quantitative calculations.

Spatial Intelligence: Ability to visualize relationships among objects arranged in different spatial positions and the ability to perceive or create visual images. For example, forming mental images of three-dimensional objects; detecting detail in objects or drawings; artistic talent for drawing, painting, sculpting, or graphic design; or skills related to sense of direction and navigation.

Musical Intelligence: Ability to appreciate or create rhythmical and melodic sounds. For example, playing, writing, or arranging music.

Interpersonal (Social) Intelligence: Ability to relate to others, to accurately identify others' needs, feelings, or emotional states of mind; and the ability to effectively express emotions and feelings to others. For example: skills involving interpersonal communication and emotional expression; ability to accurately "read" the feelings of others, or meet the emotional needs of others.

Intrapersonal (Self) Intelligence: Ability to self-reflect, become aware of, and understand one's own thoughts, feelings, and behavior. For example: capacity for personal reflection, emotional self-awareness, and self-insight into personal strengths and weaknesses.

Bodily–Kinesthetic (Psychomotor) Intelligence: Ability to use one's own body skillfully and to acquire knowledge through bodily sensations or movements. For example: skill at tasks involving physical coordination; ability to work well with hands; mechanical skills; talent for building models and assembling things; or skills relating to technology.

Naturalist Intelligence: Ability to carefully observe and appreciate features of the natural environment. For example: keen awareness of nature or natural surroundings; ability to understand causes or consequences of events occurring in the natural world.

Source: Howard Gardner (1993). *Frames of Mind: The Theory of Multiple Intelligences.*

Personal
Experience

I have an assistant (Rhonda) that has been working with me for many years. Indeed, she will be kind enough to give me feedback and input on this personal story and everything else in this book. She will also point out that including her name in this book isn't what she would consider helpful to the readers or to her. In other words, she likes being the quiet mover and shaker. Rhonda is an interesting intellectual person who is very much an introvert. She is a strong visual learner (many have said that she has a photographic memory). She pays a lot of attention to the little details that many of us extroverts leave open. Thank goodness! By the way when you read this, it sounds a lot better because of Rhonda.

—Aaron Thompson, *Professor of Sociology and co-author of this text*

Learning Styles: Individual Differences in Preferred Ways of Learning

W̲ORDS OF
̲ISDOM

"Minds differ still more than faces."

VOLTAIRE, 18TH-CENTURY FRENCH PHILOSOPHER, HISTORIAN, AND POET

In contrast to multiple intelligences, which refer to differences in learning abilities or talents, learning styles refers to differences in learning *preferences* i.e., different ways in which individuals prefer to perceive (receive or take-in) information and process information (deal with information once it has been received). For instance, individuals differ in terms of whether they prefer to acquire information by listening to it (auditory learning style), seeing an image or diagram of it (visual learning style), or physically touching and manipulating it (kinesthetic learning style). Individuals may also vary in terms of whether they prefer to receive information in a form that is very structured and orderly, or in an unstructured form that allows them the freedom to explore, play with, and restructure it in their own way.

After information has been received, individuals may also differ in terms of how they prefer to process or deal with it. For instance, some individuals like to think about it on their own, while others may prefer to talk about it with someone else, make an outline of it, or draw a picture of it.

Personal
Experience

In my family, whenever something needs to be assembled or set up (e.g., a ping-pong table or new electronic equipment), I've noticed that my wife, my son, and myself have different learning styles in terms of how we prefer to go about doing it. I like to read the manual's instructions carefully and completely before I even attempt to touch anything. My son prefers to look at the pictures or diagrams in the manual and uses them as models to find all the parts; then he begins to assemble those parts. My wife seems to prefer not to look at the manual at all. Instead, she likes to figure things out as she goes along by grabbing different parts from the box and trying to assemble parts that fit together—like piecing together pieces of a jigsaw puzzle.

—Joe Cuseo, *Professor of Psychology and co-author of this text*

There are specially designed tests that you can take to assess your individual learning style and how it compares with others. A popular learning styles instrument that may be available on your campus is the *Learning Styles Inventory (LSI)* (Dunn, Dunn, & Price, 1990), which was originally developed by David Kolb, a professor of philosophy (Kolb, 1976; 1985). It is based on how individuals differ with respect to the following two key elements of the learning process:

---

1. How Information Is Perceived (Taken in)

Concrete Experience
Learning through direct involvement
or personal experience

Reflective Observation
Learning by watching or observing

2. How Information Is Processed (Dealt with after it has been taken in)

Abstract Conceptualization
Learning by thinking about things
and drawing logical conclusions

Active Experimentation
Learning by taking chances
and trying things

Figure 2.7 Two Key Elements of the Learning Process

When these two dimensions are crisscrossed to form intersecting lines, four sectors (areas) are created, each of which represents a different learning style, as shown in Figure 2.8.

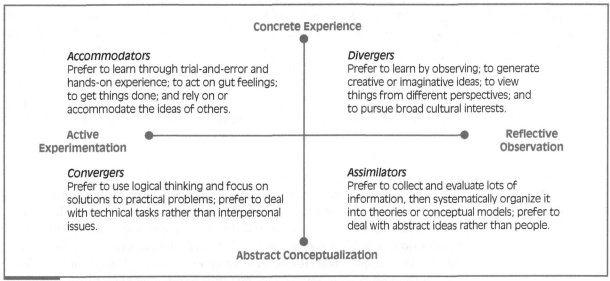

Figure 2.8 Learning Styles Measured by the Learning Styles Inventory (LSI)

Pause for Reflection

Look at the four styles in Figure 2.8.

Which one of these styles do you think best reflects your most preferred way of learning?

Do you see your learning style to be more compatible with certain academic subjects than others?

People in the medical field are most often found to be convergent thinkers.
Copyright © 2009. Under license from
Shutterstock, Inc.

Research indicates that students majoring in different fields tend to display differences in the four learning styles measured by the Learning Styles Inventory (Svinicki & Dixon, 1987). For instance, "assimilators" are more frequently found to major in mathematics and natural sciences (e.g., chemistry and physics), possibly because these subjects stress reflection and abstract thinking. In contrast, academic fields where "accommodators" tend to be more frequently found are business, accounting, and law, perhaps because these fields involve taking practical action and making concrete decisions. "Divergers" are more often attracted to majors in the fine arts (e.g., music, art, drama), humanities (e.g., history, literature) or social sciences (psychology, political science), possibly because these fields emphasize different viewpoints and multiple perspectives. In contrast, "convergers" are more likely to be found in fields like engineering, medicine, and nursing, probably because these fields focus on finding specific solutions to practical and technical problems (Kolb, 1976). When college and university faculty were asked to identify the learning styles emphasized by their academic field, this same pattern of relationships between learning styles and academic fields was found (Biglan, 1973; Carnegie Commission on Higher Education, cited in Svinicki & Dixon, 1987).

Personal Experience When I was teaching a psychology course that was required for students majoring in nursing and social work, I first became aware that students in different academic fields may have different learning styles. I noticed that some students in class seemed to lose interest (and patience) when we got involved in lengthy class discussions about controversial issues or theories, while others seemed to love it. On the other hand, whenever I lectured or delivered information for an extended period of time, some students seemed to lose interest (and attention), while others seemed to get "into it" and took great notes. After one class period that involved quite a bit of class discussion, I thought about the students who seemed to be most involved in the discussion that day and the students who seemed to drift off or lose interest. I realized that the students who did most of the talking and seemed most enthused during the class discussion were the students majoring in social work. On the other hand, most of the students who appeared disinterested or a bit frustrated were the nursing majors.

When I began to think about why this happened, it dawned on me that the nursing students were accustomed to gathering factual information and learning very practical skills in their major courses, and this was the learning style they were expecting to use in my psychology course. The nursing majors felt more comfortable with structured class sessions in which they received lots of factual, practical information from the professor. On the other hand, the social work majors were more comfortable with unstructured class discussions because courses in their major often emphasized debating social issues and hearing different viewpoints or perspectives.

I left class that day with the following question on my mind: Did nursing majors and social work students select their major because the style of learning emphasized by the major tended to "match" their preferred learning style?

—Joe Cuseo, *Professor of Psychology*
and co-author of this text

The Engineering and Humanities majors settle their differences in the Fine Arts quad!

The research on the relationship between learning styles and academic majors may have practical implications for you. If you are thinking about majoring in a particular field, it is important to consider how your learning style aligns with the style of learning emphasized by that field. If the match seems to be close or a good fit, then it should result in a satisfying and successful "marriage" between you and your major.

We recommend taking a trip to the Learning Center or Career Center on your campus, where you can take a test designed to assess your learning style. Even if the results do not help you choose a major or confirm the major you have already chosen, it will help you become more aware of your particular learning style. Gaining this self-knowledge alone should promote your academic success because research shows that just becoming more self-aware of your learning style can improve your academic performance in college courses (Claxton & Murrell, 1988).

WORDS OF WISDOM

"In order to succeed, you must know what you are doing, like what you are doing, and believe in what you are doing."

WILL ROGERS, AMERICAN ACTOR, HUMORIST, AND NATIVE AMERICAN

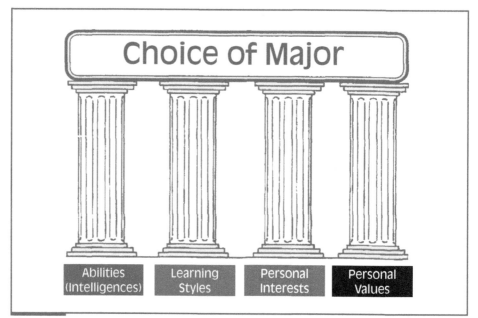

Figure 2.9 Personal Characteristics That Provide an Effective Foundation for Choice of a College Major

Pause for Reflection

In addition to taking formal tests to assess your learning style, you can gain some awareness of your learning styles through some simple introspection or self-examination. Take a moment to complete the following sentences. How you complete these sentences may trigger additional self-insight into your learning style.

I learn best if ....

I learn most from ....

I enjoy learning when ....

Personality Types: Individual Differences in Personal Traits or Characteristics

One of the most well known categories of personality types was created by psychologist, John Holland (1985). He identified the following six types as being most relevant to and individual's career choice:

Realistic: practical, physical, hands-on, tool-oriented

Investigative: analytical, intellectual, scientific, explorative

Artistic: creative, original, independent, chaotic

Social: cooperative, supporting, helping, healing/nurturing

Enterprising: competing, leading, persuading

Conventional: detailed, organized, clerically-minded

The *Vocational Preference Inventory (VPI)*, is a career test that has been developed to help individuals decide what career(s) are most compatible with their particular personality type (Holland, 1997).

Another frequently used personality test is the *Myers–Briggs Type Indicator (MBTI)* (Myers, 1976; Myers & McCaulley, 1985), which is based on the personality theory of psychologist Carl Jung. It consists of four dimensions, each of which has a pair of opposite traits or preferences, along which people vary on a scale or continuum from lower to higher. The four dimensions and opposite traits are illustrated in Figures 2.10 and 2.11.

Pause for Reflection

As you read the following scales, place a mark along the line where you think you fall with respect to these traits. For example, place a mark in the middle of the line if you think you are midway between these opposite traits, or place a mark at the far left or far right if you think you lean very strongly toward the trait listed on either end.

Extraversion Prefer to focus on "outer" world of persons, actions, or objects	*Introversion* Prefer to focus on "inner" world of thoughts and ideas
Sensing Prefer interacting with the world directly through concrete, sensory experiences	*Intuition* Prefer dealing with symbolic meanings and imagining possibilities
Thinking Prefer to rely on logic and rational thinking when making decisions	*Feeling* Prefer to rely on human needs and feelings when making decisions
Judging Prefer to plan for and control events	*Perceiving* Prefer flexibility and spontaneity

Figure 2.10 Traits and Learning Styles Measured by the Myers–Briggs Type Indicator (MBTI)

Pause for Reflection

Identify someone you know who has a very different personality than you. Look at the four pairs of personality traits listed in Figure 2.10, on which one(s) do your differ?

What do you think caused these differences to develop in the first place?

It has been found that college students who score differently on the MBTI prefer to write in different ways (Jensen & Ti Tiberio, as cited in Bean, 2001), as seen in Figure 2.11.

This research suggests that there is a relationship between an individual's personality traits and preferred writing style. Thus, it may be important to keep in mind when choosing or confirming your major that different academic fields emphasize different styles of writing. Some fields place heavy emphasis on writing that is structured and tightly focused (e.g., science and business), while other fields encourage writing with personal style, flair, or creativity (e.g., English and art). How your writing style meshes with the style emphasized by different academic fields may be a key factor to consider when making decisions about your college major.

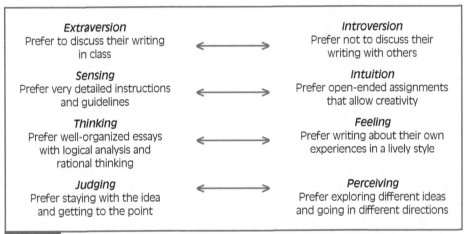

Figure 2.11 Students with Each MBTI Learning Style Have a Preferred Style of Writing

Summary

America is rapidly becoming a more racially and ethnically diverse nation. Currently, the minority population in the U.S. is at an all-time high, and by the middle of the 21st century, the minority population will comprise more than 50 percent of America's total population, making minorities the "new majority." As a result of this increasing diversity, "intercultural competence" —the ability to understand cultural differences and to interact effectively with people from different cultural backgrounds—has become an important skill for success in today's world.

Among the diversity of ethnic groups found in the United States, *American Indians* are the only ethnic group that can truly be called "native" Americans. American Indians have contributed much to the history of the United States, including the names of approximately one-half of it states.

Hispanics represent the largest minority population in the United States, and they are also the fastest growing minority group. By the middle of the 21st century, Hispanics will account for one-third of the American population.

In contrast to other racial ethnic groups who chose to come to the United States, the vast majority of *African Americans* were brought to America against their will to perform forced labor or be sold as slaves. Today, African Americans now enjoy the same personal rights as Whites in the United States. However, black Americans continue to face institutional racism—a more subtle and indirect form of racism that is rooted in organizational policies and practices that disadvantage people of color. For example, African American males earn less than white Americans, even if they have attained exactly the same level of education.

Asians are defined by the U.S. Census Bureau as a single "race." However, Asians come from multiple countries and origins. Asians are America's second-fastest growing group (after Hispanics), and after Spanish, the most widely spoken non-English language in the U.S. is Chinese.

Women do not represent a minority group in terms of their percentage of the American population; however, similar to ethnic and racial minorities, they have faced significant prejudice and discrimination throughout history. Women still face wage discrimination, as evidenced by the fact that females with graduate degrees earn only slightly more than males with a high school diploma, and women in the same profession as men (e.g., physicians) earn less than their male counterparts.

There are more than a half million same-sex couples residing in the United States, and 6–9 million children in America who currently live in households headed by two gay or lesbian parents. *GLBT* people continue to face prejudice and discrimination; for example, the majority of GLBT college students report they conceal their sexual orientation or gender identity to avoid intimidation and discrimination.

Socioeconomic status (SES) is defined primarily by income level and level of education. People of color have lower average levels of income and are more likely to live in poverty than whites. Although there is more racial and ethnic diversity among college students today than at any other time in the history of the United States, the level of educational attainment of Native Americans, African Americans, and Hispanics remains consistently lower than those of Whites and Asians.

There is substantial *religious* diversity in America; all of the world religions are represented in the United States. Approximately 90% of Americans report having a religious preference, the majority of whom report being Christians or Jews. The majority of Americans also report that they are tolerant of other religions and do not believe that their religion is the only path to salvation.

Human diversity also comes in the form of *generational* differences. A generation refers to a group or cohort of individuals born during a particular historical period, whose personal characteristics may be shaped by key events that took place in the world during the historical period in which they lived. To date, the following generations have been identified:

a. Traditional (Silent) Generation: born during the years 1922–1945
b. Baby Boomer Generation: born during the years 1946–1964
c. Generation X: born during the years 1965–1980
d. Generation Y (Millennials): born during the years 1981–2002

Regardless of one's group membership, humans display individual diversity. Each individual within a group has personal characteristics that make him or her unique. Due to different genetic make-up and different personal experiences, individuals within the same group will differ from one another in a large variety of ways which include: personal interests, values, self-concept, self-esteem, self-efficacy, learning styles, intelligences (aptitudes or talents), and personality traits (emotional and social characteristics).

Diversity in the United States is here to stay. Diversity is increasing and will continue to increase throughout the current century. Understanding its history, current forms, and future direction is critical to understanding our society and our role in it. The ability to communicate with and relate to diverse groups of people has become an essential skill for success in today's world.

Chapter 2 Exercises

Name

_____

Date

_____

2.1 Family Ties

Answer the following questions to the best of your ability:

a. What is the race or ethnicity of your father, mother, and grandparents?

b. How strongly do your family members identify with their race or ethnicity?

c. How strongly do you identify with your race or ethnicity?

d. How do your views of other racial or ethnic groups differ from those of your parents and grandparents?

(Adapted from *American Public Works Association Diversity Resource Guide*, pg. 19.)

2.2 Community Ties

a. What was the majority ethnic group in the neighborhood where you grew up?

b. How much exposure did you have to other racial or ethnic groups during your elementary and high school years?

c. If you had contact with other racial ethnic or racial groups, where did this contact typically take place?

2.3 Personal Idols and Role Models

a. My personal hero is . . .

b. The most important issue facing our country today is . . .

c. For me, the historical figure that has had the most positive influence on America was . . .

Do you think that your answers to any the above questions were influenced by your membership in any of the groups you identified with in Exercise 1.1?

2.4 Cross-Cultural Curiosity

Write down (in question form) one thing you have always wondered about, or would like to know more about, the following groups of people:

a. Native Americans (American Indians)

b. Hispanic Americans (Latinos)

c. African Americans

d. Asian Americans

e. Elderly (senior citizens)

f. Gays or lesbians

Would you feel comfortable approaching a member of each of these groups to ask your question about their culture? Why or why not?

2.5 Cross-Cultural Interview

Find a student, faculty member, or an administrator on campus whose cultural background is different from yours, and ask if you could interview that person about his or her culture. Use the following questions in your interview:

a. How is "family" defined in your culture, and what are the traditional roles and responsibilities of different family members?

b. What are the traditional gender (male/female) roles associated with your culture? Are they changing?

c. What is the culture's approach to time?
(e.g., Is there an emphasis on punctuality? Is doing things fast valued or frowned upon?)

d.   What are your culture's staple foods or favorite foods?

e.   What cultural traditions or rituals are highly valued and commonly practiced?

f.   What special holidays are celebrated?

The Benefits of Experiencing Diversity

3

Purpose

In Chapters 1 and 2, diversity was defined and described. This chapter moves beyond the question of what diversity is to the question of why diversity is beneficial. The primary purpose of this chapter is to increase your awareness of the multiple benefits of diversity, which, in turn, should increase your enthusiasm and motivation for experiencing diversity.

Activate Your Thinking

What advantage(s) would there be to experiencing diversity for a member of a majority group who has never been a victim of prejudice or discrimination?

W̲ORDS OF
I̲SDOM

"Empirical evidence shows
that the actual effects on
student development of
emphasizing diversity and
of student participation
in diversity activities are
overwhelmingly positive."

ALEXANDER ASTIN, *WHAT MATTERS
IN COLLEGE*

Diversity Promotes Self-Awareness

Learning from people with diverse backgrounds and experiences sharpens your self-knowledge and self-insight by allowing you to compare and contrast your life experiences with others whose life experiences differ sharply from your own. By stepping outside yourself to view the differences and similarities you share with other people, you take a step toward viewing yourself from a new perspective. You move beyond an egocentric viewpoint to take the multiple perspectives of other people and other times; you acquire a reflective mirror that allows you to view yourself from a comparative perspective. This *comparative perspective* gives you a new reference point for viewing your own life, placing you in a position to see more clearly how your unique cultural background has influenced the development of your personal beliefs, values, and lifestyle.

You see what is distinctive about yourself, and how you may be uniquely advantaged or disadvantaged. For instance, by learning about the limited opportunities there are for people to attend college in many countries today, and the limited opportunities there were for certain groups of people in our own country some time ago, you become immediately aware of the opportunity that you have today to participate in higher education and reach your full potential—regardless of your race, gender, age, or prior academic record. This is truly a distinctive privilege that should neither be overlooked nor taken for granted.

When students around the country were interviewed about their diversity experiences in college, many of them reported that these experiences enabled them to learn more about themselves. Some said that their interactions with students from different races and ethnic groups produced "unexpected" or "jarring" self-insights (Light, 2001).

STUDENT PERSPECTIVE

"I remember that my self-image was being influenced by the media. I got the impression that women had to look a certain way. I dyed my hair, wore different clothes, more makeup . . . all because magazines, TV, [and] music videos 'said' that was beautiful. Luckily, when I was 15, I went to Brazil and saw a different, more natural beauty and came back to America more as myself. I let go of the hold the media image had on me."

FIRST-YEAR COLLEGE STUDENT

"Variety is the spice of life, O'Toole; but at this firm conformity is the meat and potatoes."

© Patrick Hardin. Reproduction rights obtainable from www.CartoonStock.com

Diversity Stimulates Social Development

When you interact with people from a variety of groups, you widen your social circle by expanding the pool of people with whom you can interact and form relationships. Just as we seek variety in what we eat to stimulate our taste buds, seeking variety in the people with whom we interact stimulates our social development. In fact, research indicates that students who have more diversity experiences in college report higher levels of satisfaction with their college experience (Astin, 1993).

Also, by widening the range of people with whom you interact, you gain greater social self-confidence and are more able to adapt to new people and new situations (Miville, Molla & Sedlacek, 1992). You strengthen your ability to relate to people with diverse experiences and interests, and you are able to dialogue with others on a wide variety of topics. This social versatility makes you a more interesting (and interested) person who is less likely to be left out of conversations or have the topic of conversation "go over your head." Last, diversifying your perspectives through interaction with diverse cultural groups is a stimulating experience; it reduces your risk of becoming bored (and boring).

WORDS OF **W**ISDOM

"Variety is the spice of life."
AMERICAN PROVERB

"Viva la difference!"
(Long live difference!)
FAMOUS FRENCH SAYING

Pause for Reflection

What three skills do you think are most important for success in any career or profession?

Diversity Enriches the Multiple Perspectives Developed by a Liberal Arts (General) Education

Appreciating diversity is consistent with the goals of a liberal arts education because it helps to liberate (free) you from the tunnel vision of ethnocentric and egocentric (self-centered) viewpoints, enabling you to get beyond yourself and see yourself in relation to the world around you. Just as the different subjects you take in the liberal arts curriculum open your mind to multiple perspectives, so do different experiences you have with people from multiple backgrounds. Exposure to diverse groups of people expands your consciousness by expanding your perspective beyond the narrow-focus lens of your own culture (a monocultural perspective) to a wide-focus lens for viewing multiple cultures (a multicultural perspective).

Expanding your circle of friends allows you the opportunity to expand your worldview. Copyright © 2009 by Monkey Business Images. Under license from Shutterstock, Inc.

Our perception of reality is a blending of facts (objectivity) and our interpretation of those facts (subjectivity)—which is shaped and molded by our particular cultural perspective (Paul, 1995). Viewing issues from a broader "world view" enables you to perceive "reality" and evaluate "truth" from different vantage points; this advantages your thinking by making it more comprehensive and less ethnocentric.

The key components of a world view are illustrated in the following concept map (see Figure 3.1).

WORDS OF **W**ISDOM

"Without exception, the observed changes [during college] involve greater breadth, expansion, and appreciation for the new and different."

ERNEST PASCARELLA AND PAT TERENZINI, *HOW COLLEGE AFFECTS STUDENTS*

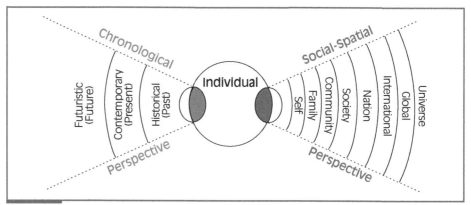

Figure 3.1 Multiple Perspectives Developed by Diversity and the Liberal Arts

In Figure 3.1, the center circle represents the *individual*. Fanning out to the right is a series of arches that encompass the *social–spatial perspective*—which includes increasingly larger social groups and more distant places, ranging from the narrowest perspective (self) to the widest perspective (universe). Diversity frees you from the narrow tunnel vision of an egocentric viewpoint and provides you with a panoramic perspective of the world, enabling you to move outside yourself and see yourself in relation to other people and other places.

To the left of the individual in Figure 3.1, there are three arches labeled the *chronological perspective*, representing the perspective of time: past (historical), present (contemporary), and future (futuristic). Diversity not only widens your perspective, it also lengthens it by stretching your vision beyond the present, enabling you to see yourself in relation to other humans who have lived before you and those who will live after you. This chronological perspective gives you the hindsight to understand where the world has been, insight into what condition the world is in now, and foresight into what direction the world may be going.

It might be said that the *social–spatial* perspective provides you with a conceptual telescope for viewing aspects of the world that are far away, while the *chronological* perspective provides you with a mental "time machine" that can be used to flash back to the past and fast forward to the future. A brief description of the specific dimensions that make up each of these two major perspectives is provided below.

WORDS OF **W**ISDOM

"Those who cannot remember the past are damned to repeat it."

GEORGE SANTAYANA, SPANISH-BORN AMERICAN PHILOSOPHER

Dimensions of the Chronological Perspective

The *historical* dimension is critical for understanding the root causes of our current human condition and world situation. Humans are products of both their social and natural history. Don't forget that our earth is estimated to be more than 4.5 billion years old and our human ancestors date back more than 250,000 years (Knoll, 2003). Thus, our current lives represent a very narrow frame of time in a very long chronological reel. Every modern convenience we now enjoy reflects the collective efforts and cumulative knowledge of diverse human groups that has accumulated over thousands of years of history. Studying the past and understanding how it is influencing the present helps us to build on our ancestors' prior achievements and avoid their previous mistakes. For example, by understanding the causes and consequences of the holocaust, we help reduce the risk of such an atrocity occurring again.

A historical perspective also makes us consciously aware of how certain groups of people have been maligned and mistreated in the past and how the consequences of that mistreatment are still being experienced today.

The *contemporary* perspective focuses on understanding the present world situation and current events that comprise today's "news." For instance, rapid technological changes are now making global communication and international interdependence a reality, which, in turn, is creating the current demand for college graduates to possess cross-cultural knowledge and intercultural skills.

The *futuristic element* of the chronological perspective focuses on looking forward and envisioning what the world will be like years from now. This perspective focuses on such questions as: Will the world be in better shape and become a better place for humans to live in it after we are gone, including our children and grandchildren? How can humans avoid short-term or shortsighted thinking and adopt a long-range vision that will enable them to anticipate, prepare for, and adapt to the future? For example, America's racial and ethnic groups, whom we now call "minorities," will be the "new majority" of the future (Glassman, 2000). Thus, the future well-being of the United States will hinge upon the ability of future Americans to appreciate and capitalize on its country's domestic diversity.

A comprehensive chronological perspective brings the past, present, and future onto a single screen. It enables us to see how the current world is a single segment in a long temporal sequence that has been shaped by events that preceded us, and how our future world will be shaped by what we do now.

To gain this comprehensive chronological perspective, Western cultures (e.g., United States and Canada) may need to modify their strong cultural tradition of taking a "monochronic" perspective—focusing intently on the present—the "here and now" and dealing with events one at a time. Western cultures may benefit from adopting the more "polychromic" perspective of Eastern cultures (e.g., India and China), which do not view time as separate and discrete segments (past, present, future) but as a continuum in which these three dimensions of time merge together as a continuous flow of interdependent events (LeBaron, 2003; Novinger, 2001).

WORDS OF WISDOM

"The future is literally in our hands to mold as we like. But we cannot wait until tomorrow. Tomorrow is now."

ELEANOR ROOSEVELT, UNITED NATIONS DIPLOMAT, HUMANITARIAN, AND WIFE OF PRESIDENT FRANKLIN D. ROOSEVELT

WORDS OF WISDOM

"We all inherit the past. We all confront the challenges of the present. We all participate in the making of the future."

ERNEST BOYER & MARTIN KAPLAN, *EDUCATING FOR SURVIVAL*

Pause for Reflection

How would you apply the information that you have just read to interpret the following statement: "We can't know where we're going until we know where we've been?"

Dimensions of the Social–Spatial Perspective

As can be seen in Figure 3.2, the first element of the social–spatial perspective is the self. Among the many goals of a college education, the one that has the longest history and most frequent emphasis is self-awareness—to "know thyself" (Cross, 1982). To do so, you need to step outside yourself and view yourself objectively. By doing so, you remove personal blinders and increase self-awareness, which is also the first step to overcoming personal biases that underlie prejudice and block diversity appreciation. (Bias and prejudice will be discussed in detail in Chapter 4.)

Self-awareness is also the first step to personal growth and future success. The "self" is composed of multiple elements or dimensions. As depicted in Figure 3.2, there are diverse dimensions of the self that join together to form the "whole person," all of which play an important role in personal development.

"It is difficult to see the picture when you are inside the frame."

AN OLD SAYING (AUTHOR UNKNOWN)

Figure 3.2 Key Elements of *Holistic (Whole-Person)* Development

Key Dimensions of the Self

Cognitive—knowledge, thoughts, and self-concept
Emotional—feelings, emotional adjustment, and mental health
Social—interpersonal interactions and relationships
Physical—bodily health and wellness
Vocational (Occupational)—career development and satisfaction
Ethical—values and moral convictions
Spiritual—beliefs about the meaning or purpose of life and the hereafter
Personal—self-concept, personal identity, and personal habits (e.g., how time and money is spent).

Pause for Reflection

Look back at the dimensions of self. Which one of these dimensions do you think represents your strongest area? Which one would you say is your weakest dimension or in most need of improvement?

We are not just thinking (intellectual) beings or working (vocational) beings; we are also social, emotional, physical, ethical, and spiritual beings. In Figure 3.2, these diverse dimensions of the self are joined or linked to represent the fact that they are interrelated and do not work independently, but interdependently to affect an individual's development and well-being (Love, & Love, 1995). For instance, our emotional state can be influenced by our social relationships (e.g., whether we feel lonely or loved); our intellectual performance can be influenced by our emotional state (e.g., whether we are relaxed or anxious); and our social relationships can be influenced by our physical condition (e.g., whether we have a positive or negative physical self-image). If one link in the chain is strengthened or weakened, other dimensions of the self are likely to be simultaneously strengthened or weakened. For example, research shows that when college students gain more knowledge, they also attain higher levels of self-esteem and greater social self-confidence (Pascarella & Terenzini, 1991, 2005).

Thus, the self is a diverse, multidimensional entity that has the capacity to develop along a variety of interdependent dimensions. Research on college students indicates that their college experience affect them in multiple ways and promotes the development of multiple dimensions of self (Bowen, 1997; Feldman & Newcomb, 1994; Pascarella & Terenzini, 1991).

Whether you experience these associated developments depends on how you go about "doing" college. For the college experience to have maximum positive impact on multiple areas of self-development, you need to take advantage of the "total" college environment. This includes not only courses in the curriculum, but also learning experiences available to you *outside the classroom*. Research consistently shows that out-of-class experiences are equally important for promoting students' overall development as the course curriculum (Kuh, 1995; Kuh et al., 1994); hence, these out-of-class learning experiences are referred to as the *co-curriculum*. The co-curriculum includes a wide variety of support services and programs on campus. Listed below are some of the key college services and programs that comprise the co-curriculum, accompanied by the primary dimensions of the self that they are designed to develop:

- Intellectual Development: Academic Advising, Learning Center, Library, Tutoring Services, Information Technology Services, Campus Speakers, Concerts, Plays, and Galleries
- Emotional Development: Counseling Services, Peer Counseling and Peer Mentoring Programs
- Social Development: Student Activities, Student Organizations, Campus Clubs, Residential-Life Programs, Commuter Programs
- Physical Development: Student Health Services, Athletics, Intramural Sports
- Spiritual Development: College Chaplain, Campus Ministry, Peer Ministry
- Ethical Development: Judicial Review Board, Academic Integrity Committee, Student Government
- Vocational Development: Career Development Services, Internships, Service Learning, Work-Study Programs, Major Fairs, Career Fairs
- Personal Development: Counseling Services, Financial Aid Services, Campus Workshops, Peer Counseling, Peer Mentoring Programs

WORDS OF WISDOM

"The research portrays the college student as changing in an integrated way, with change in any one area appearing to be part of a mutually reinforcing network or pattern of change in other areas."

PASCARELLA & TERENZINI, *HOW COLLEGE AFFECTS STUDENTS*

The above list represents just a sample of the total number of programs and services that may be available on your campus. As you can see from the length of the list, colleges and universities are armed and ready to promote your development in multiple ways.

Experiencing diversity through the curriculum and co-curriculum represents an integral element of a liberal arts education—the component of your college experience that has been intentionally designed to equip you with a broad-based, "well-rounded" learning experience, which prepares you for success in any career and prepares you for life. Research demonstrates that our quality of life depends upon attention to and integration of the different dimensions of self. For instance, people who are physically and mentally healthy, and who are most likely to achieve personal success and happiness, are typically individuals who have managed to integrate all key dimensions of the self, resulting in their development of a "well-*rounded*" person who lives a "well-*balanced*" life (Covey, 1990; Goleman, 1995; Heath, 1977).

REMEMBER: To promote your development as a "whole person," a liberal arts education relies on both the curriculum *and* co-curriculum, and requires use of the *total* college environment, including experiencing diversity inside and outside the classroom.

Perspective of the Family

Moving beyond the self, individuals comprise a larger social unit—the *family*. The people with whom you have interacted since birth certainly have played a key role in affecting the person you are today. Moreover, this influence can go both ways; the individual can also affect or influence his or her family. For example, your decision to go to college may make your parents and grandparents proud, and may influence the decision of other members of your family to attend college. Furthermore, if you are a college student with children, your graduation from college will affect your children's future welfare. Research indicates that the children of college graduates experience improved intellectual development, physical health, and economic security (Bowen, 1977, 1997; Pascarella & Terenzini, 1991, 2005).

To understand the family perspective is to appreciate diversity because individuals have joined together in multiple ways to form different types of families, such as those listed below.

- Nuclear families, which contain two spouses and one or more children
- Extended families, which include members who are related to the nuclear family (e.g., grandparents, uncles, aunts, adult children, etc.)
- Families with or without children

There are many types of families. Copyright © 2009 by Jaimie Duplass. Under license from Shutterstock, Inc.

S TUDENT
PERSPECTIVE

"Being successful is being balanced in every aspect of your life."

FIRST-YEAR COLLEGE STUDENT

- Single-parent families, which include one parent and one or more children
- Patriarchal families, in which the major authority figure and decision-maker in the family is the father
- Matriarchal families, in which the major authority figure and decision-maker in the family is the mother
- Multi-ethnic or multi-racial families, which include members from more than one race or ethnic group
- Step families, in which one or both parents are not biological parents of the children living with them
- Blended families, in which two or more siblings are not related biologically, but become members of the same family through remarriage of one of their biological parents
- Single-income families, in which there is only one breadwinner
- Families with adopted children
- Families that include children whose parents are unmarried
- Families in which the partners are gay

As the above list demonstrates, the traditional idea of a family has undergone significant change in our society.

Pause for Reflection

Which one of the above family arrangements most closely matches the one in which you were raised? In what way(s) do you think your family structure affected your personal development and the person you are today?

The chart below provides a statistical summary of familial diversity in America:

Household Types 1990–2000

	1990 Number	Percent	2000 Number	Percent
Total Households	91,947,410	100.00%	105,480,101	100.00%
Married Couple	50,708,322	55.15%	54,493,232	51.66%
With Children*	23,494,726	25.55%	24,835,505	23.55%
Without Children*	27,213,596	29.60%	29,657,727	28.12%
Female Householder, No Spouse	10,666,043	11.60%	12,900,103	12.23%
With Children*	6,028,409	6.56%	7,561,874	7.17%
Without Children*	4,637,634	5.04%	5,338,229	5.06%

(continued)

Household Types 1990–2000 *(continued)*

	1990 Number	Percent	2000 Number	Percent
Male Householder, No Spouse	**3,143,582**	**3.42%**	**4,394,012**	**4.17%**
With Children*	1,354,540	1.47%	2,190,989	2.08%
Without Children*	1,789,042	1.95%	2,203,023	2.09%
Non-Family Households	**27,429,463**	**29.83%**	**33,692,754**	**31.94%**
Living Alone	22,580,420	24.56%	27,230,075	25.82%
Two or More Persons	4,849,043	5.27%	6,462,679	6.13%

*In this table, children are people under age 18.
Source: "Census 2000" analyzed by the Social Science Data Analysis Network (SSDAN).

Multiracial Households (In rank order of the top 20)

Rank	Multiple Race Selection	Percent of Total Number	Percent of Multiple Race Population	Population
1.	White and Some Other Race	2,206,251	0.78%	32.32%
2.	White and American Indian	1,082,683	0.38%	15.86%
3.	White and Asian	868,395	0.31%	12.72%
4.	White and Black	784,764	0.28%	11.50%
5.	Black and Some Other Race	417,249	0.15%	6.11%
6.	Asian and Some Other Race	249,108	0.09%	3.65%
7.	Black and American Indian	182,494	0.06%	2.67%
8.	Asian and Hawaiian or Other Pacific Islander	138,802	0.05%	2.03%
9.	White and Hawaiian or Other Pacific Islander	112,964	0.04%	1.65%
10.	White and Black and American Indian	112,207	0.04%	1.64%
11.	Black and Asian	106,782	0.04%	1.56%
12.	American Indian and Some Other Race	93,842	0.03%	1.37%
13.	White and Asian and Hawaiian or Other Pacific Islander	89,611	0.03%	1.31%
14.	American Indian and Asian	52,429	0.02%	0.77%
15.	White and Black and Some Other Race	43,172	0.02%	0.63%
16.	Hawaiian or Other Pacific Islander and Some Other Race	35,108	0.01%	0.51%
17.	White and Asian and Some Other Race	34,962	0.01%	0.51%
18.	Black and Hawaiian or Other Pacific Islander	29,876	0.01%	0.44%
19.	White and American Indian and Some Other Race	29,095	0.01%	0.43%
20.	White and American Indian and Asian	23,766	0.01%	0.35%

Source: "Census 2000" analyzed by the Social Science Data Analysis Network (SSDAN).

The Community Perspective

Moving beyond family, individuals are also members of a larger social unit—their *community*. This wider social circle includes friends and neighbors at home, school, and work. These are communities where you can begin to take action to improve the world around you. If you want to make the world a better place, this is the place to start—for example, by trying to improve your local or college community. As will be discussed in detail in Chapter 5, volunteerism that involves service to diverse members of your community is not only an effective way to appreciate diversity; it is also an excellent way to develop your intercultural communication skills and your career prospects.

The Societal Perspective

Moving beyond community, humans are also members of a larger *society* that includes people from different regions of the country, cultural backgrounds, and social classes. Today, the United States is more ethnically and racially diverse than at any other time in history, and it will continue to grow more diverse throughout the 21st century (Torres, 2003). For example, in 1995, 75% of America's population was white; by 2050, it will shrink to 50% (U.S. Census Bureau, 2004). These demographic changes make the ability to understand, relate to, and learn from people of diverse racial and ethnic backgrounds an essential skill for success in a our multicultural society (Smith, 1997; National Association of Colleges & Employers, 2003).

The National Perspective

Individuals are not only members of a society, they are also citizens of a *nation*. To understand and appreciate the United States as a nation is to know and appreciate human diversity. America has a long and unique history of accommodating and assimilating people from different cultures; thus, diversity is a distinctive characteristic of our national identity. Let us not forget that the United States is a nation that was built and developed by members of diverse immigrant groups, many of whom came to America's shores with the hope of escaping prejudice and discrimination they were experiencing in their native countries. They came to America with the dream of gaining freedom of opportunity and building a better life for themselves and their families (Levine, 1996). Immigrants have built the foundation of America—literally. They have always done and continue to do the hardest physical labor for the least amount of pay. Despite their noble motives for coming to the United States and how hard they worked once they arrived, immigrants often faced intense discrimination until they were eventually assimilated into the dominant culture of the area in which they live. (For a brief review of America's immigration laws and attitudes see the Snapshot Summary on page 90.)

At the same time, immigrants retained pieces of their own cultural background that preserved their distinctive heritage (e.g., ethnic food stores and restaurants). These heritage-preserving practices allowed immigrants to meet their own cultural needs while, at the same time, enriched the diversity of the dominant culture into which they were assimilated. The delicious diversity of ethnic foods available in the U.S. today makes it hard to imagine how limiting and monotonous our food choices would be if we were forced to consume strictly "American" foods (e.g. cheeseburgers, hot dogs, and apple pie).

WORDS OF WISDOM

"It [liberal arts education] shows you how to accommodate yourself to others, how to throw yourself into their state of mind, how to come to an understanding of them. You are at home in any society; you have common ground with every class."

JOHN HENRY NEWMAN, ENGLISH CARDINAL AND EDUCATOR

WORDS OF WISDOM

"There is not a black America and a white America and Latino America and Asian America—there's the United States of America. Ideals of equality have gradually shaped how we understand ourselves and allowed us to form a multicultural nation the likes of which exists nowhere else on earth."

BARACK OBAMA, PRESIDENT OF THE UNITED STATES

WORDS OF WISDOM

"Give me your tired, your poor,
Your huddled masses yearning to breathe free,
The wretched refuse of your teeming shore.
Send these, the homeless, tempest-tossed to me,
I lift my lamp beside the golden door!"

MESSAGE APPEARING ON THE STATUE OF LIBERTY, ELLIS ISLAND

History of Immigration in America ⟶

In the 1790s, the U.S. first began to limit the number of immigrants allowed into the country because of the increasing number of people who were migrating to America. Listed below is a quick historical summary of steps the United States has taken to regulate or eliminate immigration.

1790: Congress passed a law that required an immigrant to live in the U.S. for 2 years before being eligible for citizenship. The number of years required to be in the U.S. increased substantially over the years. In 1795, it increased to 5 years and in 1798 it increased to 14 years.

1798: The Alien and Sedition Acts were passed. One of the laws, the Alien Act, authorized the President to expel any foreigners living in the U.S. who were deemed to be a threat to American interests. Another law, the Naturalization Act, required an individual to live in the U.S. for 14 years.

1800: The Alien Act expired.

1802: The Naturalization Act was repealed. (Today immigrants must typically live in the U.S. for 5 years before applying for citizenship.)

1840–
1930: The largest number of immigrants came to the United States during this period. Approximately 37 million made their way to America including 6 million Germans, 4.75 million Italian, 4.5 million Irish, 4.2 million from England, Scotland, and Wales, 4.2 million from Austria and Hungary, 3.3 million from Russia and the Baltic States, and 2.3 million Scandinavians.

1921: The United States established a quota system, whereby immigrants of any nationality entering the U.S. could not exceed 3% of the number of foreign- born residents of that nationality living in the United States.

1917–
1924: A series of laws were enacted to further limit the number of new immigrants. These laws established the quota system and imposed passport requirements.

1924: The National Origins Act reduced quotas for immigrants who were considered to be "less than desirable." Immigrant populations who were considered as having the ability to be "highly adaptable" to American culture were given generous quotas (i.e., immigrants from northern and western Europe), whereas other immigrant populations were given lower quotas (e.g., Russia and Italy). The National Origins Act also expanded the categories of excludable aliens, and banned all Asians—except the Japanese.

1968: An Act was passed that eliminated U.S. immigration discrimination based on race, place of birth, sex and residence. The Act also officially abolished restrictions on Asian immigration into the United States.

1976: An Act was passed that eliminated preferential treatment for residents of Western Europe.

1970–
2008: During this period of American history, most legal immigrants came from Mexico (more than 20%), the Philippines China, India, South Korea, Vietnam, and the Dominican Republic.

The majority of today's immigrants come to the United States for economic reasons, looking for employment to better their own lives and the lives of their family members (who sometimes remain in their native country). Less than 10% of immigrants choose to come to the United States for political or religious reasons.

Various reforms to immigration laws continue to take place, and the topic of immigration continues to be a hot-button issue in the United States. For example, U.S. government officials continue to struggle with how to deal fairly with the number of illegal aliens who enter and remain in America.

Source: Dinnerstein & Reimers, 2008.

The International Perspective

Moving beyond our particular country of citizenship, we are also members of an *international* world that includes multiple nations. Communication and interaction among citizens of different countries is greater than at any other time in world history, due in large part to rapid advances in electronic technology (Dryden, & Vos, 1999; Smith, 1994). Boundaries between nations are breaking down due to an increase in international travel, international trading, and multinational corporations. Today's world really is a "small world after all" and success in it requires an international perspective. By learning from and about different nations, you become much more than a citizen of your own country, you become cosmopolitan—a citizen of the world.

To gain an international perspective is to gain appreciation for the diversity of humankind. If it were possible to reduce the world's population to a "village" of precisely 100 people, with all existing human ratios remaining the same, the demographics of this village would look something like this:

60 Asians, 14 Africans, 12 Europeans, 8 Latin Americans, 5 from the United States and Canada, and 1 from the South Pacific

51 males, 49 females

82 non-whites, 18 whites

67 non-Christians, 33 Christians

80 living in substandard housing

67 unable to read

50 malnourished and 1 dying of starvation

33 without access to a safe water supply

39 lack access to improved sanitation

24 without any electricity (and of the 76 that do have electricity, most would only use it for light at night)

7 with access to the Internet

1 with a college education

1 with HIV

2 are near birth; 1 near death

5 control 32% of the entire world's wealth; all 5 are citizens of the United States

33 receive and attempt to live on just 3% percent of the village's income.

Source: State of the Village Report by Donella H. Meadows updated in Family Care Foundation, 2005.

Furthermore, as can be seen in Figure 3.3, English would not be the most common language spoken in this international village.

WORDS OF WISDOM

"I pledge allegiance to the flag of the United States of America and to the Republic for which it stands: one Nation under God, indivisible, with Liberty and Justice for all."

THE PLEDGE OF ALLEGIANCE TO THE UNITED STATES FLAG; AN OATH OF LOYALTY TO THE COUNTRY.

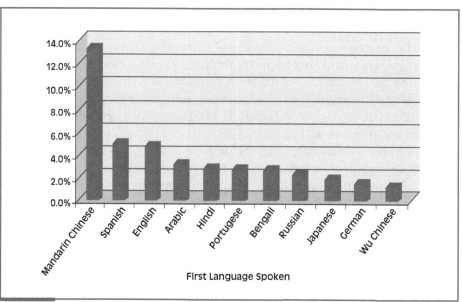

Figure 3.3 World Languages, 2005

Source: *The World Factbook*, 2008.

Pause for Reflection

What other language(s) do you wish you were able to speak? Why?

The Global Perspective

Even broader than the international perspective is the *global perspective*. This perspective goes beyond the relations between inhabitants of different nations to include all life forms that inhabit planet earth, as well as the relationships among these diverse life forms and the earth's natural resources (e.g., minerals, air, and water). Remember that humans share the earth and its natural resources with a vast array of approximately 10 million animal species (Myers, 2001) and more than 300,000 forms of vegetative life (Knoll, 2003).

Underscoring the importance of the global perspective is the contemporary issue of global warming. The earth's atmosphere is gradually thickening and trapping more heat due to a buildup of gases, which are being produced primarily by humans burning fossil fuels for industrial purposes. This increase in man-made pollution is thought to be causing temperatures to rise (and sometimes fall) around the world and to be contributing to natural disasters, such as droughts, wildfires, and dust storms (National Resources Defense Council, 2005; Joint Science Academies Statement, 2005). As inhabitants of planet earth, we need to address issues like global warming, and balance the human pursuit of industrial–technological progress with the need to preserve our earth's precious resources and the lives of our planetary cohabitants. Striking this balance may be the only way to ensure long-term survival of the diverse forms of life that inhabit our planet.

The Universal Perspective

Beyond the global perspective is the broadest of all perspectives—the *universe*. Lest we forget, the earth is one planet that shares the solar system with seven other planets. Our planet is just one celestial body sharing a galaxy with millions of other celestial bodies, which include stars, moons, meteorites, and asteroids (Encrenaz, et al., 2004).

Just as we should guard against being ethnocentric—thinking that our culture is the center of humanity, we should also guard against being geocentric—thinking that our planet is the center of the universe. All other heavenly bodies do not revolve around planet earth; our planet revolves around them. The sun doesn't rise in the east and set in the west; our planet rotates toward and away from the sun to produce our earthly experiences of day and night.

By embracing the multiple perspectives of different times, places, and persons, you are embracing the diversity associated with a liberal arts education. These diverse perspectives liberate or emancipate you from the here and now, and empower you to see view things "long ago and far away." In addition to exposing you to diverse perspectives, a liberal arts education helps you to integrate these perspectives into a meaningful whole. By combining an understanding of diversity and humanity, you are enabled to see how, as an individual, you fit into the "big picture"—the larger scheme of things. Gaining this understanding of how the perspectives of time, place, and person interrelate to form a unified whole is sometimes referred to as a *synoptic* perspective (Cronon, 1998; Heath, 1977). The word derives from a combination of two different roots: *syn*—meaning together (as in the word synthesize), and *optic*—meaning to see. Thus, a *synoptic* perspective literally means to "see things together" or to "see the whole."

Thus, there are two forms of integrated wholeness developed by the diverse perspectives of a liberal arts education: (a) understanding how different elements of the self are connected to form a *whole person*, and (b) understanding how the individual self is connected to the *whole world*.

WORDS OF WISDOM

"In astronomy, you must get used to viewing the earth as just one planet in the larger context of the universe."

PHYSICS PROFESSOR, *LEARNING TO THINK: DISCIPLINARY PERSPECTIVES* (DONALD, 2002)

WORDS OF WISDOM

"A truly great intellect is one which takes a connected view of old and new, past and present, far and near, and which has an insight into the influence of all these on one another, without which there is no whole, and no center."

JOHN HENRY NEWMAN, ENGLISH CARDINAL AND EDUCATOR, *THE IDEA OF A UNIVERSITY*, 1852

Pause for Reflection

Think about the courses you are taking this term, and look back at the different broadening perspectives developed by a liberal arts education. List what course(s) you think are developing one or more of these broadening perspectives; next to each course you have listed, note the particular perspective(s) being developed by that course. If you are unsure or cannot remember whether a course is designed to develop any of these perspectives, take a look at the course objectives or learning outcomes cited in the syllabus.

When we view ourselves as connected with others from different places and different times, we become aware of the common humanity we all share. This increased sense of connection with humankind serves to decrease our feelings of isolation or alienation (Bellah et al., 1985). In his book, *The Perfect Education*, Kenneth Eble skillfully describes this benefit of a liberal arts (general) education infused with diversity:

> It can provide that overarching life of a people, a community, a world that was going on before the individual came onto the scene and that will continue on after [s]he departs. By such means we come to see the world not alone. Our joys are more intense for being shared. Our sorrows are less destructive for our knowing universal sorrow. Our fears of death fade before the commonness of the occurrence (Eble, 1966, pp. 214–215).

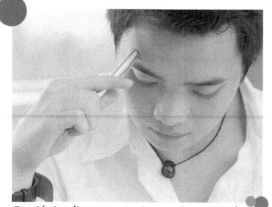

Considering diverse perspectives promotes critical thinking. Copyright © 2009 by Lorelyn Medina. Under license from Shutterstock, Inc.

Diversity Deepens Learning

A large body of research indicates that humans learn more deeply when their learning takes place in a *social* context that involves interpersonal *interaction* and *collaboration* (Cuseo, 1996; 2002). As some scholars put it, human knowledge is "socially constructed"—it is built up through interaction and dialogue with others (Bruffee, 1993). According to these scholars, our thinking is largely an "internal" (mental) representation of conversations that we have had with other people (Vygotsky, 1978). Thus, the quality and variety of our conversations with others affects the quality and complexity of our own thinking. If we have multiple conversations with humans from a rich diversity of backgrounds, the nature of our thinking becomes rich and diverse as well. Just as the quality of your physical health and performance are improved by consuming a varied and balanced diet of foods from different food groups, the quality of your mental performance is improved by helping yourself to a diverse and balanced diet of ideas acquired from different groups of people. Experiencing a rich variety of cultural perspectives serves to nourish your mind with diverse and delicious "food for thought." In contrast, when we restrict the diversity of people with whom we interact, we restrict our diet and artificially restrict the depth and breadth of our learning.

Research consistently shows that we learn more from people who are differ from us than we do from people who are similar to us (Pascarella, 2001; Pascarella & Terenzini, 2005). This result is probably best explained by the fact that learning occurs when the human brain makes a connection between something new (what you're trying to learn) with what it has already stored (what you already know) (Alkon, 1992). The greater the number and variety of learned connections that your brain has already made, the more pathways it has to build on and connect new ideas to, which leads to faster and deeper learning of new ideas.

WORDS OF WISDOM

"Knowledge is happiness, because to have knowledge —broad, deep knowledge—is to know true ends from false, and lofty things from low."

HELEN KELLER, VISUALLY AND HEARING-IMPAIRED AUTHOR, LECTURER, AND WINNER OF THE PRESIDENTIAL MEDAL OF FREEDOM.

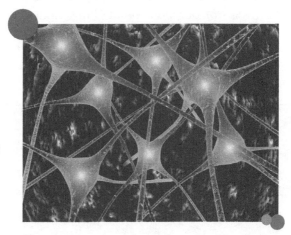

Human learning takes places when the brain connects what it is attempting to learn to an already-formed system of learned connections. The greater the number and variety of connections that exist in the brain, the more "hooks" that exist on which new ideas may be connected, thereby enabling learning to occur more rapidly and become more deeply rooted. Copyright © 2009 by Jurgen Ziewe. Under license from Shutterstock, Inc.

Furthermore, when our brain encounters something that is unfamiliar or very different than what it is accustomed to experiencing, we must stretch beyond our mental comfort zone and work harder to understand it by actively comparing and contrasting it to what we already know (Acredolo & O'Connor, 1991; Nagda, Gurin, & Johnson, 2005). This mental "stretch" requires the expenditure of extra psychological effort and energy, which serves to strengthen and deepen learning.

Thus, by interacting and collaborating with members of diverse groups of people, you create a win–win situation: you learn a lot from them and they learn a lot from you.

Diversity Elevates the Level and Quality of Thinking

Research on students who experience high levels of exposure to different dimensions of diversity in college (e.g., participate in multicultural courses and events on campus, and interact and form friendships with peers of different ethnic backgrounds) indicates these students report the greatest gains in:

- Thinking complexity: The ability to think about all parts and all sides of an issue (Gurin, 1999);
- Reflective thinking: The ability to think carefully (Kitchener et al., 2000); and
- Critical thinking: The ability to think logically (Pascarella et al., 2001).

WORDS OF WISDOM

"When all men think alike, no one thinks very much."

WALTER LIPPMANN, DISTINGUISHED JOURNALIST, AND ORIGINATOR OF THE TERM, *STEREOTYPE*.

To learn from diversity is to think with complexity and nuance. Diversity encourages multiple perspective-taking, opening your mind to see the variety and subtlety of factors that are embedded within intricate issues and difficult dilemmas. When we view the world from one cultural perspective we get a one-dimensional and incomplete understanding of any issue because it represents our one-sided (ethnocentric) viewpoint that is biased by our particular vantage point (Elder & Paul, 2002). Multicultural perspectives help us to be aware of our perceptual "blind spots" and avoid the dangers of *group think*—the tendency for tight, like-minded groups of people to think so much alike that they overlook flaws in their own thinking, which can lead them to make poor choices and faulty decisions (Janis, 1982).

A good example of how "group think" can lead to ethnocentric decisions that are ineffective (and unjust).

© 2005 Ann Telnaes and Women's eNews. Used with the permission of the Cartoonist Group. All rights reserved.

A major advantage of culture is that it helps bind people together into a tight-knit community; however our culture can also blind people from other perspectives. Since culture shapes the way we think, it can cause groups of people to view the world solely through their own cultural frame of reference (Colombo, Cullen, & Lisle, 1995). A good illustration of how our cultural perspectives can blind us, or lead to inaccurate perceptions, is optical illusions. For instance, compare the length of the two lines in Figure 3.4.

If you perceive the line on the right to be longer than the line on the left, welcome to Western culture. Virtually all Americans and people from Western cultures perceive the line on the right to be longer. Actually, both lines are equal in length. (If you don't believe it, take out a ruler and check it out.) However, people from non-Western cultures who live in environments with circular architecture rather than buildings with lines and corners, do not make this perceptual error (Segall, Campbell & Herskovits, 1966).

© 2007 JupiterImages Corporation.

The people who live in these circular huts would not be fooled by the optical illusion in Figure 3.4.

The key point underlying this optical illusion is that our cultural experiences shape and sometimes distort our perceptions of reality. We think we are seeing things objectively or "as they really are," but we are often seeing things subjectively from our limited cultural vantage point. Being open to the viewpoints of diverse people—who perceive the world from different cultural vantage points—widens our range of perception and helps us overcome our "cultural blind spots." As a result, we see and think about the world around us with greater clarity and accuracy.

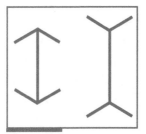

Figure 3.4
Optical Illusion

For example, learning about the fish-rich diet of Eskimos and their lower rate of cardiovascular disease helped us to discover that fish are low in saturated fat (Feskens & Kromhout, 1993) and that the natural oil in fish is high in a type of unsaturated fat, which flushes out and washes away cholesterol-forming fats from the bloodstream (Khoshaba & Maddi, 1999–2004). Thus, eating a variety of fish and adopting a diet high in unsaturated fats (and low in saturated fats) is now recommended for reducing the risk for non-genetic forms of cardiovascular disease, such as high blood pressure, heart attack, and stroke (American Heart Association, 2006). Similarly, the Chinese opened American minds to acupuncture as an effective, drug-free method of promoting pain relief, and it was Indian Buddhists who turned Americans on to the power of meditation as an effective, drug-free, stress-management strategy.

Although you may specialize in a particular field of study in college (your major), "real-life" issues and challenges are not divided neatly into specialized majors. Important and enduring issues, such as effective leadership, improving race relations, and preventing international warfare, can neither be fully understood nor effectively solved by using the thinking tools of a single

Perspective	Implication
Person	Global warming involves us on an individual level because our personal efforts at energy conservation in our homes and our willingness to purchase energy-efficient products can play a major role in solving this problem.
Place	Global warming is an international issue that extends beyond the boundaries of one's own country to all countries in the world, and its solution will require worldwide collaboration.
Time	If the current trend toward higher global temperatures caused by global warming continues, it could seriously threaten the lives of future generationsof people who inhabit our planet.
Culture	The problem of global warming has been caused by industries in technologically advanced cultures, yet the problem of rising global temperatures is likely to have its most negative impact on less technologically advanced cultures that lack the resources to respond to it (Joint Science Academies Statement, 2005). To prevent this from happening, technologically advanced cultures will need to use their advanced technology to devise alternative methods for generating energy that does not continue to release heat-trapping gases into the atmosphere.

Figure 3.5

academic major. Using one specialized field of study to understand multidimensional issues is likely to result in overly narrow, single-minded (and oversimplified) attempts to solve complex problems. A comprehensive understanding of and solution to the issue of global warming involves consideration of these four perspectives, as depicted in Figure 3.5.

For example, solutions to the current problem of global warming involve interrelationships among diverse fields of study, such as the following:

1. Ecology: understanding the intricate relationship between humans and their natural environment;
2. Physical science: research and development of alternative sources of energy;
3. Economics: cost to industry to change from existing to alternative sources of energy;
4. National politics: creating incentives or laws that encourage, regulate, and enforce changes in industry's use of energy sources; and
5. International relations: collaboration among all countries that are currently contributing to the problem to work together and contribute to its solution.

Multidimensional thinkers view issues and courses of action from multiple perspectives, such as those discussed in this chapter. For example, multidimensional thinkers ask the following types of questions:

1. How would this issue affect my personal health and wellness? (The perspective of *person*)
2. What impact would this issue have on people living in other countries? (The perspective of *place*)
3. How would future generations of people be affected by this issue? (The perspective of *time*)
4. How would this issue be interpreted or experienced by groups of people who share different social customs and traditions? (The perspective of *culture*)

STUDENT PERSPECTIVE

"To me, thinking at a higher level is when you approach a question or topic thoughtfully [and] you fully explore every aspect of that topic from all angles."

FIRST-YEAR COLLEGE STUDENT

Pause for Reflection

Think of a problem in today's world other than global warming. Look back at the four previously described perspectives associated with multidimensional thinking (person, place, time, and culture), and briefly explain how each of these perspectives may be involved in causing the problem or solving it.

Similar to global issues, personal issues and challenges that individuals face in their everyday lives are multidimensional and require perspectives and skills that go well beyond the boundaries of one particular academic field or career specialization. For example, a person's career represents just one dimension of the multidimensional self. Your career role represents merely one of many roles and responsibilities that you have in life, which include being a citizen, a consumer, a friend, a son or daughter, and possibly a spouse or parent.

REMEMBER: The multiple academic disciplines (subject areas) that you encounter in the liberal arts curriculum, coupled with the multiple perspectives you experience through diversity, will provide you with a broad base of knowledge and a versatile set of thinking tools needed to handle the multiple roles you will be required to perform throughout life.

Diversity Promotes Creative Thinking

Studies show that creative people have a wide range of knowledge and interests, and their creative products often reflect combinations of ideas drawn from multiple subject areas (Riquelme, 2002). Thus, creativity is built on a broad base of knowledge that goes beyond the boundaries of particular area of educational or professional specialization and capitalizes on connections made across different subject areas (Baer, 1993; Kaufman & Baer, 2002).

Just as experiences with different academic disciplines equips you with a broad base of knowl-

Multicultural subject matter broadens your perspective.
Copyright © 2009 by Factoria singular fotografia. Under license from Shutterstock, Inc.

WORDS OF WISDOM

"When the only tool you have is a hammer, you tend to see every problem as a nail."

ABRAHAM MASLOW, HUMANISTIC PSYCHOLOGIST, BEST KNOWN FOR HIS SELF-ACTUALIZATION THEORY OF ACHIEVING HUMAN POTENTIAL

edge and thinking styles that can be combined to create new ideas so, too, does experience with different dimensions of diversity. Diverse experiences supply you with greater breadth of knowledge and ways of thinking that can empower you to think outside the box or boundaries of your single cultural framework. Diversity expands your capacity for viewing issues or problems from *multiple* perspectives, angles, and vantage points, and these diverse vantage points work to your advantage when you encounter new problems in different contexts and situations. In contrast, limiting your number of vantage points is akin to limiting the variety of lenses or angles you can use to solve new problems, thereby limiting your creativity.

Once diverse perspectives have been acquired, they can be combined or rearranged in ways that produce unique or innovative solutions to problems. Ideas you acquire from diverse people and diverse cultures can feed off each other and "cross-fertilize," giving birth to new approaches for solving old problems. Furthermore, when you exchange ideas freely in groups comprised of people from diverse backgrounds, powerful "cross-stimulation" effects can also occur, whereby one group member's idea often triggers different ideas from other group members (Brown et al., 1998).

Your co-workers are likely to be from a broad range of cultures and ethnicities. Copyright © 2009 by Philip Date. Under license from Shutterstock, Inc.

REMEMBER: Drawing on different ideas from people of diverse backgrounds and bouncing your ideas off them is an effective way to generate energy, synergy, and serendipity—unanticipated discoveries and creative solutions.

Diversity Enhances Career Preparation and Career Success

Learning about and from diversity has a very practical benefit: It better prepares you for the world of work. Whatever career you may choose to pursue, you are likely find yourself working with employers, employees, co-workers, customers, and clients from diverse cultural backgrounds; America's workforce is now more diverse than at any other time in the nation's history and it will grow ever more diverse; the percentage of America's working-age population that are members of minority groups will jump from 34% in 2008 to 55% in 2050 (United States Bureau of Labor Statistics, 2008).

Work today also takes place in a global economy, in which there is more economic interdependence among nations, international trading (imports/exports), multinational corporations, international travel, and almost instantaneous worldwide communication—due to advances in the World Wide Web (Dryden, & Vos, 1999; Smith, 1994).

As a result of these trends, employers of college graduates are now seeking job candidates who possess international knowledge and foreign language skills (Fixman, 1990; Office of Research, 1994). Successful career performance in today's diverse workforce also requires sensitivity to human differences and the ability to relate to people from different cultural backgrounds (National Association of Colleges & Employers, 2003; Smith, 1997). A national survey of policymakers, business leaders, and employers revealed interest in college graduates who are more than just "aware" or "tolerant" of diversity; they want graduates who have actual *experience* with diversity (Education Commission of the States, 1995). These results are reinforced by a national survey of American voters, which indicate that the overwhelming majority of them agree that diversity education helps students to learn practical skills that are essential for success in today's world—such as communication, teamwork, and problem-solving skills. Almost one-half of voters also think that we should "put more emphasis on teaching people about each others' cultures, backgrounds and lifestyles" (National Survey of Voters, 1998). Thus, both employers and the American public agree that diversity education is *career preparation*. Intercultural competence has become a highly valued skill, which is essential for successful performance in today's work world.

REMEMBER: Intercultural competence is now considered to be a foundational, liberal arts skill, which, like other liberal learning skills, has two powerful qualities:

1. Transferability: intercultural competence is a portable skill that you can carry with you and transfer (apply) across a wide range of cultures, careers, and life situations; and
2. Durability: intercultural competence is an enduring skill with long-lasting value that you will be able to use continually throughout life.

Summary

This chapter identified multiple benefits associated with diversity. These benefits are listed and briefly reviewed below.

Diversity enhances self-awareness. Learning from people whose backgrounds and experiences are diverse sharpens your self-knowledge and self-insight by allowing you to compare and contrast your life experiences with others whose life experiences differ sharply from your own.

Diversity stimulates social development. Interacting with people from a variety of groups widens your social circle, and by widening the pool of people with whom you interact, you strengthen your ability to relate to people with different experiences and interests, and are better able to converse with others on a wide variety of topics.

Diversity enriches the multiple perspectives developed by a liberal arts (general) education. Diversity magnifies the power of a liberal arts education by helping to "liberate" (free) you from the tunnel vision of an ethnocentric and egocentric (self-centered) viewpoint, enabling you to move beyond yourself to gain a panoramic perspective of the world around you and a more holistic view of the multiple dimensions of self that comprise you. By integrating diversity appreciation with liberal arts education, you acquire the ability to see how you—as a whole person, fit into the "big picture"—the whole world.

Diversity deepens learning and elevates thinking. Human knowledge is socially constructed—it is built up through interpersonal interaction and dialogue with others. The quality and variety of your conversations with others deepens your learning and elevates the quality of thinking. If you have multiple conversations with humans from a rich diversity of backgrounds, the nature of our thinking becomes rich and diverse as well. Research consistently shows that we learn more from people who differ from us than we do from people who are similar to us.

Diversity promotes creative thinking. Experiencing diversity supplies you with greater breadth of knowledge and a wider variety of thinking styles that empower you to think outside the box or boundaries of a single cultural framework. Once you acquire diverse perspectives, they can also be combined or rearranged in ways that result in unique or innovative solutions to problems. Furthermore, drawing on different ideas from people of diverse backgrounds and bouncing your ideas off them is an effective way to generate energy, synergy, and serendipity—the unanticipated discovery of creative ideas.

Diversity enhances career preparation and career success. Learning about and from diversity better prepares you for today's work world. America's workforce is now more diverse than at any other time in the nation's history and it will grow increasingly diverse. Moreover, work today takes place in a global economy characterized by greater economic interdependence among nations, more international trading (imports/exports), more multinational corporations, more international travel, and almost-instantaneous worldwide communication.

As a result of these trends, employers of college graduates are now seeking job candidates who possess international knowledge, foreign language skills, sensitivity to human differences, and the ability to relate to people from different cultural backgrounds. Both employers and the American public agree that diversity education is *career preparation*.

The case for experiencing diversity is clear and compelling. Its benefits include not only the global goals of social justice, national stability, and international harmony, but also a host of educational, vocational, and personal benefits for the individual who is willing to seek out and capitalize on the power of diversity.

Chapter 3 Exercises

Name

_____

Date

_____

Planning to Infuse Diversity into Your College Education

Diversity is such an important component of a college education that it should be intentionally planned. By so doing, you can become actively involved in shaping or creating your college education in a way that it has maximum impact on your personal development and career success. Use the following exercises as a plan for infusing diversity into your college experience.

3.1 Planning for the Multiple Perspectives of a Liberal Arts Education

Use the index in your college catalog to locate the general education (liberal arts) requirements for graduation. In many cases, you will have some degree of freedom to choose from a group of courses that fulfill different requirements. You can use this freedom to infuse diversity into your general education plan. Select courses that will enable you to develop the broadening perspectives of a liberal arts education that are described previously. Use the following checklist to ensure that your overall plan is comprehensive and does not have "blind spots" (missing perspectives).

Checklist for the Multiple Perspectives of a Liberal Arts Education

Broadening Chronological Perspectives   Course developing this perspective
(See pages 82–83 for detailed description of these perspectives.)

Historical   _____

Contemporary   _____

Futuristic   _____

Broadening Social-Spatial Perspectives   Course developing this perspective:
(See pages 84–93 for further descriptions of these perspectives.)

Self   _____

Family   _____

Community   _____

Society   _____

Nation   _____

International   _____

Global   _____

Universe   _____

Name

_____

Date

_____

3.2 Planning to Develop Multiple Dimensions of the "Whole Person"

Similar to exercise 3.1, consult your college catalogue to select courses that will enable you to develop the multiple dimensions of self that are described on pages 84–86. Remember that development of your whole self also includes co-curricular learning experiences (for example, leadership and volunteer experiences) that take place outside the classroom. So, be sure to build these experiences into your plan for developing yourself as a whole person. Your *Student Handbook* probably represents the best source for information about co-curricular experiences offered by your college. The best person to contact for this information may be the Director of Student Development, Student Life, or Student Activities at your college.

Use the checklist below to be sure that your plan includes all key dimensions of holistic ("whole person") development.

Planning Checklist for Developing Multiple Dimensions of the Whole Person

Dimensions of Self *(See pages 84–86 for further description of these dimensions.)*	**Course or Co-curricular Experience Developing this Dimension of Self**
Self	_____
Intellectual (Cognitive)	_____
Emotional	_____
Social	_____
Ethical	_____
Physical	_____
Spiritual	_____
Vocational	_____
Personal	_____

3.3 Planning for Elective Courses in Diversity

In addition to courses required for general education and your major, you have *elective* courses that you are free to select from any that are listed in the college catalogue or bulletin. To ensure that some of these courses become part of your plan for infusing diversity into your college experience, review your catalogue and list elective courses that you could take to promote awareness and appreciation of diversity in each of the following areas:

Diversity across Nations **(International or Cross-cultural Courses)**

_____

_____

_____

_____

Diversity within America **(Multicultural Courses)**

_____

_____

_____

_____

3.4 Planning for Service-Learning Courses Relating to Diversity

In addition to traditional, classroom-based courses, experiential learning opportunities may be available to you in college courses that include *service learning*. These courses are designed to help you integrate or connect classroom learning with volunteer service in the local community. Service learning courses allow you to become actively involved with diversity in the local community and personally reflect on these experiences in the classroom. For example, it may be possible for you to take a sociology course that allows you to engage in volunteer service for diverse groups in the local community, reflect on these hands-on experiences via writing assignments and class discussions, and connect your volunteer experiences with material covered in the course.

Check your catalogue to identify service learning courses that have implications for promoting diversity awareness or appreciation, and list them below.

Planning List for Elective Courses in Diversity

_____

_____

_____

_____

Stumbling Blocks and Barriers to Diversity

4

Stereotypes, Prejudice, and Discrimination

Purpose

As has been documented throughout this book, human beings have a long history of displaying prejudice and discrimination toward certain groups of people preventing themselves and others from experiencing the multiple benefits of diversity. This chapter will examine the various forms of prejudice and discrimination that have plagued our society, their underlying causes, and a model for overcoming these barriers to diversity.

Activate Your Thinking

Have you ever observed or been the victim of prejudice?

If yes, what happened? Why do you think it happened? (What caused it?)

Stereotyping

The term "stereotype" derives from a combination of two word roots: (a) *stereo*—to look at in a fixed way and (b) *type*—to categorize or group together (as in the word "typical"). Thus, to stereotype is to view individuals of the same type (group) in the same (fixed) way.

In effect, stereotyping ignores or disregards a person's individuality; instead, all people who share the same group characteristic (e.g., race or gender) are viewed as having the same personal characteristics—as in the expression: "You know what they are like; they're all the same." Stereotypes involve *bias*, which literally means "slant." A bias is a belief or judgment that is slanting toward the positive or negative—before the facts are known. Positive bias results in a favorable stereotype (e.g., All Italians are great lovers or all Asians are great at Math); negative bias results in an unfavorable stereotype (e.g., all Italians are in the Mafia or all Muslims are terrorists).

Personal Experience   When I was 6 years old, I was told by another 6-year-old from a different racial group that all people of my race could not swim. Since I could not swim at that age and she could, I assumed she was correct. I asked a boy, who happened to be of the same racial group as that little girl, if that statement were true; he responded: "yes, it is true." Since I was from an area where few other African Americans were around to counteract this belief about blacks, I bought into this stereotype for a long time until I finally took swimming lessons as an adult. I am now a lousy swimmer after many lessons because I did not even attempt to swim until I was an adult. The moral of this story is that group stereotypes can limit the confidence and potential of individuals who are members of the stereotyped group.

—Aaron Thompson, *Professor of Sociology
and co-author of this text*

Pause for Reflection

1. Have you ever been stereotyped, based on your appearance or group membership? If so, how did it make you feel? How did you react?

2. Have you ever unintentionally perceived or treated someone in terms of their group stereotype rather than as an individual? What assumptions did you make about that person?

   Was that person aware of, or affected by, your stereotyping?

Whether you are male or female, don't let gender stereotypes limit your career options.

Prejudice

If virtually all members of a stereotyped group are *judged* or *evaluated* in a negative way, the result is *prejudice*. (The word prejudice literally means to "pre-judge.") Technically, prejudice may be either positive or negative; however, the term is most often associated with negative pre-judgment or *stigmatizing*—attributing inferior or unfavorable traits to people who belong to the same group. Thus, prejudice may be defined as a negative judgment, attitude, or belief about another person or group of people, which is formed before the facts are known. Stereotyping and prejudice often go hand-in-hand because individuals who are placed in a negatively stereotyped group are commonly pre-judged in a negative way.

Someone with a prejudice toward a group typically avoids contact with individuals from that group. This enables the prejudice to continue unchallenged because there is little or no chance for the prejudiced person to have positive experiences with members of the stigmatized group that could contradict or disprove the prejudice. Thus, a vicious cycle is established in which the prejudiced person continues to avoid contact with individuals from the stigmatized group, which, in turn, continues to maintain and reinforce the prejudice.

STUDENT PERSPECTIVE

When you see me, do not look at me with disgrace.

Know that I am an African-American
    Birthed by a woman of style and grace.

Be proud
    To stand by my side.

Hold your head high
    Like me.

Be proud.
    To say you know me.
    Just as I stand by you,
    proud to be me.

A POEM BY BRITTANY BEARD, FIRST-YEAR STUDENT

WORDS OF WISDOM

"See that man over there?
Yes.
Well, I hate him.
But you don't know him.
That's why I hate him."

GORDON ALLPORT, SOCIAL PSYCHOLOGIST, *THE NATURE OF PREJUDICE*

Chapter 4: Stumbling Blocks and Barriers to Diversity   113

WORDS OF WISDOM

"Let us all hope that the dark clouds of racial prejudice will soon pass away and the deep fog of misunderstanding will be lifted from our fear-drenched communities, and in some not too distant tomorrow the radiant stars of love and brotherhood will shine over our great nation."

MARTIN LUTHER KING, JR., CIVIL RIGHTS ACTIVIST AND CLERGYMAN

WORDS OF WISDOM

"The best way to beat prejudice is to show them. On a midterm, I got 40 points above the average. They all looked at me differently after that."

MEXICAN-AMERICAN STUDENT, QUOTED IN NEMKO (1988)

"A lot of us never asked questions in class before—it just wasn't done, especially by a woman or a girl, so we need to realize that and get into the habit of asking questions and challenging if we want to—regardless of the reactions of the professors and other students."

ADULT FEMALE COLLEGE STUDENT, QUOTED IN WILKIE & THOMPSON (1993)

Discrimination

Literally translated, the term discrimination means division or separation. While prejudice involves a belief or opinion, discrimination involves an *action* taken toward others. Technically, discrimination can be either negative or positive—for example, a discriminating eater may be careful about eating only healthy foods. However, the term is most often associated with a negative action that results in a prejudiced person treating another human being in an unfair way. Thus, it could be said that discrimination is prejudice put into action.

Hate crimes are an example of extreme discrimination because they are acts motivated solely by prejudice against members of a stigmatized group. For instance, victims of hate crimes may have their personal property damaged or they may be physically assaulted (e.g., "gay bashing"). Other forms of discrimination are more subtle and may take place without people being fully aware that they are discriminating. For example, there is evidence that some white, male college professors tend to interact with female students and students from ethnic or racial minority groups differently than they do with males and non-minority students. In particular, females and minority students tend to:

- receive less eye contact from the instructors,
- be called on less frequently in class,
- be given less time to respond to questions asked by instructors in class, and
- have less contact with instructors outside of the classroom (Hall & Sandler, 1982, 1984; Sedlacek, 1987; Wright, 1987).

In the vast majority of these cases, the discriminatory treatment that the female and minority students received was subtle and not done consciously or deliberately by the instructors (Green, 1989). Nevertheless, the instructors' unintended actions are still discriminatory, and they may send a message to minority and female students that their ideas are not worth hearing, or that they are not as capable as other students (Sadker & Sadker, 1994).

Pause for Reflection

Have you noticed classroom teaching behaviors or actions taken by instructors that demonstrated equal treatment of all students and demonstrated appreciation of student diversity?

What did these instructors do to convey this non-discriminatory message?

Affirmative Action: Combating Job Discrimination through Legislation

Because of the history of discrimination against women and minorities in America, affirmative action laws were passed to enhance their employment and educational opportunities. These laws were created to offer some compensation to members of groups who have been historically excluded from jobs and paid labor organizations because of their sex or race. Here is a brief summary of affirmative action legislation in America.

1964: Title VI of the Civil Rights Act was passed by Congress, which prohibited discrimination on the basis of race or sex in any programs or activities receiving federal funds. Title VII of the same act prohibited discrimination in employment.

1965: President Lyndon Johnson issued Executive Order 11246, which required employers receiving federal funds or holding government contracts to take affirmative action to ensure that individuals were selected for employment without regard to color, race, religion, or national origin.

1972: Congress passed the Equal Employment Act that amended the 1964 Civil Rights Act and extended it to cover affirmative action in colleges and universities.

It was the intention of these laws to motivate officials in majority group organizations to hire, promote, and provide equal opportunity to minorities. Since many of these organizations had historically limited hiring and promotion to members of their own (majority) group, affirmative action legislation was enacted to ensure that women and minorities were not excluded in the hiring and promotion process.

However, instead of viewing affirmative action in the manner that it was intended (creating equal opportunity), many members of work organizations interpreted these laws as forcing them to hire women and minorities. Other majority group members viewed these laws to mean that females and blacks were to be awarded jobs and promotions, even if they were not qualified. Thus, some white males believed that they were being bypassed for jobs and promotions in favor of less-qualified minorities and females.

Although majority group members may not agree with or believe in the need for affirmative action laws, these laws have changed hiring and promotion practices in a way that has led to less discrimination against women and minorities. Affirmative action legislation is a good example of how it may be easier to change discriminatory behavior than it is to change the prejudicial biased beliefs or attitudes that underlie them.

Source: Exum, cited in Thompson (1992).

Personal Experience

When I entered college in the mid 1970s, I was 6'4" and 165 lbs. with a large afro, a green leisure suit, and 4-inch white platform shoes. Colleges around the United States were starting to integrate more because of recently-passed Affirmative Action laws. Access to a college education became possible for people other than the middle and upper socioeconomic classes. Diversity on college campuses was on the rise due to affirmative action laws and the availability of financial aid.

As an African American student on a mainly white campus, I still felt somewhat isolated. The only ethnic minority instructors that I had the entirety of my undergraduate education were a South Korean and Southeast Indian. I did not have one experience with a black faculty member. Although things have changed over the years (e.g., leisure suits are gone), some things remain the same (e.g., a shortage of black faculty members). However, I feel proud to have been part of a major development in American history that allowed equal educational opportunity for students of all racial and ethnic backgrounds to attend college.

—Aaron Thompson, *Professor of Sociology and co-author of this text*

"Good News! The affirmative action ruling left all our preferences in place."

© 2003 Signe Wilkinson. Used with the permission of Signe Wilkinson and the Washington Post Writers Group in conjunction with the Cartoonist Group. All rights reserved.

Causes of Prejudice and Discrimination

There is no single or definitive answer to the question of what causes people to develop prejudice and to discriminate against other groups of people. However, research indicates that the following factors can play an influential role.

The Tendency to Favor Familiarity and Fear Strangers

It has been repeatedly shown that when humans encounter something unfamiliar or strange, they tend to experience feelings of discomfort or anxiety. In contrast, what is familiar tends to be accepted and better liked (Zajonc, 2001).

Thus, when we encounter people who are not familiar to us, experiencing some degree of discomfort is likely to occur, and it is likely to occur automatically. In fact, these feelings may be "wired into" our bodies because it was once important to the survival and evolution of our species. When we encountered strangers in our primitive past, it was to our advantage to react with feelings of anxiety and a rush of adrenaline, known as the "fight or flight" response, because those strangers may have been potential predators who could threaten or harm us (see Figure 4.1).

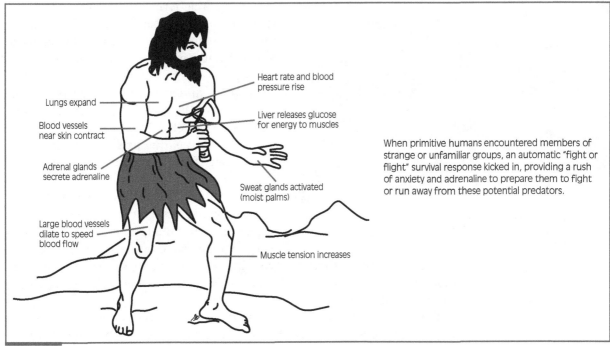

Lungs expand

Blood vessels near skin contract

Adrenal glands secrete adrenaline

Large blood vessels dilate to speed blood flow

Heart rate and blood pressure rise

Liver releases glucose for energy to muscles

Sweat glands activated (moist palms)

Muscle tension increases

When primitive humans encountered members of strange or unfamiliar groups, an automatic "fight or flight" survival response kicked in, providing a rush of anxiety and adrenaline to prepare them to fight or run away from these potential predators.

Figure 4.1 "Fight-or-Flight" Reaction

This evolutionary, fight-or-flight response may also explain why "stranger anxiety" occurs during infancy. Between about 8 and18 months of life, virtually all infants when seeing a stranger will react with anxiety (increased heart rate, breathing, crying; Papalia & Olds, 1990).

The effects of familiarity and stranger anxiety may contribute to prejudice by causing members of the same group to be positively biased toward members of their own group and to be on guard when encountering members of other groups who are less familiar or strange to us (Aronson, et al., 2005). Thus, members of minority groups are more likely to be targets of prejudice and discrimination because they are fewer in number and therefore, less familiar to the majority group.

The Influence of Segregation

Segregation may be defined as one group's decision to separate itself, either socially or physically, from another group. In human societies, people tend to organize themselves into different groups in different settings. These settings include the workplace, church or religious services, and schools. Members of minority groups are often segregated from the majority group because they are less likely to live in the same area (e.g., the same neighborhood), due to residential segregation of racial and ethnic groups, which is still common today (Massey, 2003; Tienda & Cortes, cited in Nagda, Gurin, & Johnson, 2005). Research reveals that college students, particularly white students, come from highly segregated high schools and neighborhoods (Matlock,

Segregation is an unconscious or conscious action that will limit our opportunity to learn from the diversity of society. Copyright © 2009 by Sofos Design. Under license from Shutterstock, Inc.

1997). In a long-term study of over 2,500 first-year African-American, Asian-American, Latino, and white students at the University of Michigan, it was found that students of color self-segregated, but tended to interact more with white students than the reverse. White students had the most segregated friendship patterns (Matlock, 1997).

While segregation itself is not necessarily a conscious form of deliberate prejudice or discrimination, it can lead to reduced contact between different groups of people. Continued segregation can cause a segregated group to remain "unfamiliar," and this lack of familiarity, in turn, can continue to trigger feelings of uncertainty and anxiety toward that group. Since anxiety is an unpleasant emotion, when it continues to be associated with the segregated group, it can lead to prejudice and discrimination.

Furthermore, those who are prejudiced toward the segregated group are likely to continually avoid contact with that group preventing them from experiencing and benefitting from the particular dimension of diversity (e.g., ethnic, racial, or national), that the segregated group has to offer.

Personal Experience

I was 15 years old when I first became aware that skin color really mattered to some people. I am a rabid baseball fan and my team was the San Francisco Giants. I grew up in New York during the 1950's and became a fan of the New York Giants' baseball team. When I was 8 years old, the team left New York to become the San Francisco Giants. Even though the Giants left my hometown, I still considered them to be my team. I got a lot of teasing from members of my extended Italian family about not being loyal and rooting for an out-of-town team. During one teasing episode with my cousins and uncles, I defended my team by saying that they were in first place and that I expected them to win the double-header they were going to play later that day. My 19-year-old cousin, Jimmy, interrupted me to say that the Giants' double-header was going to be cancelled that day—because of Malcolm X (black civil rights leader) was holding a meeting! Several of my older cousins and my uncles began laughing, but I couldn't figure out what was so funny. Then I suddenly got the "joke": the Giants were the team that had more Black and Latino players than any other team in baseball. The Giants were the first major-league team to have multiple players from the Dominican Republic, and had players from Puerto Rico and Cuba.

I suddenly became aware that all the teasing I received about being a Giants fan had less to do with the fact I was rooting for an out-of-town team, but because I was rooting for a "colored" team. Up to that point in time, I never thought of the Giants players as being colored; I just thought they were colorful. They had unique names (Orlando, Felipe, Mateo, and Jesus) and unique playing styles. As a young boy, I saw these players as being refreshingly different and exciting. However, this wisecrack made by my cousin that day and the reaction it produced, immediately and forever changed me from being color-blind to color-conscious. It also changed me from being a Giants fan to Giants fanatic. I was not only rooting for a team; I was rooting for a cause. Later that year, the Giants added a pitcher by the name of Masanori Murakami—the first Asian player ever to play professional baseball in America. I was proud to be rooting for the most diverse team in history. I didn't know it at the time, but I was appreciating and advocating for diversity.

Joe Cuseo, *Professor of Psychology and co-author of this text*

Pause for Reflection

Prejudice and discrimination can be subtle and may only begin to surface when the social or emotional distance between members of different groups grows closer. Rate your level of comfort (high, medium, low) with the following situations.

Someone from another racial group:

1.	Going to your school	high	medium	low
2.	Working in your place of employment	high	medium	low
3.	Living on your street as a neighbor	high	medium	low
4.	Living with you as a roommate	high	medium	low
5.	Socializing with you as a personal friend	high	medium	low
6.	Being your most intimate friend or romantic partner	high	medium	low
7.	Being your partner in marriage	high	medium	low

For any item you rated "low," why do you think it received that rating?

The Tendency toward Selective Perception and Selective Memory

Prejudice can also remain intact because facts that contradict it are often ignored through the psychological process of *selective perception*—the tendency of prejudiced people to see what they expect to see or what is consistent with already-held beliefs (Hugenberg & Bodenhausen, 2003). This can result in the prejudiced person paying closer attention to information that "proves" their prejudice and "seeing" incidents that support their viewpoint, while ignoring or overlooking information that contradicts it. Have you ever noticed that fans rooting for their favorite sports team tend to focus on and "see" the calls or decisions of referees that go against their own team, but do not seem to notice or react to calls that go against the other team? This is a classic, ev-

WORDS OF WISDOM

"We see what is behind our eyes."

CHINESE PROVERB

eryday example of selective perception. It could be said that selective perception changes the process of "seeing is believing" into "believing is seeing."

To aggravate matters, selective perception is often accompanied by *selective memory*—the tendency to remember information that is consistent with the prejudice, and to forget information that is inconsistent with it or contradicts it (Judd et al., 1991).

The twin mental processes of selective perception and selective memory can operate *unconsciously*, so people may not be fully aware that they are using them or that they are contributing to their prejudice (Baron, Byrne, & Brauscombe, 2006).

The Tendency to Mentally Categorize People into "In" and "Out" Groups

Humans tend to group people into mental categories, probably for the purpose of making their complex social world simpler to understand (Jones, 1990). While this is a natural human tendency, it can lead to stereotyping members of other groups, which blinds us to their individuality. It can also contribute to prejudice because the human tendency to categorize may result in the creation of *in*-groups ("us") and *out*-groups ("them"). One negative consequence of this type of categorization is that it contributes to *ethnocentrism*—the tendency to view one's own culture or ethnic group as the central or "normal" in-group and other cultures as marginal or "abnormal" out-groups. This tendency can, in turn, lead to prejudice and discrimination toward people whose cultural backgrounds differ from our own.

Our cultural experiences can affect our beliefs and attitudes about what is socially acceptable or "normal." For instance, in American culture, it may be socially acceptable for males to tell others of their achievements or accomplishments; however, in English and German cultures, such behavior is more likely to be perceived as immodest or immature (Hall & Hall, 1986). Failure to appreciate such cultural differences can lead to ethnocentric thinking, which fails to consider that other groups may have attitudes and behaviors that are different than our own, but which are equally acceptable and "normal" when viewed from the perspective of their particular culture. Thus, ethnocentric thinking is a form of simplistic, dualistic (black-white) thinking that can lead to the conclusion that the way things are done by the in-group ("us") is "right," and the behavior of out-groups ("them") is "wrong."

The Tendency to Perceive Members of Other Groups as More Alike than Members of Our Own Group

Studies show that humans tend to see members of groups that they are unfamiliar with as more alike in attitudes and behavior than members of their own group (Baron, Byrne, & Brauscombe, 2006). For instance, individuals perceive people older than themselves as being more alike in their attitudes and beliefs than members of their own age group (Linville, Fischer, & Salovey, 1989).

This tendency may stem from the fact that we have more experience with members of our own group; thus we have more opportunities to observe and interact with a wide variety of individuals within our group. In contrast, we have less contact with members of other groups, which narrows the range of individuals in that group we meet which may in turn lead us to conclude that individual differences among them is narrower (i.e., they are more alike in attitudes and behavior than members of our own group). This tendency to view members of other groups as being more alike in their attitudes and behaviors than members of our own group can lead to stereotyping. Even if an individual member of the group does not fit the group stereotype, he or she is likely to be dismissed as an "exception to the rule," or as an exception that "proves" the general rule (Aronson, et al., 2005).

This tendency to perceive members of other groups as being alike can be so strong that it makes it more difficult for people to detect facial differences among members of groups that we are unfamiliar with ("they all seem to look alike") (Levin, 2000). A dramatic example of this phenomenon is the case of Lenell Geter, an African American engineer, who spent over a year of his sentence in prison for a crime he never committed. Four of five non-black witnesses misidentified him for another black man who actually committed the crime and was later apprehended.

The Tendency for Majority Group Members' Attitudes to Be More Strongly Influenced by Negative Behaviors Committed by Members of Minority Groups than by Members of Their Own (Majority) Group

Studies show that if negative behavior occurs at the same rate among members of both majority and minority groups (e.g., the rate of criminal behavior in both groups is 10%), members of the majority group are more likely to develop negative attitudes (prejudice) toward the minority group than their own group (Baron, Byrne, & Brauscombe, 2006). For example, it has been found that whites in the United States tend to overestimate the crime rates of African-American men (Hamilton & Sherman, 1989).

One possible explanation why the majority group may overestimate the rate of negative minority-group behavior is the tendency of majority group members to better remember instances of negative behavior committed by minority-group members. Since minorities are more likely to be seen as different or distinctive, their behavior is more likely to stand out in the minds of majority group members, which makes it more likely that their negative behaviors will be better remembered (McArthur & Friedman, 1980). Since these negative behaviors are more likely to be retained in the minds of the majority group, they are more likely to trigger negative views of the minority group, thus increasing the possibility of prejudice.

As these findings suggest, prejudice on the part of the majority group toward minority groups is common and has produced the most extreme forms of discrimination and domination (Baron, Byrne, & Brauscombe, 2006). However, it should be noted that the majority group can also become a target for prejudice, as illustrated by the student perspective in the margin.

S TUDENT PERSPECTIVE

"My friend said that he 'hates white people because they try to dominate people of color.' I, on the other hand, feel differently. One should not blame all white people for the mistakes and prejudiced acts that white people have made. Unfortunately, my friend has yet to learn this."

STUDENT OF COLOR, QUOTED IN NAGNA, GURIN, & SOHNSON, 2005, P. 102.

The Tendency for Individuals to Strengthen Their Self-Esteem through Group Membership and Group Identity

Self-esteem—how individuals feel about themselves—can be influenced by their group membership. If people think that the group they belong to is superior, it enables them to feel better about themselves (Tafjel, 1982). Their reasoning goes something like this: "My group is superior, and since I belong to it, I am superior." This type of self-esteem building through group identification is even more likely to occur when an individual's self-esteem has been threatened or damaged by personal frustration or failure. When this happens, the person whose self-esteem has been lowered can boost it by stigmatizing and putting down members of another group (Rudman & Fairchild, 2004), or by blaming them and making them the "scapegoat" (Gemmil, 1989). For example, the person might say, "If it weren't for 'them,' we wouldn't have this problem."

Probably the most extreme example of "scapegoating" in human history took place in Nazi Germany, where Jews were blamed for the country's economic problems and became targets of the Holocaust. Studies have shown that when times are tough (e.g., when unemployment is high) and people are frustrated by failure or loss, prejudice and discrimination tend to increase (Aronson, et al., 2005).

Did You Know?

The word "scapegoat" has Biblical roots. The scapegoat was a goat released into the wilderness during the Jewish ceremony of Yom Kippur (Day of Atonement). Before the goat was set free, a high priest symbolically laid the sins of the people on its head. The word has now come to refer to a person or group of people, often innocent, who are blamed for the suffering of others or who are made to suffer in their place, usually to distract attention from the real cause.

Although the causes of prejudice are still not completely understood, we can help guard against prejudice by remaining aware of the five tendencies discussed in this section, namely:

1. The tendency to favor familiarity and fear strangers;
2. The tendency to mentally categorize people into "in" and "out" groups;

3. The tendency to perceive members of other groups as more alike than members of our own group;

4. The tendency for majority group members' attitudes to be more strongly influenced by negative behaviors committed by members of minority groups than by members of their own (majority) group;

5. The tendency for individuals to strengthen their self-esteem through group membership and group identity.

Pause for Reflection

Have you ever held a prejudice against a particular group of people?

If you have, what was the group, and how do you think your prejudice developed in the first place?

 ## Types of Stereotypes and Prejudiced Belief Systems about Group Inferiority ————————————➤ SNAPSHOT SUMMARY

Ethnocentrism: Considering one's own culture or ethnic group to be "central" or "normal," and viewing cultures that are different as "deficient" or "inferior."

> For example, claiming that another culture is "weird" or "abnormal" for eating certain animals that our culture considers unethical to eat, even though we eat certain animals that their culture considers unethical to eat.

Racism: Prejudice or discrimination based on skin color; a belief that your race is superior to another race with an expression of that belief through attitude(s) and action(s).

> For example, Cecil Rhodes (Englishman and empire builder of British South Africa), once claimed: "We [the British] are the finest race in the world and the more of the world we inhabit the better it is for the human race."
> A current example of racism is the Klu Klux Klan, an American terrorist group that believes in the supremacy of the white race, and considers all other races to be inferior.

Apartheid: An institutionalized system of "legal racism" supported by a nation's government, which is intended to maintain the government's regime. Apartheid derives from a word in the Afrikaan language, meaning "apartness." It was the official name of a national system of racial segregation and discrimination that existed in South Africa from 1948 to 1994.

STUDENT PERSPECTIVE

"I would like to change the entire world, so that we wouldn't be segregated by continents and territories."

COLLEGE SOPHOMORE

Classism: Prejudice or discrimination based on social class, particularly toward people of low socioeconomic status.

> For example, focusing only on the contributions made by politicians and wealthy industrialists to America, while ignoring the contributions of poor immigrants, farmers, slaves, and pioneer women.

Nationalism: Excessive interest and belief in the strengths of one's own nation without acknowledgment of its mistakes or weaknesses, and without concern for the needs of other nations or the common interests of all nations.

> For example, "blind patriotism" that blinds people to the shortcomings of their own nation, and views any questioning or criticism of their nation as being disloyal or "unpatriotic." (As in the slogan, "America: right or wrong" and "America: love it or leave it!")

Regionalism: Prejudice or discrimination based on the geographical region of a country in which an individual has been born and raised.

    For example, a northerner thinking that all southerners are racists.

Religious Bigotry: Denying the fundamental human right of other people to hold religious beliefs, or to hold religious beliefs that differ from one's own.

    For example, an atheist who forces non-religious (secular) beliefs on others, or a member of a religious group who believes that people who hold different religious beliefs are immoral or "sinners."

Xenophobia: Extreme fear or hatred of foreigners, outsiders, or strangers.

    For example, believing that all immigrants should be kept out of the country because they will increase the crime rate.

Anti-Semitism: Prejudice or discrimination toward Jews or people who practice the religion of Judaism.

    For example, hating Jews because they're the ones who "killed Christ."

Genocide: Mass murdering of one group by another group.

    For example, the Holocaust in World War II in which millions of Jews were murdered. Other examples include the murdering of Cambodians under the Khmer Rougher, the murdering of Bosnian Muslims in the former country of Yugoslavia , and the slaughter of the Tutsi minority by the Hutu majority In Rwanda.

Terrorism: Intentional acts of violence against civilians that are motivated by political or religious prejudice.

    For example, the September 11th attacks on the United States.

Ageism: Prejudice or discrimination based on age, particularly toward the elderly.

    For example, believing that all "old" people are bad drivers with bad judgment and bad vision.

Ableism: Prejudice or discrimination toward people who are disabled or handicapped—physically, mentally, or emotionally.

    For example, avoiding interaction with handicapped people because of anxiety about not knowing what to say or how to act around them.

Sexism: prejudice or discrimination based on sex or gender.

    For example, believing that women should not be presidents because they would be too "emotional."

Heterosexism: Belief that heterosexuality is the only acceptable sexual orientation.

    For example, using the phrase, "fag" or "queer" as an insult or put down; or believing that gays should not have the same legal rights and opportunities as heterosexuals.

Homophobia: Extreme fear and/or hatred of homosexuals.

    For example, people who create or contribute to anti-gay Web sites.

STUDENT PERSPECTIVE

"Most religions dictate that theirs is the only way, and without believing in it, you cannot enter the mighty kingdom of heaven. Who are we to judge? It makes more sense for God to be the only one mighty enough to make that decision. If other people could understand and see from this perspective, then many religious arguments could be avoided."

FIRST-YEAR STUDENT

Pause for Reflection

Look back at the stereotypes and belief systems summarized above and make a note next to each item indicating: (a) whether you have heard of this form of stereotype or prejudice, and (b) whether you have observed or experienced it.

A Model for Overcoming Bias and Appreciating Diversity

Overcoming prejudice and moving toward appreciation of diversity may be viewed as a systematic, sequential process that begins with *awareness* of human differences, followed by *acknowledgment* of any hidden biases we may have toward groups who differ from us, which leads to our *acceptance* of group differences, and culminates in our taking *action* to learn from and contribute to the diversity that surrounds us. Thus, the diversity-appreciation process may be conceived of as a cycle comprised of the following four stages:

1. **Awareness:** understanding of our personal beliefs and attitudes toward diverse groups;
2. **Acknowledgment:** how our beliefs and attitudes may have affected members of diverse groups;
3. **Acceptance:** sensitivity to and empathy for members of diverse groups; and
4. **Action:** actively reaching out and interacting with people from diverse groups (see Figure 4.2).

This process is hierarchical—i.e., each stage builds on the stage that precedes it; we cannot move to the next stage until the previous stage has been successfully completed. After all stages of the cycle are completed, we should be positioned not only to accept or tolerate diversity, but also to appreciate and learn from diversity.

Stage 1. Awareness

Research indicates that prejudice and discrimination can occur unconsciously or unintentionally (Baron, Byrne, & Branscombe, 2006). Thus, the first stage in the diversity-appreciation process is developing self-awareness about our attitudes toward diversity, particularly awareness of any stereotypes and prejudices we may have that are biasing our perception of, or behavior toward, different groups of people. At the bare minimum, we want to behave in a way that demonstrates tolerance or acceptance of diversity, and is free of prejudice or discrimination.

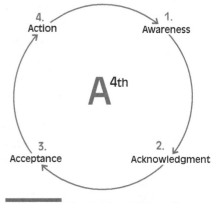

Figure 4.2 The Cycle of Diversity Appreciation

When you gain deeper self-insight into who you truly are as an individual, you gain greater awareness of your personal strengths, weaknesses, biases, and blind spots with respect to diversity. By becoming fully aware of your own beliefs and behaviors, you are demonstrating interpersonal intelligence—the ability to relate effectively to others (Gardner, 1993).

To become truly sensitive to members of other groups, we must first become fully aware of our feelings about them. As we become more aware of our feelings, we gain a greater awareness of what others feel (Goleman, 1995).

Know Thyself

Self-awareness is the first step to overcoming personal prejudices and developing intrapersonal intelligence.

This process of gaining self-awareness also involves gaining greater knowledge of our beliefs. One of the definitions of a "belief" is "something accepted as true by a group of persons" (American Heritage Dictionary, 2008). The acceptance of a belief without being aware of why a belief is held or the truth and accuracy of the "facts" on which the belief if built, can lead us to develop *bias*. Self-awareness involves asking ourselves not only what we believe about a subject, person or group, but also why we hold the belief and what evidence we have to support it. Taking time to reflect, introspect, and inspect our own biases represents the critical first stage in the process of diversity appreciation.

Many years of socialization from an early age and from a variety of agents (parents and other family members, peers, media, etc.) can strongly shape our beliefs—to such a degree that we may no longer consciously question or evaluate them. In fact, to question or challenge long-held beliefs may make us feel as if we are disregarding or disrespecting our upbringing and heritage. However, to evaluate how our beliefs have been shaped by our past experiences is to gain greater awareness and control of them. Rather than being blindly programmed by the beliefs of others, we need to be conscious of their origins and take ownership of them. For example, if you favor a particular political party, ask yourself why you favor that party? Is it because of your parents' beliefs, your friends' opinions, or by actually studying the party's platform? We should base our political party beliefs on a careful, comparative analysis of the each party's position on key issues. We may still choose the party favored by our parents or friends, but we will have made a choice based on conscious reasoning and critical thinking, rather than unconscious feelings and prior conditioning.

Similarly, becoming aware of our subtle and sometimes subconscious prejudices is the first stage toward controlling them. Reducing prejudice not only benefits those who are the targets of our prejudice, it benefits us. Research indicates that less-prejudiced people report greater satisfaction with their life (Feagin & McKinney, 2003), perhaps because they are more open to social experiences and less distrustful or fearful of other people (Baron, Byrne, & Branscombe, 2006).

Here is a simple strategy you can use to increase your conscious awareness of your feelings, beliefs, and biases about diverse groups:

- Take a moment to list all of all of the things that come to your mind about a group of people that are different than you, or a group with whom you've had very little interaction. (You can use the diversity spectrum on page 2 to identify one such group.)
- Write down all of the feelings and thoughts you have about them. Try to go very deep into the thought process to dig up all of the hidden notions you may have about the group you have chosen. Be completely honest; don't worry about whether your thoughts and feelings will be judged right or wrong, because you will not be asked to share your thoughts with anyone else. Write down what you truly believe, rather than what sounds right or seems socially acceptable.

● Once you have explored your deepest thoughts and feelings, and have recorded them in writing, honestly respond to the following question.

Pause for Reflection

Would you say that any of the beliefs and feelings represents a stereotype, negative bias, or prejudice?

If yes, why do you hold it, and how do you think you acquired it in the first place?

Once you have answered the above questions honestly, you are now ready to move on to the next stage in the cycle of diversity appreciation: *Acknowledgment*.

Stage 2. Acknowledgment

Before we can arrive at the point of appreciating differences in others, we need to acknowledge that human differences are positive and beneficial. Diversity appreciation involves the ability to recognize and value a variety of characteristics that make all people unique. In addition, it provides an atmosphere that promotes and celebrates each person as an individual and how those individuals form distinctive groups with common goals (Esty, et al., 1995).

To appreciate diversity, we must first acknowledge the diversity that surrounds us and how we can benefit from it. Acknowledging the diverse groups that make up our social environment and how their experiences differ from our own involves more than simply saying, "Live and let live" or, "We're all human, so let's come to terms with our differences and move on." These statements minimize or ignore the fact that different groups of people have had very different life experiences and continue to face different challenges. More importantly, it denies their group identity, which is an important element of their self-concept and self-esteem.

Acknowledgment also involves understanding how our thoughts and feelings may have affected the lives of others who are different than us, and how we may have affected their view of themselves. Charles Cooley, famous sociologist, coined the term "looking glass self" to capture the idea that seeing how others act toward us, or react to us (positively or negatively), is like looking in a mirror because their actions and reactions reflect back on us and affect how we view ourselves (positively or negatively) (Cooley, 1922).

Pause for Reflection

Would you say that the beliefs you've held toward the group you identified in the previous Pause for Reflection had a positive impact, negative impact, or no impact on individuals in that group?

When we honestly acknowledge how our thoughts, feelings, and actions have affected others who are different than us (particularly if the impact has been negative), we are ready to move on the next stage in the cycle of diversity appreciation: *Acceptance*.

Personal Experience I was an 11-year-old boy when I first became conscious of the ethnic group to which I belonged. One afternoon, I was comparing baseball cards with a friend of mine who was of Irish descent. As he was showing me his cards, he pulled out certain cards and said "he's good." After he pulled out the fourth or fifth card, I finally figured out what his criterion was for determining who was "good." All the cards he pulled out had Irish surnames (e.g., O'Toole, McMahon, Maloney). He certainly didn't pull out any cards that had Italian-sounding names. Later that same year, I noticed that some of my Italian classmates were being derisively called "waps" and "guineas." On one particular occasion, someone in our crowded schoolyard yelled at me: "Hey, Cuseo, you know why you don't have any freckles? It's because they'd slide right off your greasy Italian face!" Laughter then broke out among a bunch of kids who overheard the comment.

I never forgot these childhood incidents and I'm embarrassed to admit that, to this day, I root against Notre Dame sports teams because they're called the "fighting Irish" and I root against Boston's professional basketball team because they're called the Celtics. However, I'm happy to report that my best friend in college and my best friend right now is Irish. While I don't think I hold any deep-seated prejudice against the Irish, nor have I ever discriminated against them, I must admit and acknowledge that I have a bias.

Joe Cuseo, *Professor of Psychology and co-author of this text*

Stage 3. Acceptance

Acceptance involves developing sensitivity toward and empathy for others who may have been negatively affected by our biases or prejudices. In this stage, we accept that although we may not be able to fully understand the feelings of others who have been on the receiving end of prejudice, we still can sympathize with them. In short, we develop empathy, which is a critical component of emotional intelligence (Goleman, 2006).

To increase your understanding and empathy for the experiences of members of another group, imagine yourself as a member of that group, and attempt to visualize what the experience might be like. Better yet, try to place yourself in the position or situation of members of that group. For instance, spend a day in a wheelchair to experience what it is like for someone who is physically disabled, or wear blinders to experience what it's like to be visually impaired.

Personal Experience

In 1995, I had surgery in which my degenerated hip was replaced with an artificial hip. Soon after the operation, I dislocated my artificial hip, which slowed down my recovery and made it necessary for me to use a wheelchair to get around campus. This experience temporarily put me in the role of a physically handicapped person. I had always heard the best way to develop empathy for others is to literally put yourself "in their shoes" or situation. My wheelchair experience showed me that this was sage advice. Not surprisingly, I now have a deeper appreciation of why access ramps are critical for people in wheelchairs. However, what I didn't anticipate was how difficult it must be for a wheelchair-bound person to be constantly "looking up" to others and have others constantly "looking down" at them. Being 5'4" (barely), you would have thought that I, of all able-bodied people, should have been aware of this vertical challenge. But, no, I never once thought about it until I was "forced" into the role of using a wheelchair. This experience made me a firm believer in the power of role play for promoting empathy and social sensitivity.

Joe Cuseo, *Professor of Psychology and co-author of this text*

W**ords** of
Wisdom

"We need every human gift and cannot afford to neglect any gift because of artificial barriers of sex or race or class or national origin."
MARGARET MEAD, AMERICAN ANTHROPOLOGIST

Acceptance also involves realizing that our biases or prejudices have not only affected others, but ourselves as well. Prejudice not only impedes members of other groups from reaching their full potential, it also impedes our personal development and that of our society. For example, when the personal rights or freedoms of fellow citizens are threatened by prejudice and discrimination, the political stability and economic growth of any democratic nation is threatened. America's prosperity in the 21st century will require effective use of the talents and abilities of all its citizens, including those from diverse backgrounds and cultures (American Council on Education, Making the Case for Affirmative Action, 2008).

The following practices and strategies may be used to develop acceptance of individuals from diverse groups toward whom we have held biases or avoided contact.

Diversity of people and differing ideas are the foundation of creativity in the workforce. Copyright © 2009 by iofoto. Under license from Shutterstock, Inc.

WORDS OF WISDOM

"Stop judging by mere appearances, and make a right judgment."

THE BIBLE, JOHN 7:24

"You can't judge a book by the cover."

HIT RECORD, 1962, BY ELLAS BATES, A.K.A., BO DIDDLEY
(NOTE: A "BO DIDDLEY" IS A ONE-STRINGED AFRICAN GUITAR.)

"The common eye sees only the outside of things, and judges by that. But the seeing eye pierces through and reads the heart and the soul, finding there capacities which the outside didn't indicate or promise."

SAMUEL CLEMENS, A.K.A., MARK TWAIN; WRITER, LECTURER, AND HUMORIST

- Consciously avoid preoccupation with physical appearances. Go deeper and get beneath the superficial surface of appearances to view people in terms of *who* they really are and how they really act, not in terms of how they look. Remember the old proverb: "It's what's inside that counts." Judge others by the quality of their personal character, not by the familiarity of their physical characteristics.

- Make a conscious effort to perceive each person you interact with as a unique individual with a distinctive personal identity, rather than as a member of a certain group of people. Form your impressions of each person on an individual, case-by-case basis, rather than by using some general "rule of thumb."

This may seem like an obvious and easy thing to do, but remember, research shows that there is a natural tendency for humans to consider individuals who are members of unfamiliar groups as being more alike (or all alike) than members of their own group (Taylor, 2006). Thus, we may have to consciously resist this tendency to over-generalize or "lump together" people by making an intentional attempt to focus on each person's individuality.

Once we have developed the ability to perceive and understand members of diverse groups as unique individuals, we are ready to begin to make changes in our approach in dealing with them in a more positive and personal way. We are now positioned for open interaction, dialog, and friendship formation with individuals from diverse groups. We are ready to take move on to the final stage in the diversity appreciation process: *Action*.

© 2005 Grimmy, Inc. Used with the permission of Grimmy, Inc. and the Cartoonist Group. All rights reserved.

Stage 4. Action

Once we have (a) become aware of our beliefs, (b) acknowledged the effect of our beliefs on others, and (c) accepted the feelings of others, we can take action with respect to diversity. This stage in the cycle of diversity appreciation involves engaging in specific actions that will enable us to capitalize on the power of diversity to promote our own success, the success of individuals from diverse groups, and the success of our nation. Said in another way, we are now ready to climb the steps to cultural competence.

Cultural competence may be defined as moving beyond mere acceptance or tolerance of diversity to a deeper and genuine appreciation of people from diverse cultural backgrounds. Research suggests that when students focus on differences alone or have a philosophy of tolerance alone, then minority groups feel more isolated; deep, authentic appreciation of diversity can only take place when students from different groups interact with each other, and learn from one another (Smith, 1997). Someone who merely tolerates diversity might say: "Let's just get along," "live and let live," or "to each his own." Someone with cultural competence moves beyond diversity tolerance to a higher level of diversity *appreciation* by becoming genuinely interested in different cultures and eager to learn about and from the experiences of different groups of people.

Cultural competence may be characterized as an ascending stairway of ten steps that begins at the lowest and most extreme forms of resistance to diversity, escalates to progressively higher levels of diversity appreciation, and culminates in cultural competence (see Figure 4.3).

STUDENT PERSPECTIVE

"I grew up in a very racist family. Even just a year ago, I could honestly say 'I hate Asians' with a straight face and mean it. My senior AP language teacher tried hard to teach me not to be judgmental. He got me to be open to others, so much so that my current boyfriend is half Chinese!"

FIRST-YEAR COLLEGE STUDENT

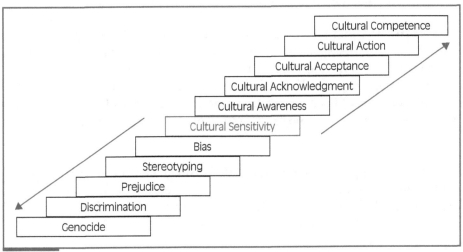

Figure 4.3 Staircase to Cultural Competence

Pause for Reflection

Cultural Sensitivity: an understanding that our internal biases have affected those around us (both those we know personally and those we do not)

Cultural Awareness: an awareness of your own cultural biases and the effects they may have on yourself and others

Cultural Acknowledgment: the act of acknowledging the differences that exist between individuals, races, and entire cultures, and viewing those differences as positive rather than negative.

Cultural Acceptance: valuing cultural differences and similarities, and viewing the differences as positive.

Cultural Action: the process of recognizing differences and responding to them in a positive manner; it represents an advanced step in the process of becoming culturally competent.

Cultural Competence: the ability to appreciate cultural differences and to interact effectively with people from different cultural backgrounds.

Looking at the definitions of each step of the staircase, which step are you on? Are you consistently moving up the stairs?

If you have not arrived at the last step of cultural competence, what actions will you take to get there?

Throughout history, humans have held beliefs about different groups that fall on the lower steps of this staircase. It should be the goal of humankind to ascend these stairs and never turn back to descend them.

REMEMBER: Don't let cultural differences get in the way of potentially rewarding relationships. The more opportunities you create to learn from others who are different than yourself, the more opportunities you create to learn about yourself. The self-knowledge you acquire by taking this step will bring you back to the first stage in the cycle of diversity appreciation, enabling you to begin a new, more advanced ascent to cultural competence.

The following and final chapter of this text will equip you with a strategic plan for appreciating diversity and for attaining cultural competence. Implementing the plan should enrich the quality of your college education and the quality of your life; it should do the same for diverse groups of people with whom you interact.

Summary

This chapter examined various forms of prejudice and discrimination that have plagued our society, identified their possible causes, and provided a model for overcoming biases that block our appreciation of diversity.

Stereotyping is often the first step in the process of developing prejudice and discrimination. To stereotype is to *view* all members of the same group in the same way. Individuality is ignored because all people who share a similar group characteristic (e.g., race or gender) are viewed as having the same personal characteristics.

If members of a stereotyped group are judged or evaluated in a negative way, the result is *prejudice*. Prejudice may be defined as a negative pre-judgment, attitude, or belief about another person or group of people, which is formed before the facts are known. Stereotyping and prejudice often go hand-in-hand because if the group stereotype is negative, individual members of the stereotyped group are then pre-judged in a negative way.

While prejudice involves a negative belief or opinion, *discrimination* involves a negative *action* that results in treating others in an unfair way. Thus, discrimination is prejudice put into action.

Research indicates that the following human tendencies play a key role in causing prejudice and discrimination.

Favoring familiarity and fearing strangers. When humans encounter what is unfamiliar or strange, they tend to experience feelings of discomfort or anxiety. In contrast, what is familiar tends to be more accepted and better liked.

Segregation of groups. When a group separates itself from another group, the result is less contact between groups, causing members of the other group to remain "unfamiliar." This lack of familiarity, in turn, can lead to feelings of uncertainty and discomfort about the other group.

Use of selective perception and selective memory. Prejudice can remain intact because facts that contradict it are often ignored through the psychological process of *selective perception*—the tendency for a person to see what he or she *expects* to see. This can result in the prejudiced person paying closer attention to information that is consistent with the prejudice and "seeing" information that supports the prejudice, while ignoring or overlooking information that contradicts it. Selective perception is often accompanied by *selective memory*—the tendency to remember information that is consistent with the prejudice, and forgetting information that is inconsistent with it, or contradicts it (Judd et al., 1991). The dual processes of selective perception and selective memory often operate *unconsciously*, so they may be used without people being fully aware that they are using them or that they are contributing to their prejudice.

Mentally categorizing people into "in" and "out" groups. To make their complex social world simpler to understand, humans tend to group people into mental categories. This tendency to categorize individuals into groups can lead to group stereotypes and contributes to prejudice by creating categories of *in*-groups ("us") and *out*-groups ("them"), whereby one's own group is seen as the "normal" in-group and other groups are viewed as "abnormal" out-groups.

Perceiving members of other groups as more alike than members of our own group. Studies show that humans tend to see members of groups that they do not belong to as more alike in attitudes and behavior than members of their own group. This tendency can lead to stereotyping members of other groups (e.g., they're all the same.) Even if an individual member of another group does not fit the group stereotype, that individual is seen as an "exception to the rule."

Majority group members' attitudes tend to be more strongly influenced by negative behaviors committed by members of minority groups than by members of their own (majority) group. Since minority group members are more likely to be seen as different or distinctive, their behavior is more likely to stand out in the minds of majority group members, which makes it more likely that any negative behaviors exhibited by a minority group member will be better remembered. Since these negative behaviors are more likely to be retained in the minds of the majority group, these memories are more likely to trigger negative views of the minority group, thus contributing to the development of prejudice.

The tendency for individuals to strengthen their self-esteem through group membership and group identity. If people think that the group they belong to is superior, it enables them to feel better about themselves. The reasoning goes like this: "My group is superior, and since I belong to it, I am superior." Thus, individuals can boost their self-esteem by claiming that other groups are inferior, which can lead to and reinforce prejudice.

Overcoming prejudice and moving toward appreciation of diversity may be viewed as a systematic, sequential process beginning with *awareness* of human differences, followed by *acknowledgment* of hidden biases toward groups who differ from us, which leads to *acceptance* of human differences and our taking *action* to learn from and through diversity. Thus, the diversity-appreciation process may be conceived of as a cycle comprised of four stages:

1. **Awareness:** our personal beliefs and attitudes toward diverse groups;
2. **Acknowledgment:** how our beliefs and attitudes have affected members of diverse groups;
3. **Acceptance:** sensitivity to and empathy for members of diverse groups; and
4. **Action:** actively reaching out and interacting with people from diverse groups.

Negative stereotypes and biases can lead to prejudice and discrimination, which, in turn, can function as blocks or barriers to diversity appreciation. Although stereotypes and biases may not always be fully conscious and blatantly intentional, we must still take the time to examine them, acknowledge them, and make a conscious and intentional attempt to overcome them. Only then can we begin to truly appreciate diversity and experience its multiple benefits.

Chapter 4 Exercises

4.1 Diversity Comfort Zones

Which one of the following students would you feel least comfortable having as a roommate?

a. Asian American

b. African American

c. Native American

d. Bisexual

Why?

You walk into a college dining hall and all the chairs are taken, except for one seat at each table. You know no one at any of the tables, and the majority of students sitting at each table are from the different groups listed below:

a. African Americans

b. Hispanic Americans

c. Women

d. International students

At which one of these tables would you feel most comfortable sitting? Why?

Source: Adapted from University of New Hampshire, 2001

135

4.2 Hidden Bias Test

Go to https://implicit.harvard.edu/implicit/demo/selectatest.html and take one or more of the *"hidden bias tests"* on the website. These tests assess subtle bias with respect to gender, age, Native Americans, African Americans, Asian Americans, religious denominations, sexual orientation, disabilities, and body weight. You can assess whether you have a bias toward any of these groups.

After you complete your self-assessment, reflect on your results by responding to the following questions:

a. Did the results reveal any bias that you were unaware of?

b. Did you think the assessment results were accurate or valid?

c. What do you think best accounts for, or explains your results?

d. If your parents and best friend took the test, how do you think their results would compare with yours?

4.3 Gender Stereotyping

Take a look at the following cartoon:

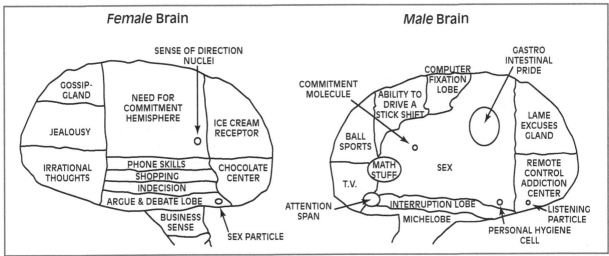

Stereotype of the male and female brain that once appeared on the Internet. Author unknown.

a. Do you find the cartoon offensive in any way?

b. Are there any elements of the cartoon that you think are definitely false or extremely exaggerated?

c. What aspects of the cartoon do you think may be generally accurate or true (if any)?

4.4 Case Study of a Hate Crime: Racially Motivated Murder

Jasper County, Texas, has a population of approximately 31,000 people, 80% of them are white, 18% black, and 2% are of other races. The county's poverty rate is considerably higher than the national average, and its average household income is significantly lower. In 1998, the mayor, president of the Chamber of Commerce, and two councilmen were black. From the outside, Jasper appeared to be a town with racial harmony, and its black and white leaders were quick to state there was racial harmony in Jasper.

However, on June 7, 1998, James Byrd, Jr., a 49-year-old African-American male, was walking home along a road one evening and was offered a ride by three white males. Rather than taking Mr. Byrd home, Lawrence Brewer (31), John King (23), and Shawn Berry (23), three individuals linked to white-supremacist groups, took Mr. Byrd to an isolated area and began beating him. They then dropped his pants to his ankles, painted his face black, chained Mr. Byrd to their truck and dragged him for approximately three miles. The truck was driven in a zigzag fashion in order to inflict maximum pain on the victim. Mr. Byrd was decapitated after his body collided with a culvert in a ditch alongside the road. His skin, arms, genitalia, and other body parts were strewn along the road, while his torso was found dumped in front of a black cemetery. Medical examiners testified that Mr. Byrd was alive for much of the dragging.

While in prison awaiting trial, Lawrence Brewer wrote letters to other inmates. In one letter, Brewer wrote: "Well, I did it and am no longer a virgin. It was a rush and I'm still licking my lips for more." Once the trials were completed, Brewer and King were sentenced to death. Both Brewer and King, whose bodies were covered with racist tattoos, had been on parole prior to the incident, and they had previously been cellmates. King had spent an extensive amount of time in prison where he began to associate with white males in an environment where each race was pitted against the other.

As a result of the murder, Mr. Byrd's family created the James Byrd Foundation for Racial Healing in 1998. On January 20, 1999, a wrought iron fence that separated black and white graves for more than 150 years in Jasper Cemetery was removed in a special unity service. Members of the Ku Klux Klan have since visited the gravesite of James Byrd several times, leaving racist stickers and other derogatory marks that have angered the Jasper community and Mr. Byrd's family.

Sources: *San Antonio Express News*, September 17, 1999, *Louisiana Weekly*, February 3, 2003, *Houston Chronicle*, June 14, 1998, Two Towns of Jasper, PBS.

Questions for Reflection and Discussion

1. What social factors (if any) do you think led to the incident?

2. Could the incident have been prevented? If yes, how? If no, why not?

3. What do you think will be the long-term effects of this incident on the town?

4. Do you think an incident such as this could occur in your hometown or near your college campus? Why?

5. If this event were to take place in your home town, how do you think members of your community would react?

4.5 Case Study of a Hate Crime: Homophobic Murder

October 7, 1998

Matthew Shepard, a 21-year-old University of Wyoming freshman, was fatally beaten a few hours after attending a planning meeting for Gay Awareness Week events on campus on October 7, 1998. Matthew was lured out of the Fireside Bar where two individuals, Aaron James McKinney and Russell Henderson, pretended to be gay and targeted him for a robbery. According to interviews with McKinney conducted by police investigators, Shepard placed his hand on McKinney's leg as they drove through Laramie. McKinney then stated, "Guess what, we're not gay. You're going to get jacked. It's Gay Awareness Week." McKinney and Henderson began beating Shepard inside the truck and drove to an isolated place in a new rural subdivision. They tied Matthew to a fence and pistol whipped him with a .357 magnum handgun. The assailants then stole Shepard's wallet and shoes and left him tied to the fence.

Approximately 18 hours after the beating had taken place, a bicyclist came upon Matthew's body which was tied to a ranch fence. Upon first glance, the bicyclist thought that Matthew was a scarecrow. A sheriff's deputy testified Matthew's wrists were tied so tight that it was difficult to cut the rope holding him. The deputy also testified Matthew's head was covered in blood, except where it had been partially washed by tears running down his face.

Matthew Shepard died five days after the attack on October 12, 1998. He never regained consciousness during the time he was hospitalized. An autopsy concluded Matthew had been hit in the head 18 times. He also sustained bruises on the back of his hands while trying to protect himself as well as bruises around the groin, an indication he had been kicked numerous times.

McKinney told girlfriend Kristin Price, "Well you know how I feel about gays" when explaining his actions that night. Rather than facing a jury trial, Henderson pleaded guilty and was sentenced to two life sentences. The two life terms were to run consecutively—life without parole in exchange for a guilty plea. McKinney was found guilty and sentenced to two life sentences in a deal brokered by Shepard's parents just as the jury was about to begin the process of hearing testimony about whether McKinney should be put to death. In exchange for the sentencing, McKinney relinquished his right to appeal.

In a statement after the sentencing at the McKinney trial, Matthew's father ended with the following: "You robbed me of something very precious, and I will never forgive you for that. May you live a long life and may you thank Matthew every day for it."

(*Source*: This information was obtained from *NY Times* articles published on the following dates: October 10, 1998, November 21, 1998, April 6, 1999, and November 5, 1999.

Questions for Reflection and Discussion

1. Why or how do you think the attackers developed such an intense hatred of gay men?

2. What, if anything, could have been done to prevent the attackers' hatred toward gays from developing in the first place?

3. What do you think the appropriate sentence should have been for this crime? Why?

4. Do you think the attackers could ever be successfully rehabilitated, educated, or treated for their homophobia?

5. Do you predict that hate crimes toward gay males are likely to decrease, remain the same, or increase in the future? Why?

6. Do you think that there are more hate crimes committed against gay males or lesbian females? If you think there is a difference, what do you think accounts for this difference?

Making the Most of Diversity in College and Beyond

5

Purpose

The primary purpose of this chapter is to supply you with a strategic plan and a set of specific action strategies for making the most of diversity, which you can use to promote your success in college and beyond.

Activate Your Thinking

What would you say is the difference between:

1. the *curriculum* and *co-curriculum*, and
2. *vicarious* learning and *experiential* learning?

Strategies for Acquiring Knowledge about Diverse Cultures

Research indicates that *active involvement* is the most powerful principle of human learning (Astin, 1993; Kuh, 2000). To maximize your success in college and life, you cannot be a passive spectator; you need to become an active agent in the learning process. Your level of active involvement increases when you increase the amount of *time* and *effort* (*energy*) you put into the learning process. Thus, learning from diversity requires that you invest both time and effort in the process of learning about diverse groups of people. Listed below are specific strategies for becoming actively involved in the diversity-learning process through the college curriculum (formal courses) and co-curriculum (out-of-class learning experiences).

Take courses that cover material relating to diversity.

You can plan to implement this strategy by reviewing your college catalog (bulletin) and identifying courses that are designed to promote understanding or appreciation of diversity. These courses may focus on diverse cultures associated with different nations (often referred to as international or cross-cultural courses), or they may focus on diverse cultures within the United States (often referred to as multicultural courses). Learning about other cultures can enable you to learn about different ethnic groups' general customs, values and styles of interpersonal interaction. However, be sure not to use these general patterns to over-generalize and stereotype individuals from these groups.

REMEMBER: While it is valuable to learn about different cultures and the common characteristics shared by members of a particular culture, individual differences exist among members of the same culture; do not assume that all individuals from the same cultural background share the same personal characteristics.

Taking courses that have an international focus helps you develop the global perspective needed for success in today's international economy and increases the attractiveness of your college transcript to potential employers (Cuseo, Fecas, & Thompson, 2007). In a national study of college students who participated in multicultural courses, it was found that students of all different racial and ethnic groups made significant gains in learning and intellectual development (Smith et al., 2003). These findings are reinforced by results from a survey of undergraduate students at Penn State University, which revealed that students who participated in multicultural courses experienced positive changes in both knowledge of, and attitudes toward diversity. For example, both white students and students of color developed more tolerant attitudes about racial and gender differences (Palmer, 2000).

It is also noteworthy that a majority of American voters support the idea that college students should be required to study different cultures; 69% agree that "courses and campus activities that emphasize diversity and diverse perspectives" have a positive effect on the education of college students (National Survey of Voters, 1998).

Strongly consider taking a foreign language course.

Courses that develop your ability to comprehend and communicate in another language are not only educationally beneficial, they also benefit your career development because research indicates that employers of college graduates are placing increasing value on employees who have foreign language skills (Fixman, 1990; Office of Research, 1994).

Taking courses relating to diversity serves to promote learning, intellectual development, and career preparation.

In class discussions and course assignments, be ready to discuss the diversity implications of whatever topic you are discussing or researching.

For instance, use multicultural or cross-cultural examples as evidence or examples to support and illustrate your points. If you have a choice about what topic to research in your courses, consider choosing topics that relate to diversity or have implications for diversity.

Engage in co-curricular experiences on campus that involve diversity.

Review your student handbook for co-curricular programs, student activities, and student clubs that promote diversity awareness and appreciation. Studies indicate that participation in diversity-related programs helps to reduce unconscious prejudice (Blair, 2002) and promote cognitive development (Pascarella & Terenzini, 2005).

What you learn from participation in diversity courses and programs also provides you with the knowledge and self-confidence to take the next step toward appreciating diversity: interpersonal contact and collaboration with people from diverse backgrounds.

Interacting and Collaborating with Members of Diverse Groups

If you have taken the time and effort to learn about diverse groups and cultures, you should feel more comfortable about interacting with people from different cultural backgrounds. Studies show that learning is maximized when students move beyond acquiring knowledge about diversity *vicariously* (through someone else) such as through lectures and readings to learning *experientially* through direct, personal contact with people from diverse

WORDS OF WISDOM

"Mere knowledge is not power; it is only possibility. Action is power; and its highest manifestation is when it is directed by knowledge."

FRANCIS BACON (1561–1626), ENGLISH PHILOSOPHER, LAWYER, AND CHAMPION OF MODERN SCIENCE

WORDS OF **W**ISDOM

"If you don't live it, it won't come out of your horn."

CHARLIE "BIRD" PARKER, FAMED AFRICAN-AMERICAN JAZZ SAXOPHONIST, COMPOSER, AND ORIGINATOR OF BEBOP

"If you do not live the life you believe, you will believe the life you live."

ANONYMOUS

STUDENT **P**ERSPECTIVE

"I am very happy with the diversity here, but it also frightens me. I have never been in a situation where I have met people who are Jewish, Muslim, atheist, born-again, and many more."

FIRST-YEAR STUDENT (ERICKSON, PETERS, & STROMMER, 2006)

groups (Nagda et al., 2003). Formal courses and programs can help you learn *about* diversity; first-hand interaction with people from different cultures and backgrounds enables you to learn directly *from* diversity. This represents a significant difference in your level of active involvement with diversity. The difference would be comparable to acquiring knowledge of another country by reading about it, as opposed to going to the country and interacting with its native citizens. Interpersonal contact with individuals from diverse groups takes you beyond multicultural or cross-cultural awareness to a higher level of learning that involves intercultural interaction, it transforms appreciating diversity from an abstract attitude or belief system into concrete action and a way of living.

Your initial comfort level when interacting with people from diverse groups is likely to depend on how much experience you have had with diversity prior to college. If you have had little or no prior contact with members of diverse groups, it may be more challenging for you to initiate interactions with diverse students on campus. However, the good news is that if you have had little or no previous experience with diversity, you have the most to gain from experiencing diversity. Research consistently shows that when humans undergo experiences that differ radically from their prior experiences, they gain the most in terms of learning and cognitive development (Piaget, 1985; Acredolo & O'Connor, 1991).

Pause for Reflection

Rate the amount or variety of diversity you have experienced in the following settings?

1. The high school you attended	High	Moderate	Low
2. The college or university you now attend	High	Moderate	Low
3. The neighborhood in which you grew up	High	Moderate	Low
4. Places where you have worked or been employed	High	Moderate	Low

Which setting had the most and least diversity? What do you think accounts for this difference?

Strategies for Meeting and Forming Friendships with People from Diverse Backgrounds

Interpersonal interaction with people who differ significantly from us represents a major step toward truly appreciating and learning from diversity; but it is a more advanced step that moves you beyond mere contact and superficial interaction to the formation of deeper relationships. Taking the step to form closer friendships with students from diverse groups serves to strengthen your learning and diversify your social life. Perhaps, most importantly, when you form friendships with individuals from diverse groups, you are taking a major step toward helping reduce prejudice among members of your own cultural group. Research indicates that when people see a member of their own group develop positive relationships with members of a group that they have held prejudice toward, their prejudice declines (Paolini, et al., 2004).

Listed below is a series of strategies for increasing the depth of your relationships with individuals from diverse groups.

Intentionally create opportunities for interaction and conversation with individuals from diverse groups by placing yourself in situations and locations where you will come in regular contact with them.

Consciously resist the natural tendency to associate only with people who are similar to you. You can do this by intentionally placing yourself in situations where individuals from diverse groups are nearby so that potential interaction can take place. Research indicates that meaningful interpersonal interactions and friendships are more likely to develop among people who are in physical proximity to one another (Latané et al., 1993). You can create this condition in the college classroom by sitting near students from different ethnic or racial groups, or by joining them if you are given the choice to select whom you will work with in discussion groups and group projects.

Studies also show that friendships form when people regularly "cross paths" and find themselves in the same places at the same times. You can capitalize on this principle to create opportunities for form friendships with individuals from diverse groups by spending as much time on campus as possible, and by spending time in places where diverse groups of people are likely to congregate (e.g., by eating your meals in the student cafeteria, and studying in the college library).

If you have the opportunity to live on campus, do so, because studies show that it helps students make social connections and increases their satisfaction with the college experience (Pascarella & Terenzini, 2005; Tinto, 1993). If you are a commuter student, try to make your college experience as similar as possible to that of a residential student; for example, spend more than just class time on campus by studying, socializing, and attending social or cultural events on campus.

Keep in mind that discrimination is defined as treating different groups unequally. If we interact exclusively with members of our own group and separate ourselves from members of another group who are different than us, we are treating these two groups unequally. We may not be doing it maliciously or consciously, but segregating ourselves from certain groups of people still qualifies as a form of discrimination. By overcoming the tendency to congregate exclusively with members of our own group, we put ourselves in a position to get to know members of different groups as individuals and develop positive relationships with them. In research on more than 1,000 students who were studied from the beginning of their first year in college through the end of their fourth year, it was found that the majority of these students became more accepting of lesbians, gay men, and bisexual people during their 4 years at college. Sixty to seventy percent of students entering with negative attitudes became more accepting, and 50% of those entering with ambivalent or uncertain attitudes displayed more positive attitudes by the end of their fourth year. When asked why their attitudes changed, the number one reason cited by students was that they had interacted with lesbians, gay men, and bisexual people and got to know them as individuals. For students who entered college with negative attitudes, contact through casual acquaintances and classmates helped students' re-examine prior stereotypes and assumptions. For students who entered college with positive attitudes, contact through close friendships with a lesbian, gay male, or bisexual person further strengthened their positive attitudes (Kardia, 1998).

Put yourself in social situations where you are likely to meet diverse people with whom you share similar interests, goals, and values.

Research supports the old proverb, "Birds of a feather flock together." People tend to form friendships with others who share similar interests, values, or goals (AhYun, 2002). When people have something in common, they are more likely to become friends because they are more likely to spend time together doing things that relate to their common interests. They are also more likely to get along with each other because they provide each other with personal validation by socially reinforcing each other's interests, beliefs, and values (Festinger, 1954).

You can find individuals from diverse groups with whom you have something in common by regularly checking your college newspaper, posted flyers on campus, and the Student Information Desk in your Student Activities Center. Keep an eye out for social events that are more likely to attract others who share your interests, values, or goals.

Also, be on the lookout for student clubs and organizations that relate to your interests and hobbies. If you cannot find one, start one of your own. By joining or forming organizations and clubs comprised of diverse people with whom you have a shared interest, you can begin to actively infuse diversity into your own social life and make the power of diversity work *for* you, rather than waiting passively and hoping it will happen *to* you.

Spend time at the multicultural center on your campus, or join a campus club or organization that is devoted to diversity awareness (e.g., international student club).

Spending time in such venues will enable you to make contact with members of groups other than your own, and clearly sends a message that you are interested in them because you have taken the initiative to come to "their turf."

Participate in a multicultural or cross-cultural retreat sponsored by your college (e.g., multicultural student services).

A retreat setting can provide a warm and comfortable environment for getting to know people at a personal level, without the everyday interference and distractions that typically take place on campus.

Take advantage of the Internet to "chat" with students from diverse groups on your campus, or with students in different countries.

Electronic communication can be a more convenient and more comfortable way to initially interact with members of diverse groups with whom you have had little prior experience. After you have communicated successfully *online*, you may then feel more comfortable about interacting with them *in person*.

Meet members of diverse groups through *FaceBook*.

You can capitalize on this electronic social networking tool to meet and interact with people from diverse groups. Created in 2004 by a college sophomore, *Facebook* is an Internet database that is the college equivalent of *MySpace*. Through it, you can network with any other college student who has an ".edu" e-mail address. Since personal information and photos are often available through the *Facebook* database, you can check for announcements of social gatherings that tend to attract students from diverse backgrounds. You may also use *Facebook* to identify campus organizations whose membership includes students from diverse racial and cultural groups.

Although *Facebook* has the potential to provide an effective avenue for meeting new people and forming diverse friendships, remember that *Facebook*, like *MySpace*, is a public domain and is available to anyone who has Internet access. For example, recent reports indicate that both schools and employers are checking students' *Facebook* and *MySpace* entries and using that information to help them decide whether to accept or reject applicants (Palank, 2006). Use good judgment about what personal information you share on your site or "wall."

If possible, participate in a study abroad or travel-study program that allows you to live in another country and interact directly with its native citizens.

In addition to gaining a global perspective from courses that emphasize international knowledge, strongly consider participating in a program that allows you to study in a different country, either for a full term or a shorter time period (e.g., January, May, or summer term). In preparation for this international experience, take a course in the language, culture, or history of the nation to which you will be traveling.

WORDS OF WISDOM

"Get involved. Don't gripe about things unless you are making an effort to change them. You can make a difference if you dare."

RICHARD C. HOLBROOKE, FORMER DIRECTOR OF THE PEACE CORPS AND AMERICAN AMBASSADOR TO THE UNITED NATIONS

"Not everything that is faced can be changed; but nothing can be changed until it is faced."

JAMES BALDWIN, RENOWNED AFRICAN-AMERICAN AUTHOR

WORDS OF WISDOM

"We make a living by what we get; we make a life by what we give."

WINSTON CHURCHILL, FORMER PRIME MINISTER OF ENGLAND AND NOBEL PRIZE-WINNING AUTHOR

Engage in volunteer experiences that may allow you to work in diverse communities or neighborhoods.

Volunteer experiences in the local community beyond the borders of your campus may allow you the opportunity to interact with diverse groups of people who may not be found in large numbers within your campus community. By engaging in volunteerism in your local community, you demonstrate *civic engagement*. Civic-minded and civically responsible people become actively engaged in their local community and try to make it the best community it can be. By stepping beyond narrow self-interest to promote the welfare of other members of your community, you demonstrate civic character, especially when volunteerism involves assisting people in need.

When you volunteer to serve others, you are also serving yourself because studies show that college students typically experience an increase in self-esteem when they engage in volunteering experiences (Zlotkowski, 2002). Additionally, they report significant gains in learning and leadership, and if the volunteer experiences involve interaction with diverse racial groups, it results in improved racial tolerance and appreciation of diversity (Astin, et al., 2000). Studies also show that those individuals who periodically devote time to doing good things for others report higher levels of personal "happiness" or personal satisfaction with their life (Myers, 1993), perhaps because of the self-satisfaction they get from knowing that they are doing something meaningful with their life.

Lastly, volunteering enables you to acquire hands-on experience in "real-life" settings. You can use your volunteer opportunities to strengthen your resume and to network with professionals outside of college who may serve as excellent resources, references, and sources for letters of recommendation. Volunteer experiences can also function as "exploratory internships" by giving you the opportunity to gain first-hand knowledge about careers that may relate to the nature of your volunteer work.

An internship is not only an effective way to gain career experience; it is also an effective way to gain experience with diversity. © JupiterImages Corporation.

Attempt to find an *internship* in a company or organization that will allow you the opportunity to work with people from diverse backgrounds and cultures.

Working in diverse social settings improves your preparation and qualifications for career entry after college. National surveys indicate that employers value college graduates who have had direct, "hands on" experience with diversity (Education Commission of the States, 1995).

Interpersonal Communication and Human Relations Skills

The ability to relate effectively with others is considered to be a major form of human intelligence, which scholars refer to as *interpersonal or social intelligence* (Gardner, 1993, 1999; Goleman, 2007). The development of your interpersonal and human relations skills is as important as the development of your academic and intellectual skills; research clearly shows that the ability to relate to others plays a pivotal role in promoting personal and professional success (Goleman, 2006, 2007). Employers of college graduates also place a high value on interpersonal communication and human relations skills in their hiring decisions (Felstead, Gallie, & Green, 2002; National Association of Colleges & Employers, 2003). Furthermore, the ability to effectively communicate with and motivate others has been found to be a key characteristic of effective leadership (Avolio, 2004).

Interpersonal intelligence is especially important when communicating with and relating to people from diverse backgrounds because cross-cultural communication that is unclear or insensitive can quickly lead to misinterpretation and termination of potentially fruitful relationships. When communicating with others from different cultures, it is imperative that we communicate clearly and sensitively. Often we are so concerned about saying the "right thing" (what to communicate) that we forget about saying it in the "right way" (how to communicate) (Du Praw & Axner, 1997).

WORDS OF WISDOM

"I will pay more for the ability to deal with people than any other ability under the sun."

JOHN D. ROCKEFELLER, AMERICAN INDUSTRIALIST, PHILANTHROPIST, AND ONCE THE RICHEST MAN IN THE WORLD

INTERCULTURAL COMMUNICATION BREAKDOWN

"I don't even know what that means."

WHITE BASKETBALL COACH COMMENTING ON AN AFRICAN AMERICAN PLAYER WHO SAID, "I'M TRYING TO FIND MY MOJO AND GET MY SWAG BACK." (*LOS ANGELES TIMES*, DECEMBER 21, 2008)

Pause for Reflection

What would you say are the most important rules or principles of good communication (verbal and nonverbal) that should be used when *communicating with someone from any culture*?

Listed below are key strategies for strengthening your interpersonal communication skills. Some of these strategies may appear to be simple and obvious; however, because they seem so simple or obvious, they can be easily overlooked, taken for granted, or used inconsistently. Don't be fooled by the seeming simplicity of the following suggestions, and don't underrate or underestimate the impact they have on the people with whom you interact. Be especially mindful of using these suggestions when you interact with people from diverse backgrounds. The more consistently you practice them, the more automatic they will become, and the better you will become at intercultural communication.

Work hard at being a good listener.

Human relations scholars report that listening attentively and sensitively is a very demanding mental task and that most people need to improve our listening skills (Nichols & Stevens, 1957; Nichols, 1995). Studies show that our listening comprehension for spoken messages is less than 50% (Nichols & Stevens, 1957; Wolvin & Coakley, 1993). This is a particularly disturbing finding because we have only one chance to understand words that are spoken to us; if we miss the meaning of a spoken message, we cannot replay it or re-read it like we can a printed message.

Since we are not actively "doing something" while listening, we can easily fall prey to passive listening, whereby we give the impression that we are totally focused on the speaker's words, but our attention is divided and part of it is actually focused on something else. We need to remain consciously aware of this tendency toward "attention drift" and make an effortful attempt to concentrate when listening to others. If we make a strong effort to listen attentively, we send others the message that they are worthy of our complete and undivided attention. This message is particularly important to send others from diverse groups because they may need greater assurance that we accept them and that we are genuinely interested in them.

Listening closely can be challenging, but it is an important interpersonal skill that lets speakers know they are worthy of your complete and undivided attention.

© JupiterImages Corporation.

Be an active listener.

One frequently recommended strategy for active listening is to periodically check our understanding of the speaker's message. "I messages" are particularly useful for this purpose (e.g., "What I hear you saying is . . ."). When the speaker finishes, you can paraphrase what you heard in your own words to be sure the message you received is consistent with the message that the speaker intended to send (e.g., "Let me check to be sure that I am following you. Are you saying that . . .?") (Donahue & Siegel, 2005). This is a particularly important strategy to employ when listening to people from other cultures because there is a greater risk that you may misinterpret the speaker's message. The strategy serves to assure you (the listener) that you have understood the message, and it assures the speaker that the message has been accurately heard and correctly interpreted. Active listening strategies also prevent "passive listening"—keeping you alert and involved in the conversation while simultaneously sending the speaker the message that you are genuinely interested in what he or she has to say.

The capacity to listen well is important for any human interaction, but it is especially important when the interaction takes place between people with different cultural backgrounds because the conversationalists may be unfamiliar with each other's verbal and nonverbal styles of communication. If we do not listen well to the ideas expressed by those who are different than us, it can send the unwanted message that we lack interest in, or respect for, their culture.

W ORDS of ISDOM

"Chi rispetta sara ripettato." (Respect others and you will be respected.)

ITALIAN PROVERB

Avoiding the Three "Egos": The Types of Person You Don't Want to Become

Good people and good friends are those who can get over themselves and get interested in others. The following types of people are more into themselves than others and, consequently, they tend to "turn off" people with whom they interact. Don't be one of them.

- **Egotist:** An egotistical person is basically *conceited*—a braggart who boasts, brags, and spends lots of conversation time talking about his or her outstanding features or personal accomplishments (sometimes to cover up feelings of personal inadequacy or low self-esteem).

- **Egoist:** An egoistic person is basically *selfish* and unwilling to share with others or help others.

- **Egocentric:** An egocentric person views the world as if he or she is always at the *center* of it (and of every conversation), showing little interest in or empathy for others. The words "me" and "I" appear with relentless frequency when an egocentric person speaks, and you may get the feeling that this person is not talking *with* you but *at* you.

An egocentric person wants to be at the "center" of (and the subject of) every conversation.

WORDS OF WISDOM

"We have been given two ears and but a single mouth in order that we may hear more and talk less."

ZENO OF CITIUM, ANCIENT GREEK PHILOSOPHER AND FOUNDER OF STOIC PHILOSOPHY

WORDS OF WISDOM

"Give every man thine ear, but few thy voice."

WILLIAM SHAKESPEARE, ENGLISH POET, PLAYWRIGHT, AND MOST QUOTED WRITER IN THE ENGLISH-SPEAKING WORLD

Be aware of the nonverbal messages you send while listening.

It has been said that 90% of communication is nonverbal because body language often communicates stronger and truer messages than spoken language (Mehrabian, 1972). Nonverbal communication is important in any human interaction, but its importance is multiplied when interaction occurs across different cultures because we are more likely to look for nonverbal cues when verbal messages are less clear or familiar to us. This is more likely to happen when we are communicating with people from a different culture, particularly if they are speaking to us in a language that is not their native language (LeBaron, 2003).

The nonverbal messages we send silently to others are often the most powerful signals. In fact, research on lying indicates that one effective strategy for detecting if someone is lying is to see whether the person's body lan-

WORDS OF WISDOM

"The most important thing in communication is to hear what isn't being said."

PETER F. DRUCKER, AUSTRIAN AUTHOR AND FOUNDER OF THE STUDY OF "MANAGEMENT"

guage fails to match the spoken language. For example, if a person says he is excited or enthusiastic about something, but his nonverbal communication indicates otherwise (e.g., eyebrows don't raise and he sits motionless), we may have reason to doubt the person's sincerity (Eckman & Friesen, 1969).

These findings suggest that using effective body language may be the best way to communicate authentic interest in the speaker's words and in the speaker. (Similarly, if we are speaking, awareness of our listeners' body language can inform us about whether we are holding or losing their interest which, in turn, should inform us about whether we should continue or stop talking.) Nonverbal messages should be avoided because they suggest disinterest in what the other person is saying, and they include finger tapping, paper shuffling, and rapid head-nodding—which sends the message that you want the speaker to hurry up and finish so you can start talking.

A good mnemonic device (memory-improvement method) for remembering the nonverbal signals that should be sent to others while listening is the acronym, SOFTEN, standing for:

S = **Smile**—periodically, but not continually because it may convey the nonverbal message that your smile is an artificial pose.

Sit Still—don't fidget and squirm because the speaker may interpret this to mean that you are feeling uncomfortable or being put on the spot (or the "hot seat") by what is being said.

O = **Open posture**—because a "closed posture" with arms crossed or hands folded together can give the speaker the impression that you are "closed minded" or passing judgment.

F = **Forward leaning**—because leaning back may send the message that you are distancing yourself emotionally from the speaker, as if you're feeling threatened by what is being said or psychoanalyzing the person saying it.

Face the speaker directly—with both shoulders lining up directly with the speaker, because turning away one shoulder suggest that you're giving the speaker the "cold shoulder."

T = **Touch**—a light touch on the arm or hand can be a good way to communicate warmth—but no rubbing, stroking, or touching in ways that could be interpreted as inappropriate by members of other cultures, or as sexual harassment by members of another gender.

E = **Eye contact**—periodically, but not continuous eye contact, which could be interpreted by members of some cultural groups as staring or glaring. For example, prolonged eye contact is considered inappropriate by working-class Hispanic and African-American cultures (Taylor, 1990). On the other hand, little or no eye contact may convey the nonverbal message that you are uncomfortable with the speaker, or that you'd like the conversation to end (much like a student who avoids eye contact with a teacher so as not to be called on in class).

N = **Nod your head**—slowly and occasionally, but not repeatedly and rapidly—because this can convey the message that you want the speaker to hurry up and finish up so you can start talking.

An interesting way to gain greater self-awareness of your nonverbal communication habits is to choose a couple of people whom you trust and know you well, and ask them to imitate your body language. Observing others mimic you can sometimes reveal nonverbal habits that you were not aware of, and which may be misinterpreted by individuals from different cultural backgrounds who are unfamiliar with your nonverbal idiosyncracies.

Sending positive nonverbal signals when listening to members of diverse groups can encourage them to become more self-confident and open to sharing their ideas and personal experiences. This not only benefits them, it benefits us as listeners, because listening to speakers who are more self-confident and open about sharing their ideas makes the challenging task of listening less difficult and more stimulating.

Be open to different topics of conversation.

Resist the temptation to be a closed-minded or selective listener who listens to others like listening to the radio—changing stations to select or "tune into" conversational topics that relate only to your personal interests or support your personal points of view, while ignoring or "tuning out" everything else.

REMEMBER: People learn best from others whose interests and viewpoints do not necessarily match their own. Ignoring or blocking out information and ideas about topics that don't immediately interest you or support your particular perspective is not only a poor social skill, it's a poor learning strategy.

It is likely that people whose background experiences are very different than our own will express viewpoints that we are unfamiliar with or don't agree with; however, you still owe them the courtesy of listening to what they have to say (rather than shaking your head, frowning, or interrupting them). This isn't just a matter of social etiquette; it's a matter of social ethics. Only after others have finished sharing their perspective or point of view should we then express our personal perspective or opinion.

Also, be sure that the opinions you express are *informed* opinions—not opinions that are rooted in personal biases or ethnocentric viewpoints. Also, be sure not to express your opinions in an *opinionated* way—stating them so strongly that it sounds like your personal point of view is the only rational or acceptable one—and all others are irrelevant or inferior (Gibb, 1961). Expressing opinions in such an opinionated fashion is likely to put an immediate end to a potentially positive exchange of ideas and, possibly, a future friendship.

REMEMBER: Our views are shaped, limited, and often biased by our particular cultural perspective. By remaining open to multiple perspectives and diverse viewpoints we create opportunities to develop personal viewpoints that are more balanced, comprehensive, and accurate.

WORDS OF WISDOM

"Seek first to understand, then to be understood."

STEPHEN COVEY, INTERNATIONAL BEST-SELLING AUTHOR OF THE BOOK, *THE SEVEN HABITS OF HIGHLY EFFECTIVE PEOPLE*

<W>ORDS OF
ISDOM</W>

"The more eyes, different
eyes, we can use to observe
one thing, the more com-
plete will our concept of this
thing, our objectivity, be."

FRIEDRICH NIETZSCHE, GERMAN
PHILOSOPHER

Pause for Reflection

On what topics do you hold strong opinions?

Do you think any of your opinions would be more acceptable to people from
some cultural backgrounds rather than others?

Human Relations Skills ("People Skills")

Interpersonal communication skill—the ability to listen and speak well when
interacting with others—is one key component of social intelligence. A second key component of social intelligence is *human relations* skills—the ability to relate to others in a sensitive and humane manner. The ability to be
sensitive to others' emotions or feelings, also known as empathy, has been
found to be more important for personal and professional success than intellectual ability (IQ; Goleman, 1995, 2006).

The following strategies may be used to improve your human relations or
"people skills."

"I have a love of words, too."

*Noticing things we have in common with members of groups who
are different than us is an excellent way to stimulate conversation
and develop future relationships.* Copyright © 2003 by Benita Epstein.
Reprinted by permission.

Make an earnest attempt to learn the names and interests of students from diverse groups.

Knowing a person's identity and personal interests enables you to establish personal rapport that may lay the foundation for further
interaction and a deeper relationship. Pay
particular attention to interests that you may
have *in common* because shared interests
can serve as a source of interesting conversations, and perhaps, lead to the development
of long-term friendships.

Remembering people's names communicates to others that you know them as individuals. It makes the person feel that he or
she is more than an anonymous face in a
crowd, but a unique individual with a distinctive identity. When you know and refer
to a person by name, you are noticing and

acknowledging their individuality. You do just the opposite when you forget a person's name, or never bother to learn it in the first place.

Despite the fact that people commonly claim they do not have a good memory for names, there is absolutely no evidence that the ability to remember names is an inherited trait that we're born with and have no control over; instead, it's a skill that can be developed through personal effort and by practicing effective learning and memory strategies, such as those discussed below.

Strategies for Remembering Names

- When you first meet someone, make a conscious effort to pay close attention to the person's name when you first hear it. While this may seem to be an obvious suggestion, it is often overlooked because, when we first meet someone, we tend to focus less on their name and more on: (a) what impression we're making on them, (b) what impression they're making on us, or (c) what we're going to say next.

- One way to improve your attention to and strengthen your memory for a new name is to use the person's name soon after you first hear it. For instance, if your friend Jack has just introduced you to Jill, you might say something like: "Jill, how long have you known Jack?" This quick rehearsal of a new name soon after we've first heard it, serves to intercept memory loss at the point in time when forgetting is most likely to occur—immediately after we acquire new information (Underwood, 1983).

- You can strengthen your memory of an individual's name by associating it with other information you've learned about the person or other information you already know. For instance, you can associate the person's name with: (a) your first impression of the individual's personality, (b) a physical characteristic of the person, (c) the topic of conversation, (d) the place where you met the person, or (e) a familiar word that rhymes with the person's name. By making a mental connection between the person's name and some other piece of information, you help to form a real, biological connection in your brain, which is the neurological basis of human memory.

- As soon as you have the opportunity, make a note of the person's name in writing. When we don't want to forget something we are sure to write it down (e.g., grocery shopping list or party invitation list). We can use the same foolproof strategy for learning names by keeping a *name journal* that includes the names of new people we meet plus some information about them (e.g., what they do and what their interests are). You could make it a goal to meet one new person every day, particularly someone from a diverse group, and make it a point to remember that person's name by recording it in your journal. It may seem that learning and remembering names is not worth all this time and effort, but it is. In business, remembering names helps to recruit and retain customers; in politics it wins votes; in education it can promote the teacher-student rapport; and when interacting with individuals from diverse groups, it rolls out the welcome mat for them to interact with you and form a relationship.

WORDS OF WISDOM

"We should be aware of the magic contained in a name. The name sets that individual apart; it makes him or her unique among all others. Remember that a person's name is to that person the sweetest and most important sound in any language."

DALE CARNEGIE, *HOW TO WIN FRIENDS AND INFLUENCE PEOPLE*, 1936

WORDS OF WISDOM

"When I joined the bank, I started keeping a record of the people I met and put them on little cards, and I would indicate on the cards when I met them, and under what circumstances, and sometimes [make] a little notation which would help me remember a conversation."

DAVID ROCKEFELLER, PROMINENT AMERICAN BANKER, PHILANTHROPIST, AND FORMER CEO OF THE CHASE MANHATTAN BANK

Refer to people by name when you greet and interact with them.

Once you have learned a person's name, be sure to refer to that person by name. For instance, saying, "Hi, Julio" will mean a lot more to Julio than simply saying "Hi" or, worse yet, saying "Hi, there"—which sounds like you're just acknowledging something "out there" that could be either a human being or an inanimate object. Continuing to use people's names after you've learned them serves to reinforce your memory of their names, and it continues to send a message to them that you haven't forgotten who they are.

REMEMBER: Developing the habit of learning and remembering names is not simply a matter of social etiquette, it is a powerful way to make others feel welcomed and validated, particularly if they are members of a minority group.

Show interest in people by remembering information about them.

W**ORDS OF**
W**ISDOM**

"All that is necessary is to take an interest in other persons, to recognize that other people as a rule are much like one's self, and thankfully to admit that diversity is a glorious feature of life."

FRANK SWINNERTON, BRITISH NOVELIST AND LITERARY CRITIC

"If we obey this law, [it] will bring us countless friends. The law is this: Always make the person feel important."

DALE CARNEGIE, *HOW TO WIN FRIENDS AND INFLUENCE PEOPLE*

Ask questions about others' interests, plans, and experiences. Pay particular attention to their answers, especially to what seems most important to them, what they care about, and what excites them (e.g., politics, sports, relationships). Introduce these topics when you have conversations with them. Try to move beyond the standard, generic questions that are routinely asked after people say "hello" (e.g., "What's goin' on?"). Instead, ask about something *specific* that you discussed with them last time you conversed (e.g., "How was that math test you were worried about last week?"). This sends a message to others that you know and care about their personal interests and priorities, and that they are also of interest and concern to you.

When you remember specific information about people, particularly people from groups that may not see themselves as having anything in common with you, it suggests to them that you are interested in them and they matter to you. Our memory often reflects our priorities—we're most likely to remember what's most important to us. So, when you remember people's names and something about them, it suggests to them that they are important to you.

Furthermore, you are likely to find that others will start showing more interest in you after you show interest in them. (Another surprising, almost contradictory thing can happen when you show interest in others: You become a person that others consider to be a great conversationalist.)

Pause for Reflection

What would you say are universal human interests—topics of conversation that would be of interest or importance to people from any cultural background?

One of my most successful teaching strategies is something I do on the first day of class. I ask my students to complete a "student information sheet" that includes their name and some information relating to their past experiences, future plans, and personal interests. I answer the same questions I ask my students by writing my answers on the board while they write theirs on a sheet of paper. (This allows them to get to know me while I get to know them.) After I've collected all their information sheets, I call out the names of individual students, asking them to raise their hand when their name is called, so I can associate their name and face. To help me remember their names, as I call each name, I very rapidly jot down a quick word or abbreviated phrase next to the student's name for later review (e.g., something about a distinctive physical feature or where the student is seated).

I save the students' information sheets, and I refer back to them throughout the term. For example, I record the student's name and strongest interest on a post-it note, and stick the note onto my class notes near topics I'll be covering during the term that relates to the student's interest. When I get to that topic in class (which could be months later), I immediately see the student's names posted by it. When I begin to discuss the topic, I mention the name of the student who had expressed interest in it on the first day of class (e.g., "Gina, we're about to study your favorite topic."). Often what happens is that students really perk up when I mention their name in association with their preferred topic; plus, they're often amazed by my apparent ability to remember their personal interests from the first day of class so much later in the term. Students rarely ask how I managed to remember their personal interests, so they are not aware of my post-it note strategy. Instead, they just think I've got extraordinary social memory and social sensitivity (which is just fine with me).

—Joe Cuseo, *Professor of Psychology*
and co-author of this text

Personal Experience

Words of Wisdom

"You can make more friends in two months by becoming interested in other people than you can in two years by trying to get other people interested in you."

DALE CARNEGIE, *HOW TO WIN FRIENDS AND INFLUENCE PEOPLE*

Be a sharing person.

When people are uncertain about how to act around others, or if they are worried about whether others will accept them, they may act in a guarded manner—concealing their true feelings and protecting themselves against the possibility of rejection. (As in the words of an old Simon and Garfunkel song: "I am a rock, I am an island; and a rock feels no pain, and an island never cries.")

This self-insulation can result in behavior that may seem distant or cool. How often have you witnessed this rapid, ritualistic interchange between two individuals?

Person A: "Hi, how's it goin'?"
Person B: "Fine, how ya' doin'?"

No real personal information is shared by either person, and chances are that neither one expects nor wants to hear about how the other person is truly feeling (Goffman, 1967). Such social rituals are understandable and acceptable when people first interact with each other. However, if these individuals continue to interact and want to move their relationship beyond a superficial level, they should move beyond these ritualistic routines and move toward mutual sharing of more personal, meaningful information.

STUDENT
SPERSPECTIVE

"How do you strengthen
your trust in a person?"
QUESTION ASKED BY A FIRST-YEAR
STUDENT

As you become more comfortable interacting with others from diverse groups, engage in some self-disclosure—disclose (share) a little more of yourself. Naturally, you want to do this gradually and in small doses, rather than by blowing others away in a tornado of private details about your personal life. Selectively and gradually sharing some things about yourself serves to show others that you trust them well enough to share a part of yourself. In turn, they will be more likely to trust you and share a part of themselves.

You can start this sharing process by noticing the things that other people share with you and follow up by sharing something about yourself that relates to the same topic or experience. Relating a similar experience of your own to an experience that someone has shared with you demonstrates empathy—ability to understand the feelings of others. This is particularly important to show others whose background experiences are different than yours. It also lets them know that you have something in common, which, in turn, encourages them to share more of themselves with you (Adler & Towne, 2001). Friendships gradually build up through this progressive process of give-and-take sharing of personal information, which is referred to by human relations specialists as the *intimacy spiral* (Cusinato & L'Abate, 1994).

Developing friendships with peers from diverse groups is an excellent way to learn from diversity and develop self-confidence in relating to people with different cultural backgrounds.

Ask people from diverse backgrounds to share their personal stories with you.

Once you have established a relationship of trust with members of diverse groups, ask them to share some of their life experiences with you—such as turning points in their life, and people in their lives who have served as role models or sources of inspiration. You could do this on an individual basis or by organizing small, informal social groups comprised of students from diverse backgrounds. Allowing others from a variety of backgrounds to share their stories may enable others to see that they have had very different personal journeys and may have overcome major obstacles to get where they are now.

Seek out the views and opinions of classmates from diverse backgrounds.

For example, during or after class discussions, ask students from different backgrounds if there was any point made or position taken in class that they would strongly question or challenge. Seeking out divergent (diverse) viewpoints has been found to be one of the best ways to develop critical thinking skills (Kurfiss, 1988).

Join or form discussion groups with students from diverse backgrounds.

You can gain access to diverse perspectives by joining groups of students who differ from you in terms of gender, age, race, or ethnicity. You might begin by forming discussion groups of students who differ in one way, but are similar in another way. For instance, form a learning group of students who have the same major as you do, but who differ with respect to race, ethnicity, or age. This strategy can give the diverse members of your group some common ground for discussion, and can raise your group's awareness that humans who are members of different groups can, at the same time, share similar educational experiences, needs, and goals.

REMEMBER: Including diversity in your discussion groups not only provides social variety, it also promotes the quality of the group's thinking by allowing its members to gain access to the diverse perspectives and life experiences of people from different backgrounds.

© Stockbyte.

Forming discussion groups with peers from diverse racial or cultural backgrounds who share an interest in the same major can provide common ground for social interaction.

For instance, older students may have a broad range of life experiences that younger students can draw upon and learn from, while younger students may bring a fresh, idealistic perspective to group discussions with older students. Also, males and females may bring different thinking styles to group discussions. Studies show that males are more likely to be "separate knowers" who tend to "detach" themselves from the concept or issue being discussed so they can analyze it. In contrast, females are more likely to be "connected knowers" who tend to relate personally to concepts and connect them to their own experiences. For example, when confronting a poem, males are more likely to ask themselves, "What techniques can I use to analyze it?" In contrast, females are more likely to ask themselves, "What is the poet trying to say to me?" (Belenky, et al., 1986, p. 101). It has also been found that females are more likely to adopt a more collaborative style during group discussions and collect the ideas of other group members; in contrast, males are more likely to adopt a competitive approach and debate the ideas of others (Magolda, 1992).

Pause for Reflection

How would you define teamwork?

What do you think are the key factors that make study groups or group projects successful?

Form collaborative learning teams.

A learning *team* is much more than a discussion group or a study group; it moves beyond discussion to collaboration (i.e., they "co-labor" [work together] as part of a joint and mutually-supportive effort to reach the same goal. Studies show that when individuals from different ethnic and racial groups work collaboratively to attain a common goal, it reduces racial prejudice and promotes interracial friendships (Allport, 1954; Amir, 1976). These positive findings may be explained by the fact that if individuals from diverse groups work collaboratively on the same team, no one is a member of an "out group" (them); instead, they are all members of the same "in group" (us) (Pratto, et al., 2000; Sidanius, et al., 2000).

Research indicates that the greatest gains in reducing prejudice and improving relationships among members of different ethnic and racial groups take place when collaboration occurs under the six conditions described in the Snapshot Summary on page 165. For example, in an analysis of multiple studies involving more than 90,000 people from 25 different countries, it was found that interaction between members of diverse groups were characterized by these six conditions and resulted in a significant reduction of prejudice (Pettigrew & Tropp, 2000). Furthermore, studies show that these same conditions are most likely to produce the largest gains in learning among team members (Slavin, 1995; Johnson, et al., 1998), particularly students of color (Posner & Markstein, 1994).

Tips for Teamwork: Creating Successful Collaborative Learning Groups

1. **Teammates should have a common goal.**
   To help your team identify and work toward a common goal, plan to produce a single, unified work product that serves as visible evidence of your group's effort and accomplishment (e.g., a completed sheet of answers to questions, a list or chart of specific ideas, or an outline). This will help keep the team focused and moving in a common direction.

2. **Teammates should have equal opportunity and individual responsibility for contributing to the team's final product.**
   For example, each member of the team should have the same opportunity to participate during group discussions and to be responsible for contributing something specific to the team's final product—such as a different piece of information (e.g., from lecture notes or reading material), a different perspective (e.g., national, global, or ethical) or a different form of thinking (e.g., application, synthesis, or evaluation).

3. **Teammates should work interdependently—that is, they should depend on or rely upon each other to achieve their common goal.**
   Similar to a sports team, each member of the collaborative learning group has a specific role to play. For instance, each member of the team may assume one of the following roles:
   - Manager: assures that the team stays focused on their goal and doesn't get off track,
   - Moderator: assures that all members have equal opportunity to contribute,
   - Summarizer: identifies what the team has accomplished and what remains to be done, or
   - Recorder: keeps a written record of the team's ideas.

   Teammates can also take on roles in which each member contributes a particular perspective to an issue that the group is addressing, as if bringing a different piece of the puzzle:
   - Time (e.g., past, present, or future)
   - Place (e.g., national, international, global)
   - Person (e.g., social, emotional, or physical dimension of self)

4. **Before beginning their work, teammates should take some time to interact informally with each other to develop a sense of team identity and group solidarity.**
   For example, teammates should have some "warm up" time to get to know each other's names and interests before tackling the learning task. Teammates need to feel comfortable with each other as persons before they can feel comfortable about sharing their personal thoughts and feelings, particularly if the team is comprised of individuals from diverse backgrounds who have little prior experience with each other.

5. **Teamwork should take place in a friendly, informal setting.**
   The context or atmosphere in which group work takes place can influence the nature and quality of interaction among group members. People are more likely to work openly and collaboratively with one another when they are in a social environment that is conducive to collaboration. For example, a living room or a lounge area provides a warmer and friendlier atmosphere than a classroom.

6. **Learning teams should occasionally change membership so that each member gets an opportunity to work with a variety of individuals from different ethnic and racial groups.**
   If someone with a prejudice toward a certain ethnic or racial group has the experience of working on multiple teams that include multiple individuals from the same racial or ethnic group, the prejudiced person is less likely to conclude that the positive experience was due to having interacted with someone who was an "exception to the rule."

When contact between people from diverse groups takes place under the above conditions, it can have the greatest impact on diversity appreciation and team learning. Working in teams under these conditions is a win–win situation: Prejudice is gradually weakened while learning is simultaneously strengthened.

Sources: Amir (1969); Allport (1979); Aronson, Wilson, & Akert (2005); Cook (1984); Sherif et al. (1961); and Wilder (1984).

> # Words of Wisdom
>
> "We are born for cooperation, as are the feet, the hands, the eyelids, and the upper and lower jaws."
>
> MARCUS AURELIUS, ROMAN EMPEROR, 161–180 A.D.

WORDS OF WISDOM

TEAM = Together Everyone Achieves More

AUTHOR UNKNOWN

Research consistently shows that we learn more from people who differ from us than we do from people who are similar to us (Pascarella, 2001; Pascarella & Terenzini, 2005). Thus, the best learning teams to join or form are those comprised of people who are dissimilar to you, or who have characteristics that are not very familiar to you. Ideal teammates are individuals who are different than you in terms of age, gender, ethnicity, race, culture or geographic backgrounds, learning styles, and personality characteristics. Such variety brings different life experiences, styles of thinking, and learning strategies to your team, which serves not only to enrich its diversity but its productivity as well. If you team-up only with friends or classmates whose interests and lifestyles are similar to your own, this homogeneity and familiarity can actually backfire and work against your team's performance. Your common experiences can cause your learning group to get off track and onto topics that have nothing to do with the learning task (for example, what you did last weekend or what you are planning to do next weekend).

REMEMBER: Seek diversity—capitalize on the advantages of collaborating with peers with varied backgrounds and lifestyles. Simply stated, studies show that you learn more from people who differ from you than you do from people who are similar to you.

Research shows that when peers work collaboratively to achieve a common goal, they display a higher level of achievement and a lower level of prejudice toward their teammates.
Copyright © by Ed Arno. Reprinted by permission of the Estate of Arnold Arno.

Pause for Reflection

Have you ever engaged in any of the following types of group learning experiences?

1. lecture note-taking teams
2. reading teams
3. writing teams
4. library research teams
5. study groups

How likely is it that you will do so in the future? Why?

Reflect on Your Experiences with Diversity

Learning deeply from diversity involves not only *action*, but also *reflection*. Personal reflection or thoughtful review is the flip side of active involvement. Both involvement and reflection are needed for learning to be complete and "deep." Active involvement is necessary to capture your *attention*—enabling you to initially "get into" the learning task and get information through your attention filter into your brain; reflection is necessary for *consolidation*—en-

"Beta" Brain-Wave Pattern Associated with a Mental State of *Active Involvement*	"Alpha" Brain-Wave Pattern Associated with a Mental State of *Reflective Thinking*

Figure 5.1 Active Involvement and Reflective Thinking Brain Waves

abling you to "step back" from the learning task and "lock in" that information into your long-term memory (Broadbent, 1970; Bligh, 2000). Researchers have discovered different brain-wave patterns are associated with each of these two essential processes of human learning (Bradshaw, 1995). As you can see in Figure 5.1, when you are actively involved in the learning process, your brain produces very rapid, irregular brain waves—known as "beta" waves—which indicate a mental state of *intense excitement*. When you slow down, "step back," and *reflect* on what you were actively involved with, your brain produces an almost opposite pattern of slow, regular or rhythmical brain waves—known as "alpha" waves—which indicate a mental state of *relaxed alertness*.

These general findings on how humans learn also apply to how students learn from diversity. Studies show that college students learn most effectively from their diversity experiences when they take time to reflect on these experiences, particularly when they record these reflections in writing (Lopez, et al., 1998; Nagda, et al., 2003).

Writing is a powerful strategy for helping us learn from any experience because it increases our level of involvement with it and our ability to carefully reflect on it. The phrase "writing-to-learn" has been coined by scholars to capture the idea that writing is not only a communication skill that is learned in English composition classes, but is also a skill that can promote learning of any academic subject or learning from any life experience. Thus, writing to learn and learning to write are complementary skills; and you can use writing not only as a channel for communicating your knowledge or ideas to others, but also as a tool for strengthening your learning (Applebee, 1981; Elbow, 1973; Murray, 1984).

Writing can also be used as a tool to develop your ability to think at higher levels. Since writing requires physical action, it implements the effective learning principle of active involvement; it essentially forces you to focus attention on your own thoughts and activate your thinking. Writing "jump starts" your thinking and elevates its quality by slowing down your thought process, allowing it to proceed in a more careful, systematic manner which makes you more consciously aware of specific details. Furthermore, the act of writing results in a visible product that you can review and use as feedback to improve the quality of your thoughts (Applebee, 1984; Langer & Applebee, 1987). In other words, writing allows you to "think out loud on paper" (Bean, 2003, p 102).

The following writing strategies are recommended to promote personal reflection and deep learning with respect to your experiences with diversity.

WORDS OF **W**ISDOM

"I write to understand as much as to be understood."

ELIE WIESEL, WORLD-FAMOUS AMERICAN NOVELIST, NOBEL PRIZE WINNER, AND HOLOCAUST SURVIVOR

WORDS OF **W**ISDOM

"How can I know what I think 'til I see what I say?"

GRAHAM WALLAS, *THE ART OF THOUGHT*, 1926

Writing in a journal is an effective way to reflect on, and learn from, your experiences with diversity. Copyright © 2009 by Darren Baker. Under license from Shutterstock, Inc.

Keep a diversity *journal*, in which you record personal reflections on diversity experiences.

When recording reflections on diversity experiences in your journal, keep the following questions in mind:

● What type of feelings or emotions did you experience?

● When and where did you experience these feelings? (What was the situation or context?)

● Why do you think you felt that way?

● Did the experience change your beliefs, attitudes, or behavior in any way? If yes, how? If no, why not?

After concluding work in collaborative learning teams and small-group discussions, take time to pause and reflect on the group experience.

Ask yourself questions that cause you to reflect on the ideas that emerged from diverse members of your group and think about what impact these ideas had on you. For instance, after group discussions you could ask yourself the following questions:

● What major differences emerged among group members during your discussion?

● What major similarities in viewpoints or background experiences did all group members share?

● Were there particular topics or issues raised during the discussion that proved equally important or relevant to all members of the group?

● Did the discussion cause me to reconsider or change any ideas that I previously held?

For additional reflection questions, see the following Snapshot Summary.

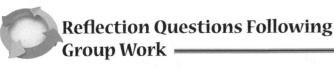

Reflection Questions Following Group Work

Group **Effectiveness/Efficiency**
- Did all members contribute *equally* to the group's work?
- Did team members listen closely to each other?
- Did I feel that working together was more *effective* than working alone? (Was the *quality* of my group's work better than what I could have produced on my own?)
- Was working in a group more *efficient* than working alone? (Did I accomplish *more in less time* than I would have by working alone?)
- What constructive *feedback* could I give members of my group in terms of what they did to *help* or *hinder* the group's progress?

Personal *Responsibility*/**Individual** *Accountability*
- How did my level of *participation* compare with those of my teammates?
- Did I do my *fair share* of the work? (Could I say that I "carried my load" or "pulled my own weight?")
- What could I do *differently* in the future to improve my personal performance or my group's collective performance?

Personal *Leadership*
- Did I take the *initiative to seek out* ideas or information from others?
- Did I *encourage* quiet or reluctant teammates to participate?
- Did I help keep the group *on track* and moving toward its goal?
- What was the strongest *skill* or greatest *contribution* I brought to the group?

Developing Leadership Skills and Taking Leadership Roles with Respect to Diversity

Effective leadership may be defined as the ability to influence people in a positive way (e.g., such as motivating your peers to do their best), or the ability to produce positive change in an organization or institution (e.g., a school, business, or political organization) (Kouzes & Posner, 1988; Veechio, 1997).

In college, you have a tremendous opportunity to influence your peers because they are making a life-changing transition to a new social environment. When people find themselves in situations they are unfamiliar with, or provides less structure and more freedom than they're accustomed to, they often look to others for cues about how to act. Research clearly indicates that peers provide a powerful source of support and direction for students in college (Feldman & Newcomb, 1969; Astin, 1993). This may be particularly true for new college students who are in the process of making a major life transition. These students are likely to look for support and direction from others whom they see as making the same transition. You may be in a position right now to step forward and have a positive influence on your peers, particularly peers who are minorities on your campus, and may be feeling isolated or marginalized. If you accept this leadership challenge, you can create a "win–win–win" scenario for three different parties:

1. Your *peers* win by benefiting from the positive leadership you provide,
2. Your *college or university* wins by having a more integrated and interactive student body, and
3. *You* win by developing leadership skills that will contribute to your personal success in college and your professional success beyond college.

Truths and Myths about Effective Leadership

Contrary to popular belief, leadership is not a single personality trait that people possess automatically and naturally (e.g., a "natural born" leader). Rather than being an inherited trait or characteristic, leadership is more often a learned behavior that reflects what we *do* or how we *act* (Reicher, Haslam, & Platow, 2007). Furthermore, leadership is not a single, "charismatic" quality that individuals possess and deploy across all situations. Instead, different types or forms of leadership are demonstrated in different situations, which scholars refer to as *situational leadership* (Fiedler, 1993). Rather than being born with leadership skill as an innate gift, leadership often represents an acquired habit that we develop through experience and use of effective strategies in specific situations or contexts.

Another misconception about leadership is that effective leaders are extroverted, bold, and aggressive (or ruthless). While these traits may have characterized some famous or notorious political leaders, many effective leaders are not aggressive, dominant, or power hungry; instead, they display their leadership in subtle, sensitive, and caring ways. Leaders don't always roar; they may be "quiet leaders" who lead with subtle strength and a soft voice. Or they may lead without doing much talking at all; they lead by example—by being role models who model positive behaviors, skills, and achievements that others may imitate or emulate.

Thus, the bottom line on leadership is that it is displayed in multiple styles and in multiple situations (Locke, 1991). This means that you have the potential to demonstrate leadership in a way that reflects your particular leadership style and assume leadership in circumstances where you feel most comfortable. Thus, an important first step toward becoming an effective leader is to become aware of your special leadership strengths or skills (Bennis, 1989), as well as the situations in which your leadership style may be best applied (Zaccaro, Foti, & Kenny, 1991). Self-awareness is also important for enabling you to prioritize your leadership efforts so that you do not spread yourself too thin by taking on too many different leadership roles and responsibilities. Effective leaders strive for quality, not quantity, by limiting themselves to those leadership roles and situations that best match their leadership interests and talents.

Words of Wisdom

"Be the change you want to see in the world."

MAHATMA GANDHI, INDIAN NATIONAL LEADER

Words of Wisdom

"Know thyself, and to thine own self be true."

PLATO, ANCIENT GREEK PHILOSOPHER

Pause for Reflection

In what situations have you displayed leadership or do you think you have leadership potential?

Leadership Situations and Roles for College Students

The ways in which you can demonstrate leadership are almost limitless. However, most leadership roles in college may be grouped into four general categories: (1) academic leadership, (2) organizational leadership, (3) social and emotional leadership, and (4) civic leadership.

Academic Leadership

You can demonstrate leadership in the classroom by modeling intellectual curiosity and academic motivation—for example, by being highly attentive and participating in class and by contributing insightful questions or comments during class discussions. Additional academic leadership roles you can assume on campus include:

1. being a peer tutor in your college's academic-support center,
2. serving as a peer-teaching assistant for a college course, or
3. forming learning and study groups.

You can provide academic leadership in any of these roles without necessarily being intellectually gifted or brilliant, but by simply being knowledgable, reliable, and available as a resource for your peers. For example, you can demonstrate academic leadership with respect to diversity during *class discussions*, by ensuring that the ideas of minority students are included, heard, and respected, and by encouraging and reinforcing the contributions of students who may be reluctant to speak up because of their minority status. Including members from diverse races and cultures in a discussion group has great potential to reduce prejudice, but only if each member's cultural identity and perspective is sought out and brought into the discussion, rather than isolating or ignoring them (Baron, Byrne, & Brauscombe, 2006).

Instead of taking over and controlling conversations with monologues, effective discussion leaders exert their positive influence by allowing participants from all groups an equal opportunity to engage in dialogue, and by encouraging equal exchange of ideas from all members of their team.

WORDS OF WISDOM

"The classroom can provide a 'public place' where community can be practiced."

SUSANNE MORSE, AUTHOR, *RENEWING CIVIC CAPACITY: PREPARING COLLEGE STUDENTS FOR SERVICE AND CITIZENSHIP*

WORDS OF **W**ISDOM

"The nation's future depends upon leaders trained through wide exposure to that robust exchange of ideas which discovers truth out of a multitude of tongues."

WILLIAM J. BRENNAN, FORMER SUPREME COURT JUSTICE

"To lead, one must follow."

LAO TZU, ANCIENT CHINESE PHILOSOPHER AND FOUNDER OF TAOISM—A PHILOSOPHY THAT EMPHASIZES THOUGHT BEFORE ACTION

Organizational Leadership

You can also demonstrate leadership by organizing and motivating groups of people to work for worthy political causes (e.g., by developing co-curricular programs on campus that are sensitive to the needs and interests of minority students). This type of leadership also involves such activities as initiating clubs and directing student organizations, effectively delegating tasks and responsibilities, maintaining group cohesiveness and cooperation, and keeping groups on track and moving toward a common goal. Specific leadership roles you can assume that serve these purposes include:

1. student government,
2. college committees and task forces, and
3. volunteer work in the local community.

Since effective organizational leadership involves the ability to produce positive change in an organization or institution, it begins with gaining knowledge about the organization or institution to which you belong and the people who comprise it. Learn how your institution is organized and its decisions are made. By learning how "the system" works, you can "work the system," making it work for your leadership cause. Gaining organizational knowledge will enable you to navigate and utilize the system's decision-making channels. For example, become familiar with your college's table of organization or organizational flow chart, which shows the chain of command and decision-making authority from top to bottom. Also, be familiar with the student organizations and leadership opportunities that exist at your college by reviewing your *Student Handbook*. (We encourage you to complete the exercise at the end of this chapter.)

By assuming leadership in a student organization, you can provide leadership for diversity by organizing campus events that promote diversity awareness and appreciation. For instance, to promote awareness and tolerance of groups with alternative sexual orientation and lifestyles, you could invite a panel of representatives from a chapter of the *Parent and Friends of Lesbians and Gays (PFLAG)*. This is an international organization with almost 300 chapters in the United States, including at least one in every state. The organization consists of "parents, families and friends of lesbian, gay, bisexual and transgender persons" and their goal is to "celebrate diversity and envision a society that embraces everyone, including those of diverse sexual orientations and gender identities" (PFLAG, 2006). Trained panelists from this organization typically speak briefly about their experiences and then field questions from the audience. (To locate a chapter of PFLAG in your geographical area, go to: http://www.pflag.org/Find_a_Chapter.68.0.html.)

To ensure that your peers give sufficient forethought and afterthought to a campus visit from this group, ask your peers to bring one or two questions to ask the panelists in advance of their presentation. After the presentation, ask your peers to reflect on how they felt about the experience, what they learned from it, and what unanswered questions they may still have about it.

When I was in college in the 1970s, students were re-energized by the fact that the Vietnam war was over, the Civil Rights Movement had achieved many opportunities for women and minorities, and financial aid had produced a large, diverse student body. Opportunity for student leadership across my campus was rampant. For me, deciding what leadership role I wanted to be a part of became the biggest decision of my freshman year. I decided to run for senator in our Student Government since I only could handle one co-curricular activity at a time. I understood my limits with school and work. However, I did become a member of the resident hall council because I had a job as a Residential Hall Assistant. In my second year, I became the president of the sophomore class. In my junior year, I became the president of the Black Student Union and the leadership drum kept beating through my senior year. My collegiate years as a leader taught me how to maneuver through society after college by being a good citizen and a thriving professional. Moreover, it taught me how to make goals and follow a path to successfully achieve those goals in college and beyond. Now as a college professor, I serve as the advisor to many student organizations including the Student Government Association. In addition, I have been or am currently a member of many community boards and professional organizations. These experiences have assisted me in moving up the ladder in organizations where I have worked. Being a student leader not only contributed to my success in college, it prepared me for success in life.

—Aaron Thompson, *Professor of Sociology and co-author of this text*

Personal Experience

Social and Emotional Leadership

You can demonstrate this form of leadership by (a) modeling responsible social behavior, (b) making others feel welcome—particularly members of minority groups, (c) drawing out people who may be shy and including them in conversations and activities, and (d) being an empathic listener who provides a sensitive "sounding board" for others. Effective leaders work to understand the needs, values, and viewpoints of those they are leading (Reichter, Haslam, & Platow, 2007). Specific social and emotional leadership *roles* that you may assume on campus include:

Becoming a resident assistant is one way to demonstrate social and emotional leadership. © JupiterImages Corporation.

1. student leader for new-student orientation,
2. resident assistant in campus housing,
3. peer mentor,
4. peer counselor,
5. peer minister, or
6. peer mediator.

(Check your *Student Handbook* for a description of all the leadership roles available to you on your campus.)

Effective leadership often involves communicating and relating effectively to others, whether they may be members of majority or minority groups. Successful leaders do not dominate dialogue and discussion, but when they do speak, they employ effective oral communication strategies that enable them to express their ideas efficiently and persuasively. They also communicate with social sensitivity, which enables them to effectively mediate and resolve interpersonal disagreements before they develop into full-blown conflicts. For example, effective leaders know their constituents names and interests (Hogan, et al., 1994), and they are good listeners (Johnson & Bechler, 1998). Although being a dynamic and eloquent speaker can be helpful in certain leadership roles, leaders are often effective not because of their spectacular oratory skills, but because of their outstanding interpersonal and human relations skills. Thus, effective interpersonal communication and human relations skills such as those discussed earlier in this chapter, will not only improve your social life, they will develop your leadership potential for diversity by enabling you to relate effectively with people from diverse backgrounds and promote harmonious relations among them.

If you have made the effort to develop friendships with members of diverse groups, it is likely that they will come to you for advice or assistance about diversity-related issues. Listed below are some key strategies for providing effective social and emotional support to peers who seek your help on personal issues related to prejudice or discrimination.

Words of Wisdom

"A friend in need is a friend indeed."

QUINTUS ENNIUS, ROMAN POET, THIRD-CENTURY B.C.; REGARDED AS THE "FATHER OF LATIN POETRY"

Words of Wisdom

"A friend is a person with whom I may be sincere. Before him, I may think aloud."

RALPH WALDO EMERSON, AMERICAN AUTHOR, PHILOSOPHER, AND ORATOR

- Be a good listener and lend an empathic ear. Just providing a sounding board and letting others bounce their thoughts and feelings off you can often result in a solution bouncing right back to them. An effective leader helps others gain self-insight and find solutions to their own problems. By simply giving others the opportunity to express their feelings, to get their concerns out in the open, and to think out loud, you can lead them to discover an effective solution on their own. Show authentic concern for other people's feelings. For example, instead of asking the routine question, "How's it going?" ask the person, "How are you feeling?" Studies show that when people discuss or share their feelings with others, it helps them feel understood and feel better about themselves (Reis & Shaver, 1988). Thus, you may help them by doing little more than listening in a concerned and compassionate way. Showing concern for others not only helps them feel more comfortable about sharing information with you, it creates more opportunities for you to learn from and about the diverse people you meet.

- Be sure not to dismiss or minimize the person's feelings. Avoid saying things like, "Oh, don't worry about it, everything will be alright" or, "You'll get over it." Comments like these make it sound like the person's feelings are unjustified or exaggerated (e.g., "you're making a mountain out of a mole hill"); such comments may also send the message that you are doubting or discounting the legitimacy of the person's feelings.

- If you have experienced a similar problem (e.g., being stereotyped) and have dealt with it effectively, share your experience. Sharing a similar experience of your own can help others feel that their issue is not "weird" and enable them to feel more optimistic or self-confident about dealing with it. However, be sure not to begin the process by saying: "I know how you feel." Although this statement may be well intended, it is presumptuous to say that you know how someone else feels because it is impossible to get into that person's head and know exactly what he or she is feeling or experiencing, particularly if that person comes from a different cultural background and has had very different life experiences than you.

- Ask questions that will help the person clarify the problem and identify options for solving it. Often we can provide better help by knowing what questions to ask than by knowing what answers to give. Good questions help launch others on a quest for their own solution by clarifying the issue and by generating viable options. For example, ask questions such as, "Could it be that . . . ?" "Do you think that . . .?" "What might have . . .?"

In contrast, questions you want to avoid are "trapping questions," such as: "What are you going to do about it?" "What if somebody finds out?" "Will you get in trouble?" Pelting others with prying questions like these is likely to elevate their anxiety about the issue that they came to you, causing them to leave feeling worse off than they did before they came to you for help.

- If supportive listening and questioning are not enough to help solve the person's problem or resolve the issue, work with the person to generate specific solutions. Brainstorming can serve as an effective method for generating possible solutions to personal problems and issues. (Key steps in the brainstorming process are summarized in the following box.)

The Process of Brainstorming ➡

Key steps:

1. Generate and list as many solutions and ideas as you possibly can and write them down without stopping to judge or evaluate them. Studies show that worrying about whether an idea is "correct" often blocks creativity (Basadure, Runco, & Vaga, 2000). So, let your imagination run free, and don't worry yet about whether the ideas you generate are impractical, unrealistic, or outrageous.

2. Use the ideas on your list as a springboard to generate additional ideas. In other words, use your listed ideas to "trigger" new ideas or "piggyback" on them to create combined ideas.

3. After you run out of ideas, review and evaluate the list of ideas you've generated and eliminate those that you think are least effective.

4. From the remaining list of ideas, choose what you think is the best idea or best combination of ideas.

➡

An effective helper is someone who helps others brainstorm their options, and the pros and cons of those options, but does not make the decision for them. When people seeking help ultimately make their own choice, they "own" that decision and the action they take on it serves to bolster their sense of self-control and self-efficacy. They are also more likely to become independent thinkers with greater self-confidence in their ability to solve their own problems, and become less dependent on others to solve their problems for them.

WORDS OF WISDOM

"When I ask you to listen to me and you begin to tell me why I shouldn't feel that way, you are trampling my feelings."

—RAY HOUGHTON, MD FROM POEM "PLEASE, JUST LISTEN!" BY RAY HOUGHTON, MD, ORIGINALLY APPEARING IN *TEEN TIMES* NOV/DEC 1979. COPYRIGHT © 1979 BY FAMILY, CAREER, & COMMUNITY LEADERS OF AMERICA (FCCLA). REPRINTED BY PERMISSION.

- If the person cannot make a decision after all options have been identified, deliver your advice as a concerned friend, not as an expert authority. For instance, before beginning to give your advice, introduce it by saying, "This is just a suggestion . . ." or, "I wonder if this might . . ." Offer your recommendations as reasonable possibilities rather than as sure-fired solutions. The last thing you want to do is give the impression that you are performing psychoanalysis on the person by saying things like, "What your problem is . . ." or, "What you need to do is . . ." Statements such as these can make the person feel like a patient who is helplessly dependent on you for your expert diagnosis and treatment.

- If the problem is extremely serious (e.g., the person has been a victim of a hate crime), encourage the person to seek professional assistance from a campus professional—such as an advisor, counselor, or multicultural specialist. You can take your encouragement one step further by helping the person take the specific steps necessary to get professional assistance by:
  1. helping the person identify what questions to ask the professional;
  2. helping the person find contact information for the professional (e.g., phone number);
  3. helping the person "connect" with the professional (e.g., encouraging the person to phone the professional, or walking with the person to the professional's office);
  4. complimenting the person for being open and willing to seek help; and
  5. following up later by asking if the professional assistance proved helpful.

- Last and most importantly, if peers come to you for help or assistance with personal issues relating to diversity, any information they share with you should remain confidential. This respects their right to privacy, reinforces their trust in you, and increases the likelihood they will come to you again if they need advice.

WORDS OF WISDOM

"Emollit Mores Nec Sinit Esse Feros"

("LEARNING HUMANIZES CHARACTER AND DOES NOT PERMIT IT TO BE CRUEL.")

MOTTO OF THE UNIVERSITY OF SOUTH CAROLINA

Pause for Reflection

Do you find that your peers frequently come to you for advice or assistance? If yes, why do you think they do?

Civic Leadership

You can have a positive influence on your peers by being a good *citizen* in your community. Good citizens model what it means to live in a democratic society by demonstrating:

1. Civility: being respectful of and sensitive to the rights of others; interacting with fellow citizens or community members in a humane and compassionate manner, and
2. Civic Responsibility: being willing to step up and confront others who disrespect, dehumanize, or violate the rights of fellow citizens.

When you take a leadership role with respect to preserving civility and exercising civic responsibility, you are demonstrating civic character.

REMEMBER: When you take a leadership role by modeling appreciation of diversity and confronting prejudice expressed by others, you are taking a stand for social justice, human rights, and equal opportunity for all human beings.

Listed below are major ways in which you can demonstrate civic leadership and civic character in college and beyond.

Serve as a community builder by identifying common themes that cut across the experiences of people from diverse backgrounds.

Look for common denominators—themes of unity that underlie diversity. For example, regardless of their particular group membership, all humans live in communities, develop relationships, have emotional needs, and undergo life experiences that affect their self-esteesm and personal identity. Individuals from diverse ethnic and racial groups share many common characteristics as a result of their being citizens of the same country, persons of the same gender, or members of the same generation.

As you look to capitalize on diversity, do not overlook the unity that transcends human differences; you can build on this unity to create community. Focusing exclusively on diversity without detecting the underlying similarities that lie beneath our obvious differences may aggravate feelings of separation and division among diverse groups. In fact, some research shows that when diversity education focuses on differences alone, minority groups are likely to feel even more isolated (Smith, 1997). To minimize this risk, you need to dig below the surface and unearth the common ground from which our differences grow. Raising your fellow students' consciousness of universal themes that unite different groups of people under the common umbrella of humanity can help ensure that focusing on diversity will not foment divisiveness. One strategy for doing so is to begin discussions of diversity by identifying commonalities—before launching into a discussion of your differences. For example, before beginning a discussion of cultural differences, you might first discuss the common elements of all cultures (e.g., language, family, artistic expression, traditions). This initial identification of similarities may help defuse feelings of separateness and create a common ground upon which a non-defensive discussion of diversity can be built.

REMEMBER: Diversity represents an opportunity for you to develop your civic character and leadership.

WORDS OF WISDOM

"Americanism is a question of principles, of idealism, of character: it is not a matter of birthplace or creed or line of descent."

THEODORE ROOSEVELT, AMERICAN SOLDIER, PRESIDENT, AND NOBEL PRIZE WINNER

By embracing human variety while highlighting our common humanity, you become a leader by building bridges of unity across islands of diversity. Research shows that effective leaders enable different individuals to see themselves as members of the same group, and see that when they work together for the group's best interest, they are also working individually for their own best interest (Bass & Riggio, 2005).

Take a stand against prejudice on campus by constructively disagreeing with those who make stereotypical statements or prejudicial remarks.

WORDS OF **W**ISDOM

"Put your creed into your deed."

RALPH WALDO EMERSON

"Happiness is when what you think, what you say and what you do are in harmony."

MAHATMA GANDHI, NON-VIOLENT CIVIL RIGHTS LEADER WHO LED STRUGGLE TO FREE INDIA FROM COLONIAL RULE

By saying nothing, you may avoid conflict, but your silence may be perceived by others to mean that you agree with people who make prejudicial remarks. Studies show that when members of the same group observe another member of their group making prejudiced comments, the group's prejudice tends to increase, probably due the pressure of group conformity (Stangor, Sechrist, & Jost, 2001). In contrast, if a person's prejudicial remark is challenged by a member of one's own group, particularly by a member who is liked and well respected, the person's prejudice tends to decrease, as does prejudice held by other members of the group (Baron, Byrne, & Brauscombe, 2006). Thus, by taking a leadership role and not remaining silent when people make prejudiced remarks, you not only help reduce one person's prejudice, you may also reduce the prejudice of all others who heard you challenge their remarks.

REMEMBER: By being open to diversity and opposed to prejudice, you demonstrate civic character. You become a role model whose actions visibly demonstrate to your fellow student citizens that diversity has both educational and ethical value. It's not only the *smart* thing to do; it's also the *right* thing to do.

Although you are expected to vote as a citizen of a nation, American citizens between the ages of 18 and 24 have the lowest voter turnout.

Under license from Shutterstock, Inc.

Exercise your right to vote, and when you do vote, be mindful of political leaders who are committed to equal rights, social justice, and advancing our understanding and appreciation of diversity.

It is noteworthy that American citizens between the ages of 18 and 24 have the lowest voter-turnout rate of any age group that is eligible to vote (Cummings, 2002). If you are a student in this age group who has not yet exercised your right to vote, get involved in the voting process because this is the process that is the lifeblood of a democratic nation. Informed voting also exemplifies one of the original purposes of a liberal arts education—to educate citizens and empower them with the knowledge and critical thinking skills needed to choose their leaders wisely. In a democracy, people are liberated from uncritical dependence on, and blind obedience to, a dictator or autocrat; instead, power rests with the people because they select (elect) their own leaders. To ensure that a democracy runs successfully and political freedom is preserved, citizens in a democratic nation must be *well educated* so they can ask intelligent questions of potential political leaders and make wise choices about whom they elect as their leaders and lawmakers (Bishop, 1986; Cheney, 1989).

Having the privilege of being a citizen in a free country brings with it the responsibility of participating in your country's governance through the process of voting. As a democracy, the United States is a nation that has been built on a foundation of equal rights and freedom of opportunity, that is guaranteed by its constitution.

REMEMBER: When the personal rights and freedoms of any group of citizens are threatened by prejudice and discrimination, the political stability and survival of any democratic nation is threatened. Thus, diversity and democracy go hand-in-hand; by appreciating the former, you preserve the latter.

W**ORDS** OF **W**ISDOM

"Knowledge will forever govern ignorance; and a people who mean to be their own governors must arm themselves with the power which knowledge gives."

JAMES MADISON, 4TH PRESIDENT OF THE UNITED STATES, AND CO-SIGNER OF THE AMERICAN CONSTITUTION AND BILL OF RIGHTS

Pause for Reflection

Did you vote in the last presidential election?

If no, why not?

If yes, what would you say was the major reason or issue that led you to vote for the candidate of your choice?

Summary

A deep appreciation of diversity can only be attained through active involvement in the process of learning about diverse cultures and through direct interaction with diverse groups of people. Key strategies for becoming involved in the diversity-learn process discussed in this chapter are summarized below.

Take courses relating to diversity, and engage in co-curricular experiences on campus that involve diversity. Research indicates that students who participate in multicultural and cross-cultural courses report greater gains in learning and greater satisfaction with the college experience. Participation in co-curricular programs relating to diversity has been found to reduce unconscious prejudice and promote cognitive development.

W**ORDS** OF **W**ISDOM

"General [liberal arts] education is intimately concerned with democratic processes and with the needs of a democratic society and always has been."

GEORGE MILLER, AUTHOR, *THE MEANING OF GENERAL EDUCATION*

WORDS OF WISDOM

"A progressive society counts individual variations as precious since it finds in them the means of its own growth. A democratic society must, in consistency with its ideal, allow intellectual freedom and the play of diverse gifts and interests."

JOHN DEWEY, U.S. EDUCATOR, PHILOSOPHER, AND PSYCHOLOGIST

Interact and collaborate with members of diverse groups. If you have taken the time and effort to learn about the culture of diverse groups, you should feel more comfortable about interacting with people from different cultural backgrounds. Studies show that learning is maximized when students move beyond acquiring knowledge about diversity vicariously from lectures and readings—to *experiencing* diversity through direct, interpersonal contact with people from diverse groups.

Intentionally create opportunities for interaction and conversation with individuals from diverse groups by placing yourself in situations and locations where you will come in regular contact with them. Spend as much time as you can on campus and spend it in places where diverse groups of people are likely to congregate. Research indicates meaningful interactions and friendships are more likely to develop among people who find themselves in physical proximity to one another.

Engage in volunteer experiences that allow you to work in diverse communities or neighborhoods. Volunteer experiences in the local community that extends beyond the borders of your campus may allow you the opportunity to interact with diverse groups of people who may not be found in large numbers within your campus community.

Find an internship in a company or organization that enables you to work with people from diverse backgrounds and cultures. Working in a diverse social setting will improve your preparation and qualifications for career entry after college. National surveys indicate that employers value college graduates who have had direct, hands-on experience with diversity (Education Commission of the States, 1995).

Develop your interpersonal communication and human relations skills. These skills are important when interacting with people in general. They are particularly important when interacting with people from different cultural backgrounds because they lack familiarity and previously shared experiences, which can easily lead to communication breakdowns that short-circuit potentially fruitful interactions and relationships.

Form learning teams with students from diverse backgrounds. Research consistently shows that we learn more from people who are dissimilar to us than we do from people who are similar to us, and we learn best from others whose experiences and viewpoints do not necessarily match our own.

Reflect on personal experiences with diversity. Learning deeply from diversity requires both action and reflection. Writing is an effective strategy for promoting reflection on diversity experiences because it slows down the thought process and provides a visible product of our thinking which can be reviewed later and used to prompt further reflection on our experiences.

Take a leadership role with respect to diversity. Leadership roles in college may be grouped into four general categories:

1. **Academic leadership**—for example, forming diverse learning groups;
2. **Organizational leadership**—for example, serving on diversity or multi-cultural committees;
3. **Social and emotional leadership**—for example, serving as an orientation-group leader for new students;
4. **Civic leadership**—for example, publicly challenging peers who make prejudicial comments or engage in discriminatory behavior.

This chapter outlined a comprehensive, strategic plan for appreciating diversity and attaining intercultural competence. Implementing this plan should enrich the quality of your college education and the quality of your personal life; it will do the same for all diverse groups of people with whom you interact.

Chapter 5 Exercises

Name

_____

Date

_____

5.1 Intercultural Interview

1. Identify a person on campus who is a member of an ethnic or racial group that is unfamiliar to you and ask that person for an interview. During the interview, ask the following questions:

    a. What does "diversity" mean to you?

    b. Who would you cite as positive role models, heroes, or sources of inspiration in your life?

    c. What would you say have been the major influences and turning points in your life?

    d. What prior experiences have affected your current viewpoints or attitudes about diversity?

    e. What societal contributions made by your culture would you like others to be aware of and acknowledge?

    f. What do you hope will never again be said about your ethnic or racial group?

2. If you were the interviewee instead of the interviewer, how would you have answered the above questions?

3. What do you think accounts for the differences (and similarities) between your answers and those provided by your interviewee?

5.2 Diversity Leadership Scenarios

1. You are with a group of friends when someone in the crowd begins telling a joke that includes a derogatory term for African Americans. You do not feel comfortable in the situation. What would you do?

2. Your parents have invited you home for the holidays, but when you ask if your gay/lesbian friend can also attend, they say no. How would you respond to your parents? Would you still go home and leave your friend who has nowhere else to go for the holidays?

3. Your daughter wants to play football but the coach has told you only boys are allowed to play on the team. Would you explain to your daughter that she is not allowed to play football? Or would you try to get her on the team anyway?

4. Your daughter wants to play little league baseball. When you go to sign her up, you are told that little league baseball is only for boys, but she could play softball with the other girls. Your little girl is heartbroken and only wants to play baseball. What would you say or do?

Source: University of New Hampshire, 2001

5.3 Identifying *Leadership* Opportunities at Your College or University

1. Consult your *Student Handbook* and list the student organizations and leadership opportunities that are available on your campus.

2. Which one of the student organizations and leadership opportunities on your campus best *matches* your particular leadership talents, skills, or interests?

3. Which one of the student organizations do you think has the most potential for promoting diversity appreciation?

4. Do you see yourself assuming a leadership role with respect to diversity in any organizations, positions, or situations on campus? Why?

5. In what areas or aspects of college life do you think diversity leadership is most needed on your campus?

References

Acredolo, C. & O'Connor, J. (1991). On the difficulty of detecting cognitive uncertainty. *Human Development, 34,* 204–223.

Adherents.com *Major religions of the world ranked by number of adherents* Retrieved July 27, 2008, from http://www.adherents.com/Religions_By_Adherents.html.

Adherents.com *Largest religious groups in the United States of America* Retrieved July 27, 2008, from http://www.adherents.com/rel_USA.html.

Adler, R. B. & Towne, M. (2001). *Looking out, looking in: Interpersonal communication* (10th ed.). Orlando, FL: Harcourt Brace.

AhYun, K. (2002). Similarity and attraction. In M. Allen, R. W. Preiss, B. M. Gayle, & N. A. Burrell (Eds.), *Interpersonal communication research* (pp. 145–167). Mahwah, NJ: Erlbaum.

Alkon, D. L. (1992). *Memory's voice: Deciphering the brain-mind code.* New York: HarperCollins.

Allport. G. W. (1954). *The nature of prejudice.* Cambridge, MA: Addison-Wesley.

Allport, G. W. (1979). *The nature of prejudice* (3rd ed.). Reading, MA: Addison-Wesley.

America.gov (2008). *Survey finds Americans are religious, tolerant, nondogmatic* Retrieved August 28, 2008, from http://www.america.gov/st/diversity-english/2008/June/200806261547511CJsamohT0.6362116.html.

American Council on Education (2008). *Making the case for affirmative action* Retrieved October 25, 2008, from http://www.acenet.edu/bookstore/descriptions/making_the_case/works/research.cfm.

American Heart Association (2006). *Fish, levels of mercury and omega-3 fatty acids* Retrieved Jan. 13, 2007, from http://americanheart.org/presenter.jthml?identifier=3013797.

American Heritage Dictionary of the English Language (4th ed.) (2008). Boston: Houghton Mifflin.

American Public Works Association Diversity Resource Guide (2001). Retrieved June 25, 2006, from http://www.apwa.net/Documents/About/Board/DiverGuideVol1.pdf.

Amir, Y. (1969). Contact hypothesis in ethnic relations. *Psychological Bulletin, 71,* 319–342.

Amir, Y. (1976). The role of intergroup contact in change of prejudice and ethnic relations. In P. A. Katz (Ed.), *Towards the elimination of racism* (pp. 245–308). New York: Pergamon Press.

Applebee, A. N. (1981). *Writing in the secondary school.* Urbana, Ill.: National Council of Teachers of English.

Applebee, A. N. (1984). Writing and reasoning. *Review of Educational Research, 54*(4), 577–596.

Aronson, E., Wilson, T. D., & Akert, R. M. (2005). *Social psychology* (5th ed.). Upper Saddle River, NJ: Pearson/Prentice Hall.

AsianNation.org. *14 important statistics about Asian Americans* Retrieved July 27, 2008, from http://www.asian-nation.org/14-statistics.shtml.

Asian Nation.org. *The first Asian Americans* Retrieved July 27, 2008, from http://www.asian-nation.org/first/shtml.

Astin, A. W. (1993). *What matters in college?* San Francisco: Jossey-Bass.

Astin, A. W., Vogelgesang, L. J., Ikeda, E. K., & Yee, J. A. (2000). *How service-learning affects students*. Higher Education Research Institute, University of California, Los Angeles.

Avolio, B. J. (2005). *Leadership development in balance: Made/born*. Mahwah, NJ: Lawrence Erlbaum Associates.

Baer, J. M. (1993). *Creativity and divergent thinking*. Mahwah, NJ: Lawrence Erlbaum Associates.

Baron, R. A., Byrne, D., & Brauscombe, N. R. (2006). *Social psychology* (11th ed.). Boston: Pearson.

Basadur, M., Runco, M. A., & Vega, L. A. (2000). Understanding how creative thinking skills, attitudes, and behaviors work together. *Journal of Creative Behavior, 34*(2), 77–100.

Bass, B. M. & Riggio, R. E. (2005). *Transformational leadership* (2nd ed.). Mahwah, NJ: Lawrence Erlbaum Associates.

Bean, J. C. (2001). *Engaging ideas: The professor's guide to integrating writing, critical thinking, and active learning in the classroom*. San Francisco: Jossey-Bass.

Bean, J. C. (2003). *Engaging ideas*. San Francisco: Jossey-Bass.

Belenky, M. F., Clinchy, B., Goldberger, N. R., & Tarule, J. M. (1986). *Women's ways of knowing: The development of self, voice, and mind*. New York: Basic Books.

Bellah, R. N., Madsen, R., Sullivan, W. M., Swidler, A., & Tipton, S. M. (1985). *Habits of the heart: Individualism and commitment in American life*. Berkeley: University of California Press.

Bennis, W. (1989). *On becoming a leader*. Reading, MA: Addison-Wesley.

Biglan, A. (1973). The characteristics of subject matter in different academic areas. *Journal of Applied Psychology, 57*, 195–203.

Bishop, S. (1986). Education for political freedom. *Liberal Education, 72*(4), 322–325.

Blair, I. V. (2002). The malleability of automatic stereotypes and prejudice. *Personality & Social Psychology Review, 6*(3), 242–261.

Bligh, D. A. (2000). *What's the use of lectures*. San Francisco: Jossey-Bass.

Bowen, H. R. (1977). *Investment in learning: The individual and social value of American higher education*. San Francisco: Jossey-Bass.

Bowen, H. R. (1997). *Investment in learning: The individual and social value of American higher education* (2nd ed.). Baltimore: The Johns Hopkins Press.

Bradshaw, D. (1995). Learning theory: Harnessing the strength of a neglected resource. In D.C.A. Bradshaw (Ed.), *Bringing learning to life: The learning revolution, the economy and the individual* (pp. 79–92). London, UK: The Falmer Press.

Bridgeman, B. (2003). *Psychology and evolution: The origins of mind*. Thousand Oaks, CA: Sage.

Broadbent, D. E. (1970). Review lecture. *Proceedings of the Royal Society of London B*, 333–350.

Brown, T. D., Dane, F. C., & Durham, M. D. (1998). Perception of race and ethnicity. *Journal of Social Behavior & Personality, 13*(2), 295–306.

Bruffee, K. A. (1993). *Collaborative learning: Higher education, interdependence, and the authority of knowledge*. Baltimore: Johns Hopkins University Press.

Caplan, P. J. & Caplan, J. B. (1994). *Thinking critically about research on sex and gender*. New York: HarperCollins College Publishers.

Central Intelligence Agency (2008). *The World Factbook* Retrieved July 27, 2008, from https://www.cia.gov/library/publications/the-world-factbook/print/xx.html.

Censusscope.org *United States household and family structure* Retrieved October 2, 2008, from http://www.censusscope.org/us/chart_house.html.

Censusscope.org *United States multiracial profile* Retrieved October 2, 2008, from http://www.censusscope.org/us/chart_multi.html.

Cheney, L. V. (1989). *50 hours: A core curriculum for college students*. Washington, D.C.: National Endowment for the Humanities.

Chronicle of Higher Education (2003, August 30). Almanac 2003–04. *The Chronicle of Higher Education, 49*(1). Washington, D.C.: Author.

Cianciotto, J. (2005) *Hispanic and latino same-sex couple households in the United States: A Report from the 2000 Census.* New York: The National Gay and Lesbian Task Force Policy Institute and the National Latino/a Coalition for Justice.

Clark, K. (2007). *Defining white privilege* Retrieved February 6, 2007, from http://www.whiteprivilege.com.

Claxton, C. S. & Murrell, P. H. (1988). *Learning styles: Implications for improving practice*. ASHE-ERIC Educational Report No. 4. Washington D.C.: Association for the Study of Higher Education.

Colombo, G., Cullen, R., & Lisle, B. (1995). *Rereading America: Cultural contexts for critical thinking and writing*. Boston: Bedford Books of St. Martin's Press.

Cook, S. W. (1984). Cooperative interaction in multiethnic contexts. In N. Miller & M. B. Brewer (Eds.), *Groups in contact: The psychology of desegregation*. New York: Academic Press.

Cooley, C.H. (1922). *Human nature and the social order*. New York: Scribner's.

Covey, S. R. (1990). *Seven habits of highly effective people* (2nd ed). New York: Fireside.

Cronon, W. (1998). "Only connect": The goals of a liberal education. *The American Scholar* (Autumn), 73–80.

Cross, K. P. (1982). Thirty years passed: Trends in general education. In B. L. Johnson (Ed.), *General education in two-year colleges* (pp. 11–20). San Francisco: Jossey-Bass.

Cummings, M. C. (2002). *Democracy under pressure* (9th ed.). Belmont, CA: Wadsworth.

Cuseo, J. B. (1996). *Cooperative learning: A pedagogy for addressing contemporary challenges and critical issues in higher education*. Stillwater, OK: New Forums Press.

Cuseo, J. B. (2002). *Igniting student involvement, peer interaction, and teamwork: A taxonomy of specific cooperative learning structures and collaborative learning strategies*. Stillwater, OK: New Forums Press.

Cuseo, J. B., Fecas, V., & Thompson, A. (2007). *Thriving in college: Research-based strategies for academic success and personal development*. Dubuque, IA: Kendall/Hunt.

Cusinato, M. & L'Abate, L. (1994). A spiral model of intimacy. In S. M. Johnson & L. S. Greenberg (Eds.), *The heart of the matter: Emotion in marital therapy*. New York: Brunner/Mazel.

Dang, A. & Frazer, S. (2004) *Black same-sex households in the United States: A Report from the 2000 Census*. New York: National Gay and Lesbian Task Force Policy Institute and the National Black Justice Coalition.

Dinnerstein, L. & Reimers, D. (2008) *Immigration* Retrieved August 25, 2008, from http://encarta.msn.com/text_761566973___0/Immigration.html.

Donahue, J. & Siegel, M. E. (2005). *Are you really listening: Keys to successful communication*. South Bend, IN: Ave Maria Press.

Donald, J. G. (2002). *Learning to think: Disciplinary perspectives*. San Francisco: Jossey-Bass.

Driscoll, E. V. (2008). Bisexual species. *Scientific American Mind, 19*(3), 68–73.

Dryden, G. & Vos, J. (1999). *The learning revolution: To change the way the world learns*. Torrance, CA & Auckland, New Zealand: The Learning Web.

Dunn, R., Dunn, K., & Price, G. (1990). *Learning style inventory*. Lawrence, KS: Price Systems.

Du Praw, M. & Axner, M. (1997). *Toward a more perfect union in an age of diversity: Working on common cross-cultural communication challenges* Retrieved September 27, 2008, from http://www.pbs.org/ampu/crosscult.html.

Eble, K. E. (1966). *A perfect education*. New York: Macmillan.

Eckman, P. & Friesen, W. V. (1969). Nonverbal leakage and clues to deception. *Psychiatry, 32*, 88–106.

Education Commission of the States (1995). *Making quality count in undergraduate education*. Denver, CO: ECS Distribution Center.

Elbow, P. (1973). *Writing without teachers*. New York: Oxford University Press.

Encrenaz, T., Bibring, J.-P., Blanc, M., Barucci, M.-A., Roques, F., & Zarka, P. (2004). *The solar system*. Berlin, Germany: Springer.

Erickson, B. L., Peters, C. B., & Strommer, D. W. (2006). *Teaching first-year college students*. San Francisco: Jossey-Bass.

Etsy, K., Griffin, R. & Hirsch, M. S. (1995). *Workplace diversity*. Adams Media Corporation: Holbrook, MA.

Feagin, J. & Feagin, C. (2003). *Racial and ethnic relations*. Upper Saddle River, NJ: Prentice Hall.

Feagin, J. R. & McKinney, K. D. (2003). *The many costs of racism*. Lanham, MD: Rowman & Littlefield.

Feldman, K. A. & Newcomb, T. M. (Eds.) (1969). *The impact of college on students*. San Francisco: Jossey-Bass.

Feldman, K. A. & Paulsen, M. B. (Eds.) (1994). *Teaching and learning in the college classroom*. Needham Heights, MA: Ginn Press.

Felstead, A., Gallie, D., & Green, F. (2002). *Work skills in Britain 1986–2001* Retrieved December 22, 2006, from http://www.kent.ac.uk/economics/staff/gfg/WorkSkills1986–2001.pdf.

Feskens, E. J. & Kromhout, D. (1993). Epidemiologic studies on Eskimos and fish intake. *Annals of the New York Academy of Science, 683*, 9–15.

Festinger, L. (1954). A theory of social comparison processes. *Human Relations, 7*, 117–140.

Fiedler, F. E. (1993). The leadership situation and the black box in contingency theories. In M. M. Chemers & R. Ayman (Eds.), *Leadership theory and research* (pp. 2–28). New York: Academic Press.

Fixman, C. S. (1990). The foreign language needs of U.S.-based corporations. *Annals of the American Academy of Political and Social Science, 511*, 25–46.

Gallup (2005, March 15). *Religious tolerance score edge up in 2004: More Americans positive about other faith traditions* Retrieved Nov. 21, 2008, from http://www.gallup.com/poll/15253/Religious-Tolerance-Score-Edged-2004.aspx.

Gardner, H. (1993). *Multiple intelligences: The theory of multiple intelligences* (2nd ed.). New York: Basic Books.

Gardner, H. (1999). *Intelligence reframed: Multiple intelligences for the 21st century*. New York: Basic Books.

Gemmil, G. (1989). The dynamics of scapegoating in small groups. *Small Group Behavior, 20*, 406–418.

Gibb, J. R. (1961). Defensive communication. *The Journal of Communication* (September) *11*, p. 3.

Glassman, J. K. (2000, June 9). The technology revolution: Road to freedom or road to serfdom? *Heritage Lectures*, No. 668. Washington, D.C.: The Heritage Foundation.

Goffman, E. (Ed.) (1967). *Interaction ritual: Essays in face-to-face behavior*. Chicago: Aldine.

Goleman, D. (2006). *Emotional intelligence: Why it can matter more than IQ*. New York: Bantom Books.

Goleman, D. (2007). *Social intelligence: The new science of human relationships*. New York: Bantom Books.

Green, M. G. (Ed.) (1989). *Minorities on campus: A handbook for enhancing diversity*. Washington, D.C.: American Council on Education.

Gurin, P. (1999). New research on the benefits of diversity in college and beyond: An empirical analysis. *Diversity Digest* (spring). Retrieved November 21, 2008, from http://www.diversityweb.org/Digest/Sp99/benefits.html.

Gutman, H. G. (1975). *Work, culture & society*. New York: Vintage.

Hall, E. T. & Hall, M. R. (1986). *Hidden differences: How to communicate with the Germans*. Hamburg, West Germany: Gruner & Jahr.

Hall, R. M. & Sandler, B. R. (1982). *The classroom climate: A chilly one for women*. Association of American Colleges' Project on the Status of Women. Washington, D.C.: Association of American Colleges.

Hall, R. M. & Sandler, B. R. (1984). *Out of the classroom: A chilly campus climate for women*. Association of American Colleges' Project on the Status of Women. Washington, D.C.: Association of American Colleges.

Hamilton, D. L. & Sherman, S. J. (1989). Illusory correlations: Implications for streotype theory and research. In D. Bar-Tal, C. F. Graumann, A. W. Kruglanski, & W. Stroebe (Eds.), *Stereotyping and prejudice: Changing conceptions* (pp. 59–82). New York: Springer-Verlag.

Heath, H. (1977). *Maturity and competence: A transcultural view*. New York: Halsted Press.

Hogan, R., Curphy, G. J., & Hogan, J. (1994). What we know about leadership: Effectiveness and personality. *American Psychologist, 49*, 493–504.

Holland, J. L. (1997). *Making vocational choices: A theory of vocational personalities and work environments*. Lutz, FL: Psychological Assessment Resources.

Hugenberg, K. & Bodenhausen, G. V. (2003). Facing prejudice: Implicit prejudice and the perception of facial threat. *Psychological Science, 14*, 640–643.

Institute of International Education (2001). *Open doors* Retrieved July 7, 2005, from http://www.opendoorsweb.org/2001%20Files/layout_htm.

Jablonski, N. G. & Chaplin, G. (2002). Skin deep. *Scientific American* (October), 75–81.

Janis, I. L. (1982). *Groupthink: Psychological studies of policy decisions and fiascoes*. (2nd ed.). Boston: Houghton Mifflin.

Johnson, D., Johnson, R., & Smith, K. (1998). Cooperative learning returns to college: What evidence is there that it works? *Change, 30*, 26–35.

Johnson, S. D. & Bechler, C. (1998). Examining the relationship between listening effectiveness and leadership emergence: Perceptions, behaviors, and recall. *Small Group Research, 29*(4), 452–471.

Joint Science Academies Statement (2005). *Global response to climate change* Retrieved August 29, 2005, from http://nationalacademies.org/onpi/06072005. pdf.

Jones, W. T. (1990). Perspectives on ethnicity. In L. V. Moore (Ed.), *Evolving theoretical perspectives on students* (pp. 59–72). San Francisco: Jossey-Bass.

Judd, C. M., Ryan, C. S., & Parke, B. (1991). Accuracy in the judgment of in-group and out-group variability. *Journal of Personality and Social Psychology, 61*, 366–379.

Kardia, D. (1998). Student attitudes toward gay and lesbian issues: The impact of college. *Diversity Digest* (summer). Retrieved from http://www.diversityweb.org/Digest/Sm98/attitudes.html.

Kaufman, J. C. & Baer, J. (2002). Could Steven Spielberg manage the Yankees?: Creative thinking in different domains. *Korean Journal of Thinking & Problem Solving, 12*(2), 5–14.

Khoshaba, D. M. & Maddi, S. R. (1999–2004). *HardiTraining: Managing stressful change*. Newport Beach, CA: The Hardiness Institute.

Kitchener, K., Wood, P., & Jensen, L. (2000, August). *Curricular, co-curricular, and institutional influence on real-world problem-solving*. Paper presented at the annual meeting of the American Psychological Association, Boston.

Knoll, A. H. (2003). *Life on a young planet: The first three billion years of evolution on earth*. Princeton, NJ: Princeton University Press.

Kolb, D. A. (1976). Management and learning process. *California Management Review, 18*(3), 21–31.

Kolb, D. A. (1985). *Learning styles inventory*. Boston: McBer.

Kosmin, N. A., Mayer, E., & Keyser, A. (2002). *American religious identification survey, 2001*. New York: City University of New York, Graduate Centre.

Kouzes, J. M. & Posner, B. Z. (1988). *The leadership challenge: How to get extraordinary things done in organizations*. San Francisco: Jossey-Bass.

Kuh, G. D. (1995). The other curriculum: Out-of-class experiences associated with student learning and personal development. *Journal of Higher Education, 66*(2), 123–153.

Kuh, G. D. (2000). Setting the bar high to promote student learning. In G. S. Blimling, E. J. Whitt, & Associates, *Good practice in student affairs: Principles to foster student learning* (pp. 67–90). San Francisco: Jossey-Bass.

Kuh, G. D., Douglas, K. B., Lund, J. P., & Ramin-Gyurnek, J. (1994). *Student learning outside the classroom: Transcending artificial boundaries*. ASHE-ERIC Higher Education Report, No. 8. Washington, D.C.: George Washington University, School of Education and Human Development.

Kurfiss, J. G. (1988). *Critical thinking: theory, research, practice, and possibilities*. ASHE-ERIC, Report No. 2. Washington, D.C.: Association for the Study of Higher Education.

Langer, J. A. & Applebee, A. N. (1987). *How writing shapes thinking*. NCTE Research Report No. 22. Urbana, IL: National Council of Teachers of English.

Lancaster, L. and Stillman, D. (2002) *When generations collide*. New York, NY: Harper Collins.

LeBaron, M. (2003). *Bridging cultural conflicts: New approaches for a changing world*. San Francisco: Jossey-Bass.

Levin, D. T. (2000). Race as a visual feature: Using visual search and perceptual discrimination tasks to understand face categories and the cross-race recognition deficit. *Journal of Experimental Psychology: General, 129*(4), 559–574.

Levine, L. W. (1996). *The opening of the American mind: Canons, culture, and history*. Boston: Beacon Press.

Light, R. J. (2001). *Making the most of college: Students speak their minds*. Cambridge, MA: Harvard University Press.

Linville, P. W., Fischer, G. W., & Salovey, P. (1989). Perceived distributions of the characteristics of in-group and out-group members: Empirical evidence and a computer simulation. *Journal of Personality and Social Psychology, 57*, 165–188.

Locke, E. A. (1991). *The essentials of leadership*. New York: Lexington Books.

Lopez, G. E., Gurin, P., & Nagda, B. A. (1998). Education and understanding structural causes for group inequalities. *Journal of Political Psychology, 19*(2), 305–329.

Lott, B. (2002). Cognitive and behavior distancing from the poor. *American Psychologist, 57*, 100–110.

Luhman, R. (2007). *The sociological outlook*. Lanham, MD: Rowman & Littlefield.

Magolda, M. B. B. (1992). *Knowing and reasoning in college*. San Francisco: Jossey-Bass.

Massey, D. (2003). *The source of the river: The social origins of freshmen at America's selective colleges and universities*. Princeton, NJ: Princeton University Press.

Matlock, J. (1997). Student expectations and experiences: The Michigan study. *Diversity Digest* (summer). Retrieved November 21, 2008, from http://www.diversityweb.org/Digest/Sm97/research.html.

Mayer, J. D. & Salovey, P. (1997). What is emotional intelligence? In P. Salovey & D. Sluyter (Eds). *Emotional development and emotional intelligence: Implications for educators* (pp. 3-31). New York: Basic Books.

McArthur, L. Z. & Friedman, S. A. (1980). Illusory correlation in impression formation: Variations in the shared distinctiveness effect as a function of the distinctive person's age, race, and sex. *Journal of Personality and Social Psychology, 39*, 615–624.

Mehrabian, A. (1972). *Nonverbal communication*. Chicago: Adline-Atherton.

Miville, M. L., Molla, B., & Sedlacek, W. E. (1992). Attitudes of tolerance for diversity among college students. *Journal of the Freshman Year Experience, 4*(1), 95–110.

Molnar, S. (1991). *Human variation: race, type, and ethnic groups* (3rd ed.). Englewood Cliffs, NJ: Prentice-Hall.

Murray, D. M. (1984). *Write to learn* (2nd ed.). New York: Holt, Rinehart, & Winston.

Myers, D. G. (1993). *The pursuit of happiness: Who is happy—and why?* New York: Morrow.

Myers, D. G. & McCaulley, N. H. (1985). *Manual: A guide to the development and use of the Myers-Briggs Type Indicator*. Palo Alto, CA: Consulting Psychologists Press.

Myers, I. B. (1976). *Introduction to type*. Gainesville, FL: Center for the Application of Psychological Type.

Myers, N. (1997). The rich diversity of biodiversity issues. In M. L. Reaka-Kudla, D. E. Wilson, & E. O. Wilson (Eds.), *Biological diversity II: Understanding and protecting our biological resources* (pp. 125–134). National Academic of Sciences, Washington, D.C.: Joseph Henry Press.

Nagda, B. R., Gurin, P., & Johnson, S. M. (2005). Living, doing and thinking diversity: How does pre-college diversity experience affect first-year students' engagement with college diversity? In R. S. Feldman (Ed.), *Improving the first year of college: Research and practice* (pp. 73–110). Mahwah, NJ: Lawrence Erlbaum Associates.

Nagda, B. R., Gurin, P., & Lopez, G. E. (2003). Transformative pedagogy for democracy and social justice. *Race, Ethnicity, & Education, 6*(2), 165–191.

National Association of Colleges and Employers (NACE) (2003). *Job Outlook 2003 survey*. Bethlehem, PA: Author.

National Committee on Pay Equity. *The wage gap over time: in real dollars, women see a continuing gap* Retrieved October 1, 2008, from http://www.pay-equity.org/info-time.html.

National Council of La Raza (2007). *Twenty of the most frequently asked questions about Hispanics in the U.S.* Retrieved from http://www.nclr.org.

National Gay and Lesbian Task Force Summit and Hearing (2005). *Make room for all: diversity, cultural competency, & discrimination in aging America* Retrieved October 1, 2008, from http://www.agingasourselves.org/pdf/MakeRoomForAllNGLTF.pdf.

National Resources Defense Council (2005). *Global warming: A summary of recent findings on the changing global climate* Retrieved Nov. 11, 2005, from http://www.nrdc.org/global/Warming/fgwscience.asp.

National Survey of Voters, Autumn 1998 Overview Report Conducted by DYG, Inc. Retrieved July 15, 2004, from http://www.diversityweb.org/research_and_trends/research_evaluation_impact/campus_community_connections/national_poll.cfm.

National Wellness Institute (2005). *The six dimensional wellness model* Retrieved August 11, 2006, from http://www.nationalwellness.org/SitePrint.ph?id=391&tier name=Free%20Resource%20.

National Women's Law Center. *Congress must act to close the wage gap for women* Retrieved October 1, 2008, from http://www.pay-equity.org/PDFs/PaycheckFairnessAct_2007.pdf.

National Women's History Project. *Living the legacy: the women's rights movement 1848–1998* Retrieved October 1, 2008, from http://www.legacy98.org/move-hist.html.

NativeAmericans.com *Facts about American Indians today* Retrieved July 23, 2008, from http://www.nativeamericans.com/today.htm.

NativeAmericans.com *Native American languages* Retrieved July 23, 2008, from http://www.nativeamericans.com/NativeAmericanLanguages.htm.

Nemko, M. (1988). *How to get an Ivy League education at a state university*. New York: Avon.

Nicholas, R. W. (1991). Cultures in the curriculum. *Liberal Education, 77*(3), 16–21.

Nichols, R. G. & Stevens, L. A. (1957). *Are you listening?* New York: McGraw-Hill.

Novinger, T. (2001). *Intercultural communication: A practical guide*. Austin, TX: University of Texas Press.

Obama, B. (2006). *The audacity of hope: Thoughts on reclaiming the American dream*. New York: Three Rivers Press.

Office of Research (1994). *What employers expect of college graduates: International knowledge and second language skills*. Washington, D.C.: Office of Educational Research and Improvement (OERI), U.S. Department of Education.

Oller, D. K. (1981). Infant vocalizations: Exploration and reflectivity. In R. E. Stark (Ed.), *Language behavior in infancy and early childhood* (pp. 85–104). New York: Elsevier/North-Holland.

Palank, J. (2006, July 17). *Face it: 'Book' no secret to employers* Retrieved August 21, 2006, from http://www.washtimes.com/business/20060717-12942-1800r.htm.

Palmer, B. (2000). The impact of diversity courses: Research from Pennsylvania State University. *Diversity Digest* (winter) Retrieved from http://www.diversityweb.org/Digest/W00/research.html.

Paolini, S., Hewstone, M., Cairns, E., & Voci, A. (2004). Effects of direct and indirect cross-group friendships on judgments of Catholics and Protestants in Northern Ireland: The mediating role of an anxiety reduction mechanism. *Personality and Social Psychology Bulletin, 30*, 770–786.

Papalia, D. E. & Olds, S. W. (1990). *A child's world: Infancy through adolescence* (5th ed.). New York: McGraw-Hill.

Pascarella, E. T. (2001). Cognitive growth in college: Surprising and reassuring findings from The National Study of Student Learning. *Change* (November/December), pp. 21–27.

Pascarella, E., Palmer, B., Moye, M., & Pierson, C. (2001). Do diversity experiences influence the development of critical thinking? *Journal of College Student Development, 42*, 257–291.

Pascarella, E. & Terenzini, P. (1991). *How college affects students: Findings and insights from twenty years of research.* San Francisco: Jossey-Bass.

Pascarella, E. T. & Terenzini, P. T. (2005). *How college affects students: A third decade of research* (volume 2). San Francisco: Jossey-Bass.

Paul, R. W. & Elder, L. (2002). *Critical thinking: Tools for taking charge of your professional and personal life.* Upper Saddle River, NJ: Pearson Education.

Peoples, J. & Bailey, G. (2008). *Humanity: An introduction to cultural anthropology* (8th ed.). Belmont, CA: Wadsworth.

Pettigrew, T. F. & Tropp, L. R. (2000). Does intergroup contact reduce prejudice? Recent meta-analytic findings. In S. Oskamp (Ed.), *Reducing prejudice and discrimination* (pp. 93–114). Mahwah, NJ: Lawrence Erlbaum Associates.

PFLAG (2006). *Vision, mission and strategic goals* Retrieved January 14, 2009, from http://community.pflag.org/Page.aspx?pid=237.

Piaget, J. (1985). *The equilibration of cognitive structures: The central problem of intellectual development.* Chicago, IL: University of Chicago Press.

Pinker, S. (1994). *The language instinct.* New York: HarperCollins.

Pope, R. L., Miklitsch, T. A., & Weigand, M. J. (2005). First-year students: Embracing their diversity, enhancing our practice. In R. S. Feldman (Ed.), *Improving the first year of college: Research and practice* (pp. 51–72). Mahwah, NJ: Lawrence Erlbaum Associates.

Posner, H. & Markstein, J. (1994). Cooperative learning in introductory cell and molecular biology. *Journal of College Science Teaching, 23*, 231–233.

Postsecondary Education Opportunity (2001). *Enrollment rates for females 18 to 34 years, 1950–2000.* Number 113 (November). Washington, D.C.: Center for the Study of Opportunity in Higher Education.

Pratto, F., Liu, J. H., Levin, S., Sidanius, J., Shih, M., Bachrach, H., & Hegarty, P. (2000). Social dominance orientation and the legitimization of inequality across cultures. *Journal of Cross-Cultural Psychology, 31*, 369–409.

Public Broadcasting Service (2008). *Diversity timeline from 1600 to present* Retrieved December 8, 2008, from http://www.pbs.org/itvs/testofcourage/diversity4.html.

Rankin, S. (2003) *Campus climate for gay, lesbian, bisexual and transgender people: A national perspective.* New York: The National Gay and Lesbian Task Force Policy Institute.

Reicher, S. D., Haslam, A., & Platow, M. J. (2007). The new psychology of leadership. *Scientific American Mind, 18*(4), pp. 22–29.

Reis, H. T. & Shaver, P. (1988). Intimacy as an interpersonal process. In S. W. Durck (Ed.), *Handbook of personal relationships* (pp. 367–389). New York: Wiley.

Riquelme, H. (2002). Can people creative in imagery interpret ambiguous figures faster than people less creative in imagery? *Journal of Creative Behavior, 36*(2), 105–116.

Rose, S. & Hartmann, H. (2004). *Still a man's labor market: the long-term earnings gap*. Washington, D.C.: The Institute for Women's Policy Research.

Rudman, L. A. & Fairchild, K. (2004). Reactions to counter-stereotypic behavior: The role of backlash in cultural stereotype maintenance. *Journal of Personality and Social Psychology, 87*, 157–176.

Ruffins, P. (1996) *Ten myths, half-truths and misunderstandings about black history* Retrieved August 8, 2008, from http://www.diverseeducation.com/artman/publish/printer_7469.shtml.

Sadker, M. & Sadker, D. (1994). *Failing at fairness: How America's schools cheat girls*. New York: Charles Scribner's Sons.

Schneider, E. C., Zaslavsky, A. M., & Epstein, A. M. (2002). Racial disparities in the quality of care for enrollees in Medicare managed care. *Journal of the American Medical Association, 287*, 1288–1294.

Sedlacek, W. (1987). Black students on white campuses: 20 years of research. *Journal of College Student Personnel, 28*, 484–495.

Segall, M. H., Campbell, D. T., & Herskovits, M. J. (1966). *The influence of culture on visual perception*. Indianapolis: Bobbs-Merrill.

Shapiro, S. R. (1993). *Human rights violations in the United States: A report on U.S. compliance*. Human Rights Watch, American Civil Liberties Union. New York, NY.

Sherif, M., Harvey, D. J., White, B. J., Hood, W. R., & Sherif, C. W. (1961). *The Robbers' cave experiment*. Norman, OK: Institute of Group Relations.

Sidanius, J., Levin, S., Liu, H., & Pratto, F. (2000). Social dominance orientation, anti-egalitarianism, and the political psychology of gender: An extension and cross-cultural replication. *European Journal of Social Psychology, 30*, 41–67.

Slavin, R. E. (1995). *Cooperative learning* (2nd ed.). Boston: Allyn & Bacon.

Smith, D. (1997). How diversity influences learning. *Liberal Education, 83*(2), 42–48.

Smith, D. G., Guy L., Gerbrick, G. L., Figueroa, M. A., Watkins, G. H., Levitan, T., Moore L. C., Merchant, P. A., Beliak, H. D., & Figueroa, B. (1997). *Diversity works: The emerging picture of how students benefit*. Washington, D.C.: Association of American Colleges and Universities.

Smith, R. L. (1994). The world of business. In W. C. Hartel, S. W. Schwartz, S. D. Blume, & J. N. Gardner (Eds.), *Ready for the real world* (pp. 123–135). Belmont, CA: Wadsworth Publishing.

Stangor, C., Sechrist, G. B., & Jost, J. T. (2001). Changing racial beliefs by providing consensus information. *Personality and Social Psychology Bulletin, 27*, 484–494.

Stein, M. T., Perrin, E. C., & Potter, R. J. (2004). A difficult adjustment to school: The importance of family constellation. *Journal of Developmental Behavioral Pediatrics, 25*(5), S65–68.

Svinicki, M. D. & Dixon, N. M. (1987). The Kolb model modified for classroom activities. *College Teaching, 35*(4), 141–146.

Tafjel, H. (1982). *Social identity and intergroup behavior*. Cambridge, England: Cambridge University Press.

Taylor, O. T. (1990). *Cross-cultural communication: An essential dimension of effective education*. Chevy Case, MD: The Mid-Atlantic Center.

Taylor, S. E., Peplau, L. A., & Sears, D. O. (2006). *Social psychology* (12th ed.). Upper Saddle River, NJ: Pearson/Prentice-Hall.

Thompson, A. (2007). Boy, you better learn how to count your money in R. Luhman *Sociological Outlook* (8th ed.). Lanham: MD: Rowman & Littlefield Publishers.

Thompson, A. (2009). *White privilege* in H. Greene & S. Gabbidon *Encyclopedia of race and crime*. Thousand Oaks, CA: Sage.

Tinto, V. (1993). *Leaving college: Rethinking the causes and cures of student attrition* (2nd ed.). Chicago: University of Chicago Press.

Torres, V. (2003). Student diversity and academic services: Balancing the needs of all students. In G. L. Kramer & Associates, *Student academic services: An integrated approach* (pp. 333–352). San Francisco: Jossey-Bass.

Underwood, B. J. (1983). *Attributes of memory*. Glenview, IL: Scott, Foresman, & Company.

University of New Hampshire Office of Residential Life (2001). *The hate that hate produced* Retrieved January 8, 2007, from http://www.unh.edu/residential-life/diversity/kn_article6.pdf.

U.S. Census Bureau (2008). *An older and more diverse nation by midcentury* Retrieved August 20, 2008, from http://www.census.gov/Press-Release/www/releases/archives/population/012496.html.

U.S. Census Bureau (2008). *U.S. Hispanic population surpasses 45 million, now 15 percent of total* Retrieved September 15, 2008, from http://www.census.gov/Press-Release/www/releases/archives/population/011910.html.

U.S. Census Bureau American Community Survey (2006).

U.S. Census Bureau Current Population Survey's Annual Social and Economic Supplement (2008).

U.S. Department of Education, National Center for Education Statistics. (2008). Digest of Education Statistics, 2007 (NCES 2008-022), Chapter 3.

U.S. Diplomatic Mission to Germany. *Hispanic Americans* Retrieved October 1, 2008, from http://usa.usembassy.de/society-hispanics.htm.

Veechio, R. (1997). *Leadership*. Notre Dame, IN: University of Notre Dame Press.

Vygotsky, L. S. (1978). Internalization of higher cognitive functions. In M. Cole, V. John-Steiner, S. Scribner, & E. Souberman (Eds. & Trans.), *Mind in society: The development of higher psychological processes* (pp. 52–57). Cambridge: Harvard University Press.

Wheelright, J. (2005). Human, study thyself. *Discover* (March), pp. 39–45.

Wilder, D. A. (1984). Inter-group contact: The typical member and the exception to the rule. *Journal of Experimental Psychology, 20*, 177–194.

Wilkie, C. J. & Thompson, C. A. (1993). First-year reentry women's perceptions of their classroom experiences. *Journal of the Freshman Year Experience, 5*(2) 69–90.

Wolvin, A. D. & Coakley, (1993). *Perspectives on listening*. Norwood, NJ: Ablex Publishing.

Wright, D. J. (Ed.) (1987). *Responding to the needs of today's minority students*. New Directions for Student Services, No. 38. San Francisco: Jossey-Bass.

Zaccaro, S. J., Foti, R. J., & Kenny, D. A. (1991). Self-monitoring and trait-based variance in leadership: An investigation of leader flexibility across multiple group situations. *Journal of Applied Psychology, 76*, 308–315.

Zajonc, R. B. (2001). Mere exposure: A gateway to the subliminal. *Current Directions in Psychological Science, 10*, 224–228.

Zlotkowski, E. (Ed.) (2002). *Service-Learning and the First-Year Experience: Preparing students for personal success and civic responsibility*. (Monograph No. 34). Columbia, SC: University of South Carolina, National Resource for the First-Year Experience and Students in Transition.

Glossary

Diversity-Related Terms and Concepts

Ableism: prejudice or discrimination toward people who are disabled (i.e., who are physically, mentally, or emotionally handicapped).

Affirmative action: laws enacted to enhance employment and educational opportunities for groups of people who have experienced a long history of exclusion from jobs and paid labor organizations because of their group membership (e.g., women and minorities).

Ageism: prejudice or discrimination toward a certain age group, particularly the elderly.

Anthropocentric: the belief that humans are at the center of the world and that human needs take precedence over all other life forms and natural resources found on planet earth.

Anti-Semitism: prejudice or discrimination toward Jews or people who practice Judaism.

Apartheid: an institutionalized system of "legal racism" supported by a nation's government, which is intended to maintain the government's regime. (Apartheid derives from a word in the Afrikaan language, meaning "apartness.") It was the official name of a national system of racial segregation and discrimination that existed in South Africa from 1948 to 1994.

Baby Boomer Generation: people born during the years 1946–1964 who were influenced by events such as the Vietnam War, Watergate, and the human rights movement.

Bias: a predisposition toward viewing something positively or negatively before the facts are known.

Blended family: two or more siblings who are not related biologically, but who become members of the same family through remarriage of one of their biological parents.

Civic character: taking a leadership role with respect to promoting civility and civic responsibility.

Civic responsibility: willingness to step up and confront others who disrespect, dehumanize, or violate the rights of fellow citizens and members of their community.

Civility: displaying respect for the rights of fellow citizens or community members, and interacting with them in a humane and compassionate manner.

Classism: prejudice or discrimination based on social class, particularly toward people of lower socioeconomic status.

Cohort: a group sharing the same characteristic, such as a group of people born during the same historical period.

Connected knower: a learning style characterized by a preference for relating personally to the concept or issue being discussed and connecting it with one's own experiences.

Cosmopolitan: having worldly knowledge (literally, "a citizen of the world").

Cross-cultural: occurring between or across different cultures.

Cultural acceptance: valuing cultural differences and similarities, and viewing the differences as positive.

Cultural action: the process of recognizing differences and responding to them in a positive manner; it represents an advanced step in the process of becoming culturally competent.

Cultural acknowledgment: the act of acknowledging the differences that exist between individuals, races, and entire cultures, and viewing those differences as positive rather than negative.

Cultural awareness: an awareness of your own cultural biases and the effects they may have on yourself and others.

Cultural competence: the ability to appreciate cultural differences and to interact effectively with people from different cultural backgrounds.

Cultural sensitivity: an understanding that our internal biases have affected those around us, both those we know personally and those we do not.

Culture: a distinctive pattern of beliefs and values that are learned by a group of people who share the same social heritage, traditions, and style of living (e.g., language, fashion, food, art, music, values, beliefs, etc.).

Discrimination: unequal and unfair treatment of a person or group of people; discrimination is prejudice put into action.

Diversity: the variety of differences that exist among people who comprise humanity (the human species).

Domestic diversity: cultural differences that exist within the same nation.

Education attainment: the highest level of education achieved by a person or group of people.

Egocentric: to view the world as if one is at the center of it, showing little interest in or empathy for others.

Egoistic: to be *selfish* and unwilling to share with others or help others.

Egotistic: conceited and lacking humility.

Empathy: sensitivity to the emotions and feelings of others.

Ethnic group (Ethnicity)**:** a group of people sharing the same cultural characteristics, which have been learned or acquired through shared social experiences.

Ethnocentrism: considering one's own culture or ethnic group to be "central" or "normal," and viewing cultures that are different as "deficient" or "inferior."

Extended family: relatives of a nuclear family (e.g., grandparents, uncles, aunts, adult children, etc.).

Generation: a group or cohort of individuals born during the same historical period who, as a result of being exposed to the same historical events, may develop similar personal characteristics, values, and attitudes.

Generation X: people born during the years 1965–1980 who were influenced by events such as Sesame Street, MTV, AIDS, and soaring divorce rates.

Generation Y (Millennials)**:** people born between 1981–2002 who were influenced by events such as the 9/11 terrorist attack on the United States, the shooting of students at Columbine, and the collapse of the Enron Corporation.

Genocide: mass murdering of a certain group of people that is motivated by prejudice.

Geocentric: thinking that earth is the center of the universe and that the sun and other heavenly bodies revolve around our planet.

GLBT: Gay, lesbian, bisexual and transgender.

Global perspective: a viewpoint that encompasses all nations and all life forms that inhabit planet earth, as well as the relationship between these diverse life forms and the earth's natural resources.

Groupthink: the tendency for tight, like-minded groups of people to think so much alike that they overlook flaws in their own thinking, which can lead to poor group decisions.

Hate crime: an extreme, aggressive act of discrimination that is motivated solely by prejudice (e.g., vandalism, assault, or genocide).

Hate group: an organization whose primary purpose is to stimulate prejudice, discrimination, and hostility toward groups of people based on ethnicity, race, religion, social categories, etc. (e.g., Ku Klux Klan, Neo Nazis, White Supremacists).

Heterosexism: belief that heterosexuality is the only acceptable sexual orientation.

Holistic perspective: viewing the self as a "whole person" made up of multiple components, including intellectual, emotional, social, physical, and spiritual dimensions.

Homophobia: extreme fear and/or hatred of homosexuals.

Human relations skills: the ability to relate to others in a socially sensitive and humane manner.

Humanity: the universal aspects of the human experience that are shared by all people, regardless of their particular cultural background.

Individuality: differences among individuals within the same group.

Intercultural communication: communication that takes place between members of different cultures.

Interdependence: a style of collaborative teamwork in which group members rely upon each other to achieve a common goal.

International diversity: cultural differences that exist between different nations.

Interpersonal communication skills: the ability to listen and speak well when interacting with others.

Interpersonal intelligence (Social intelligence): the ability to understand, empathize, and relate to other people.

Institutional racism: a subtle form of racism that is rooted in organizational policies and practices that disadvantage certain racial or ethnic groups (e.g., race-based discrimination in mortgage lending, housing, and bank loans).

Intimacy spiral: a process through which intimacy or closeness between two people is built up gradually through mutual sharing of personal information.

"Jim Crow" laws: formal and informal laws created by whites after the abolition of slavery to continue their control over Black labor.

Learning styles: individual differences in preferred ways of learning—i.e., personal preference for the way in which information is taking in or received, and the way in which information is processed once it has been received.

Liberal arts education: the component of a college education that is designed to "liberate" or free learners from the tunnel vision of ethnocentric and egocentric (self-centered) viewpoints, to emancipate them from uncritical dependence on authority figures, and to equip them with critical thinking skills needed to make wise personal and political choices.

Looking-glass self: how people act and react to an individual (positively or negatively) reflects back on that individual and affects the person's self-concept or self-esteem (positively or negatively).

Majority group: a group whose membership accounts for more than one-half of the population and/or maintains societal power (dominant group).

Matriarchal family: a family in which the major authority figure and decision-maker is the mother.

Minority group: a group whose membership accounts for less than one-half of the population and/or have less societal power (subordinate group).

Multicultural: cultural differences that exist within the same society.

Multiple intelligences: different talents or abilities that individuals display, which can vary from person to person.

Multiple perspective-taking: viewing an issue from multiple angles and vantage points, including the perspectives of time (e.g., past, present, or future), place (e.g., national, international, or global), and person (e.g., social, emotional, or physical dimension of self).

Multiracial family: a family comprised of members from more than one race.

Nationalism: excessive interest and belief in the strengths of one's own nation without acknowledgment of its mistakes or weaknesses, without concern for the needs of other nations or the common interests of all nations.

Non-Western cultures: non-European cultures, such as Asian, African, Indian, Latin American, and Middle Eastern.

Nuclear family: a family consisting of two spouses and one or more children.

Opinionated: stating opinions so strongly that one's personal point of view is made to seem as if it is the only rational or acceptable one, while all others are irrelevant or inferior.

Over-represented group: a group whose percentage (proportion) of a specific population is higher than its percentage of the general population. For example, the majority of Americans who live below the poverty line are people of color, yet people of color represent a minority of the overall (general) population in America.

Patriarchal family: a family in which the major authority figure and decision-maker is the father.

Personality traits: individual differences in temperament, emotional characteristics, or social tendencies (e.g., introvert/extrovert).

Prejudice: a negative prejudgment of a person or group of people.

Privilege: an advantage given to, or enjoyed by, a person or group of people.

Race: a group of people who have been socially categorized on the basis of some distinctive physical traits, such as skin color or facial characteristics. Currently, the U.S. Census Bureau categorizes people into three races: White, Black, and Asian.

Racism: prejudice or discrimination based on skin color; a belief that your race is superior to another race with an expression of that belief through attitude(s) and action(s).

Redlining: term coined in the late 1960s to describe the practice of marking a redline on a map to indicate an area where banks would not invest or lend money, which often were neighborhoods inhabited predominantly by African Americans.

Regionalism: prejudice or discrimination based on the geographical region in which an individual was born and raised.

Religious bigotry: denying the fundamental human right of other people to hold religious beliefs, or to hold religious beliefs that differ from one's own.

Scapegoat: a person or group of people who is blamed—without good reason—as being responsible for causing frustration or failure experienced by the accuser.

Segregation: the decision of a group to separate itself, either socially or physically, from another group.

Selective listening: selecting or "tuning into" conversational topics that relate only to the listener's personal interests or that support the listener's personal viewpoints, and "tuning out" everything else.

Selective memory: tendency to remember information that is consistent with one's beliefs, while forgetting information that is inconsistent with it or contradicts it.

Selective perception: tendency to "see" what is consistent with one's beliefs, while failing to see what contradicts it.

Separate knower: a learning style characterized by "detaching" oneself from the concept or issue being discussed in order to analyze it objectively.

Sexism: prejudice or discrimination based on sex or gender.

Silent Generation (Traditional Generation): people born during the years 1922–1945 who were influenced by events such as the Great Depression and World War I and II.

Single-parent family: a family consisting of one parent and one or more children.

Situational leadership: leadership demonstrated in specific situations or contexts, rather than as a general personality characteristic that is displayed in all situations.

Social identity: the group or groups an individual identifies with, which shape or influence one's personal identity.

Social stratification: divisions of society into higher to lower layers (strata) or subgroups based on level of income, education, and occupational status.

Socialization: characteristics that have been learned through social experiences.

Society: a group of people organized under the same social system (e.g., same system of government, justice, and education).

Socioeconomic Status (SES): stratification of groups of people into social classes based primarily on their *income* level and level of *education*.

Step family: a family in which one or both parents are not the children's biological parents.

Stereotyping: viewing members of the same group in the same way, such that all individuals in the same group (e.g., same race or gender) are viewed as having the same personal characteristics.

Stigmatizing: attributing inferior or unfavorable traits to people who belong to the same group.

Synoptic perspective: a broad viewpoint that encompasses multiple perspectives (e.g., time, place, and person) and integrates them to form a unified whole.

Terrorism: intentional acts of violence toward civilians, which are motivated by political or religious prejudice.

Under-represented group: a group whose percentage (proportion) of a specific population represents less than its percentage of the general population. For example, the percentage of women in the specific field of engineering is far less than the percentage of women in the general population.

Western culture (Western civilization): cultures of European origin.

Xenophobia: extreme fear or hatred of foreigners, outsiders, or strangers.

Index

Strangers, fearing, 116–117
Student government, 172
Student Handbook, 172–173
Student leader, 173
Study groups, 171
Subgroups, 7
Swinnerton, Frank, 160
Switching group identity, 25–26

T

Take leadership role with respect to diversity, 180
Task forces, 172
Teammates, 165
   common goal, 165
   interacting informally, 165
   interdependently connected, 165
Teamwork
   setting, 165
   tips for, 165
Technology, as component of culture, 6
The Tenth Muse Lately Sprung Up in America, 42
Terenzini, Pat, 81
Terrorism, 124, 206
Thinking, 64–65
   complexity, 96
   diversity and, 96–99
Thompson, Aaron, 4, 13, 47, 51, 55, 58, 112, 116, 173
Thorpe, Jim, 29
Ties, family, 69–70
Time, 98, 146
   as component of culture, 6
Timeline, historical events, 48–51
Title VI of Civil Rights Act, 115
Tool-oriented personality type, 63
Traditional Generation, 53
Twain, Mark, 130
Tzu, Lao, 172

U

Unconscious, 120, 133
Under-represented group, 207
Universal perspectives, 93–94
U.S. News and World Report, 13

V

Viva Zopata, 32
Vocational development, 85
Vocational Preference Inventory, career test, 63
Volunteer experiences, 180
Volunteer work, 172
Voting, 178–179
VPI. *See Vocational Preference Inventory*

W

Wage gaps, 39–40
Wallas, Graham, 167
Weaver, Robert, 35
West Side Story, 32
Wharton, Edith, 42
Wheatley, Phillis, 35
Who Would Have Thought It?, 31
Whole person, 93
   multiple dimensions of, 105–106
Whole person development, elements of, 84
Wiesel, Elie, 167
Wilson, Harriet, 35
Women, 38–42, 66
   earnings of, 40
   famous firsts by, 42
Wong, Anna May, 38
Woodhull, Victoria Claflin, 42
The World Factbook, 2008, 51
World languages, 92
World religions, 52

X

Xenophobia, 124, 207

Y

Young, Andrew, 35